ANGLO-SPANISH CONFRONTATION ON THE GULF COAST DURING THE AMERICAN REVOLUTION

WILLIAM S. COKER
ROBERT R. REA
EDITORS

Proceedings of the
GULF COAST HISTORY
AND HUMANITIES CONFERENCE

Volume IX

Sponsoring Institutions and 1981
Board of Directors:

Escambia County School Board
James M. Moore
Historic Pensacola Preservation Board
James W. Moody, Jr., *General Chairman*
Russell E. Belous
B. Lynne Robertson
Pensacola Junior College
Grace E. Earnest, *Treasurer*
Ted Carageorge
Glenn H. Costen
The University of West Florida
Jane E. Dysart, *Secretary*
William S. Coker
Yolanda Reed
Administration of Conference
William S. Coker, *Program Chairman*
Robert R. Rea (Auburn University), *Program Co-Chairman*
Jane E. Dysart *Local Arrangements*
Yolanda Reed, *Printed Program*
Nancy Brown, *Program Design*

The 1981 Conference was cosponsored by the
Gálvez Celebration Commission of Pensacola
Executive Committee
J. Earle Bowden, *General Chairman*
William S. Coker, *Chairman, History and Heritage Committee*
Joe Rubel, *Chairman, Activities Committee*
Rosilan H. Dodson, *Executive Director*
Roxanne Bonifay, *Secretary*
Ginger Bass
Mike Green
David Nebel
Norman Simons

ANGLO-SPANISH CONFRONTATION ON THE GULF COAST DURING THE AMERICAN REVOLUTION

WILLIAM S. COKER
ROBERT R. REA
EDITORS

INDEX BY POLLY COKER

PENSACOLA, FLORIDA

GULF COAST HISTORY AND HUMANITIES CONFERENCE

1982

HUDSON BRANCH

No portion of this book may be reproduced by any means without the express consent of the Gulf Coast History and Humanities Conference.

Copyright 1982 by the Gulf Coast History and Humanities Conference.

Library of Congress Cataloging in Publication Data

Anglo-Spanish confrontation on the Gulf Coast during the American Revolution.

(Proceedings of the Gulf Coast History and Humanities Conference ; v. 9)
Includes edited papers from the Ninth Gulf Coast History and Humanities Conference held May 7-8, 1981 in Pensacola, Fla.
Includes bibliographical references and index.
1. Gulf States—History—Revolution, 1775-1783—Congresses. 2. Gulf States—History—To 1803—Congresses. I. Coker, William S. II. Rea, Robert Right, 1922- . III. Gulf Coast History and Humanities Conference (9th : 1981 : Pensacola, Fla.) IV. Series: Gulf Coast History and Humanities Conference. Proceedings of the Gulf Coast History and Humanities Conference ; v. 9.
E230.5.G83A53 1982   976'.02   82-15664
ISBN 0-940836-16-5
ISBN 0-940836-17-3 (pbk.)

CONTENTS

List of Illustrations and Maps vii
Introduction viii

The Legacy of Spain
A.P. Nasatir 1

The Cuban Fishing Ranchos: A Spanish Enclave within British Florida
James W. Covington 17

Anglo-Spanish Commerce in New Orleans during the American Revolutionary Era
Robin F.A. Fabel 25

The Creek Confederacy in the American Revolution: Cautious Participants
Michael D. Green 54

Hamstrung by Penury: Alexander Cameron's Failure at Pensacola
James H. O'Donnell III 76

The Anglo-Spanish Contest for the Gulf Coast as Viewed from the Townsquare
Kathryn Holland 90

José de Ezpeleta and the Siege of Pensacola
Francisco de Borja Medina Rojas 106

José Solano and the Spanish Navy at the Battle of Pensacola
Eric Beerman 125

French and Spanish Military Units in the 1781 Pensacola Campaign
Jack D. L. Holmes 145

*Loyalist Resistance after Pensacola: The Case of
James Colbert*
Gilbert C. Din 158

*The Queen's Redoubt Explosion in the Lives of
William A. Bowles, John Miller and William Panton*
J. Leitch Wright, Jr. 177

Spanish Historians and the Gulf Coast Campaigns
Light T. Cummins......................................194

Index 206

LIST OF ILLUSTRATIONS AND MAPS

Following Page

Participants in the Conference xiv
Caricature for Gálvez Celebration and Conference xiv
The Gulf Coast Region during the Revolutionary Era xiv
The Lower Mississippi Valley during the Revolutionary
   Era xiv
Creek Country — 1780 54
Little Tallassee or The Hickory Ground 54
Don José de Ezpeleta y Galdeano 117
The Mobile-Pensacola Area, 1780-1781 117
Plan of Pensacola Area, 1781 117
Plan of the Spanish Encampment . . . British
   Fortifications . . . and Pensacola 117
Don José de Solano y Bote 124
Reconstructed Uniform of the Navarra Regiment 151
Reconstructed Uniform of Four Units at Pensacola in
   1781 151

INTRODUCTION

The Ninth Gulf Coast History and Humanities Conference met in Pensacola on May 7 and 8, 1981, in conjunction with the weeklong Gálvez Bicentennial Celebration. Those dates, May 7-8, were historically significant for Pensacola, and, indeed, for the entire Gulf Coast. The events which took place at Pensacola, May 7-8, 1781, led directly to the return of the Floridas to Spain two years later. The conference even produced a little of the dramatic. At the Friday morning session on the 8th, one of the participants looked at his watch — it was 9:30 — and announced that at that same hour two hundred years ago an explosion had rocked the Queen's Redoubt. That explosion caused by a hot shot from a Spanish mortar which had rolled into the powder magazine, turned out to be the most crucial cannon shot during the two month-long siege of Pensacola, March 9-May 8, 1781. The Spaniards quickly captured the redoubt and turned its cannon on the remaining British fortifications, the Prince of Wales Redoubt and Fort George. Within a few hours the bombardment of those positions led to the British capitulation. The formal surrender of Pensacola on May 10, climaxed the Anglo-Spanish confrontation which had begun some years earlier.

This Gulf Coast conference, one of several devoted to some aspect of the southeastern Spanish Borderlands, attracted a number of Borderlands historians. Professor Herbert Eugene Bolton, considered the "father" of Spanish Borderlands history, must surely have smiled from his seat among that circle of distinguished historians at Clio's feet, when he observed three of his former students among those present. Professors Abraham P. Nasatir and Donald E. Worcester served on the program, while Professor Alfred Barnaby Thomas attended the conference. It was the first time in more than fifty years that Nasatir and Thomas had met. Both studied under Bolton at the University of California in the late 1920s and, along with Worcester, became distinguished apostles of the "Boltonlands" school.

Introductions should, in our opinion, serve at least two purposes: to set the stage for the information which follows, and to acknowledge the contributions of those who gave unstintingly of their time and effort to the cause. For some of our readers who may not be familiar with the Anglo-Spanish conflict on the Gulf Coast and in the Mississippi Valley during the American Revolution, we have included a brief survey of the period. The papers in the text expand upon or fill in much that is not said here.

In 1763 with the end of the French and Indian War, Britain had eliminated France as a colonial power in North America. Spain lost Florida but received French Louisiana west of the Mississippi River including the Isle of Orleans and the city of New Orleans, which lay south of the lakes (Borgne, Ponchartrain, and Maurepas and the Iberville River) and east of the Mississippi. Britain acquired everything else east of the Mississippi and north of the lakes. The British occupied Florida in 1763, but it was 1766 before Antonio de Ulloa arrived to take charge of Louisiana for Spain.

In 1764 Britain divided Florida into two colonies, East Florida and West Florida. East Florida, with its capital at St. Augustine, included all of the territory east of the Apalachicola River and south of the colony of Georgia. Until 1769, St. Marks (*San Marcos de Apalache*) was East Florida's principal gulf outlet. West Florida extended from the Apalachicola-Chattahoochee Rivers to the Mississippi. The Gulf of Mexico and the line of lakes that separated the Isle of Orleans from British territory was its southern boundary. The northern boundary was set at $32°28'$ North Latitude, or a line from the mouth of the Yazoo River to the Chattahoochee. West Florida included Pensacola, the capital; Mobile, Manchac, Baton Rouge, and Natchez, as its principal towns or villages.

British, mostly Scottish, merchants and traders along the east bank of the Mississippi, and from Mobile and Pensacola, built a lucrative trade with the former French subjects of Louisiana and the few Spaniards and Anglos that came to the colony after 1766. For the most part, Spanish officials tended to look the other way about this illegal British trade but occasionally confiscated the goods and ships which were sold at auction much to the dismay of the merchants involved. At the same time, Spaniards from Cuba fished and traded with the Indians in the Florida keys and along the Gulf Coast as far north as the Apalachicola River. British officials were not happy with this arrangement, but did little to interfere since British merchants were also trading in Havana and other Spanish Gulf and Caribbean ports. There matters rested until the outbreak of the American Revolution in 1775.

At first the American colonists were forced to go it alone. But, in 1778, France joined the Americans in the war against Britain and recognized the independence of the thirteen colonies. France wanted revenge for her losses to the British in 1763. Spain also wanted revenge not only for her losses in 1763, but for those in 1713 as well when Britain acquired Gibraltar. As early as 1776, however, France and Spain both advanced funds for the manufacture of arms and munitions for the colonies. The money was funneled through a fictitious French firm. Later Spain used the commercial house of Diego de Gardoqui and Sons of Bilbao to ship materiel to Havana and New Orleans for the Americans. For fear of the precedent it would set for her own American colonies, Spain was reluctant to recognize American independence. After efforts to negotiate a settlement of her grievances with Great Britain had failed, Spain declared war in 1779. Exactly what date that took place and whether Spain soon after also recognized American independence is still a matter of debate.

Colonel Bernardo de Gálvez, the young Governor of Louisiana, who had already befriended the Americans on several occasions, learned of the declaration of war before his opponent, General John Campbell, in West Florida. Gálvez had planned for this eventuality and was prepared to take the offensive against the British. In August of 1779, Gálvez moved his army out of New Orleans and captured Fort Bute at Manchac, and Fort New Richmond at Baton Rouge. In the terms of capitulation the British commander, Lieutenant Colonel Alexander Dickson, gratuitously included British Fort Panmure at Natchez. Thus by September of 1779, the east bank of the Mississippi River was Spanish. In January of 1780, Gálvez led an expedition out of New Orleans against Mobile. After much difficulty in navigating the pass into Mobile Bay, the Spanish forces laid siege to Fort Charlotte commanded by Captain Elias Durnford. Efforts by General Campbell to reinforce Mobile from Pensacola failed, and Durnford surrendered to Gálvez on March 14. That left only Pensacola in British hands.

Gálvez planned to move against Pensacola soon after the fall of Mobile. But for several reasons—not enough troops, indecision about whether to attack by sea or land, and/or knowledge that the British had a large force of Indian warriors ready to defend Pensacola—the Spaniards decided to try it another day. That fall, Gálvez gathered his forces at Havana and another expedition for the Pensacola campaign got underway in mid-October, only to be scattered by a violent hurricane. Finally, in late February of 1781, a fourth expedition with reinforcements from Spain left Havana. Supported by troops and ships from New Orleans and

Mobile, the siege of Pensacola commenced in March. For the next two months, aided by additional Spanish and French assistance from Havana, the Spaniards slowly but surely tightened the noose around General Campbell's neck. Campbell had elected to fight a defensive rather than an offensive war. Most historians have agreed that Campbell put up a dismal defense, although in all fairness to him, the British had already written West Florida off as a lost cause. The only British attempt to bring supplies and reinforcements for Pensacola arrived after the siege began and could not be landed. The formal surrender precipitated by the explosion in the Queen's Redoubt, came on May 10, 1781. Thus in three campaigns Gálvez had conquered British West Florida and the Spanish victories heavily influenced the British to retrocede the Floridas to Spain in 1783.

As these events transpired in the lower Mississippi Valley and on the Gulf Coast, the Americans and Spaniards sparred and clashed with the British in the upper Mississippi Valley. Fernando de Leyba and his successor at St. Louis, Francisco Cruzat, managed to prevent the British from taking St. Louis, while General George Rogers Clark successfully carried the fight against the British in the Illinois country. The situation in that area, however, remained much more in doubt until the end of the war than it did in West Florida.

Because Bernardo de Gálvez was the most important single figure in the Anglo-Spanish conflict, some historians may wonder why no separate paper was devoted to him. For one thing, so much had already been written about Gálvez, that no effort was made to solicit such a paper. For obvious reasons Pensacola did not celebrate the Gálvez bicentennial until 1981, but similar celebrations had begun in Louisiana in 1979, and in Alabama in 1980. Those earlier events as well as Pensacola's celebration, produced some new articles and books about Gálvez. Thus for those who would prefer more on Gálvez, we apologize and refer you to James A. Servies, *The Siege of Pensacola, 1781: A Bibliography* (Pensacola: The John C. Pace Library, 1981), which is the latest and most complete bibliography on the subject to date.

All of the papers delivered at the conference had as their central theme the Anglo-Spanish confrontation on the Gulf Coast or in the Mississippi Valley. To be sure the individual subjects covered a wide range and not all of them pertained directly to the American Revolutionary era, 1775-1783. The papers as presented here are not in the same order in which they were read at the conference. We decided to begin this volume with the overview of the Anglo-Spanish conflict prepared by Nasatir. As he explained, his concentration on the upper Mississippi Valley merely mirrored his own years of research and writing on that topic. The next two chapters, those by Covington and Fabel, reveal the commercial interests, rivalry, and conflict between Spain and Great Britain which began not long after 1763. Chapters 4-6 by Green, O'Donnell, and Holland concern the Indians and their participation or lack thereof during the war years. Why, for example, with literally thousands of Indian warriors within their beck and call did the British have only a few hundred present in Pensacola in 1781, and practically none at Mobile the previous year? The papers by Borja Medina and Beerman discuss the role of two of the major military figures present at Pensacola during all or part of the siege: José de Ezpeleta and José de Solano. Next, Holmes reviews the various Spanish and French military units including those from Mexico which served under the overall command of Bernardo de Gálvez. Din and Wright deal with events which transpired largely after the Pensacola campaign. Din's study of James Colbert shows that not all British sympathizers in the West laid down their arms on May 10, 1781. Some carried on the war against the Spaniards for nearly two years afterwards. Wright explains how that fatal explosion in the Queen's Redoubt affected the lives of three men, only one of whom was at Pensacola at the time. These three: William Augustus Bowles, John Miller, and William Panton, played a significant role in the events which took place in the Floridas during the last two decades of the eighteenth century. Finally Cummins surveys how Spanish historians have looked at the Anglo-Spanish war in West Florida.

It is unfortunate that economic constraints prevented the publication of the papers in their entirety, and did not enable us to include the remarks of the commentators. For several reasons but primarily because of their length—some papers ran 50-70 pages—the papers have been considerably revised and shortened by the editors. A note or two is also necessary in regard to the editing. A number of names particularly Indian names, but some French and Spanish names too, are variously spelled. Since it is difficult if not impossible to say which spelling is correct, we have retained the spelling of most of those names as given by the authors. Some papers contained only the last name of a particular person. In such cases, please check the index for the complete name, if it is known. Footnote format with some exceptions has been standardized. After some thought, we elected not to include a separate bibliography. Our thanks to Polly Coker for preparing the index and for much typing and retyping of the manuscript.

The session chairmen and commentators, all noted for their expertise in Spanish Borderlands, Military, or Gulf Coast history, helped make the conference an outstanding success. The chairmen included: Dr. Paul E. Hoffman, Louisiana State University, Baton Rouge; Dr. Ted Carageorge, Pensacola Junior College; General Edwin H. Simmons (USMC Ret.), Director of Marine Corps History, and President of the American Military Institute; and Dr. John K. Mahon, Professor of History at the University of Florida, and in 1981 President of the Florida Historical Society.

The commentators were: Dr. Donald E. Worcester, Professor Emeritus, Texas Christian University; Dr. Robert D. Bush, then of the Historic New Orleans Collection, and now Director of the Wyoming State Department of Archives and History; Dr. Ralph Lee Woodward, Tulane University; and Dr. Thomas D. Watson, McNeese State University. These gentlemen provided incisive and instructive comments and analyses of the papers.

On several occasions we mentioned the Gálvez Bicentennial Celebration. We are particularly indebted to the Gálvez Celebration Commission of Pensacola, Mr. J. Earle Bowden, chairman, and the other members of the Commission for cosponsoring the Gulf Coast conference, and for the substantial financial support it furnished the conference and for the publication of this volume. A grant from the State of Florida sponsored by the Honorable W.D. Childers, President of the Florida Senate, and the entire West Florida legislative delegation, enabled the Commission to provide such support.

We would be remiss in not acknowledging the continued support, financial and otherwise, from the four organizations which have been the sponsors of the Gulf Coast History and Humanities Conference from its inception: the Escambia County School Board, Historic Pensacola Preservation Board, Pensacola Junior College, and the University of West Florida. The Board of Directors of the Conference, composed of representatives from these institutions, also contributed above and beyond . . . to help make the conference a great success.

We would also like to thank Auburn University for its assistance in the typing of the first revised copy of the proceedings. Without such support we would still be a long way from publication.

A special note of appreciation is also due Mary Takach, Sandra Gentry, Tracy Spikes, and the Board of Trustees of the Pensacola Museum of Art, for permitting us to hold our meetings in their facilities.

Three of the maps used in this volume were borrowed from Vol. VII in the Gulf Coast Conference series, *The Military Presence on the Gulf Coast*. Professor Jerome F. Coling prepared those maps which we modified for inclusion here.

William S. Coker, University of West Florida
Robert R. Rea, Auburn University

Dr. Ted Carageorge[2]

Dr. Paul E. Hoffman[2]

Ms. Kathyrn Holland[1]

Dr. Robin F. A. Fabel[1]

PARTICIPANTS IN THE NINTH GULF COAST HISTORY AND HUMANITIES CONFERENCE

PARTICIPANTS IN THE NINTH GULF COAST HISTORY AND HUMANITIES CONFERENCE, PENSACOLA, FLORIDA. MAY 7-8, 1981.

1. Dr. Light T. Cummins[1]
2. Dr. Thomas D. Watson[3]
3. Dr. Eric Beerman[1]
4. Dr. Gilbert C. Din[1]
5. Dr. James W. Covington[1]
6. Dr. James H. O'Donnell, III[1]
7. Dr. Ralph Lee Woodward[3]
8. Dr. Robert R. Rea[4]
9. B/Gen. Edwin H. Simmons (USMC,Ret.)[2]
10. Fr. Francisco de Borja Medina Rojas, S.J.[1]
11. Dr. Robert D. Bush[3]
12. Dr. John K. Mahon[2]
13. Dr. Donald E. Worcester[3]
14. Dr. J. Leitch Wright, Jr.[1]
15. Dr. Jack D. L. Holmes[1]
16. Dr. Michael D. Green[1]
17. Dr. William S. Coker[4]
18. Dr. Abraham P. Nasatir[1]

[1]Read Paper   [3]Commentator
[2]Chaired a Session   [4]Program Co-Chairmen

Caricature by J. Earle Bowden, Editor, Pensacola *News-Journal*, advertising the Gálvez Celebration and the Gulf Coast Conference.

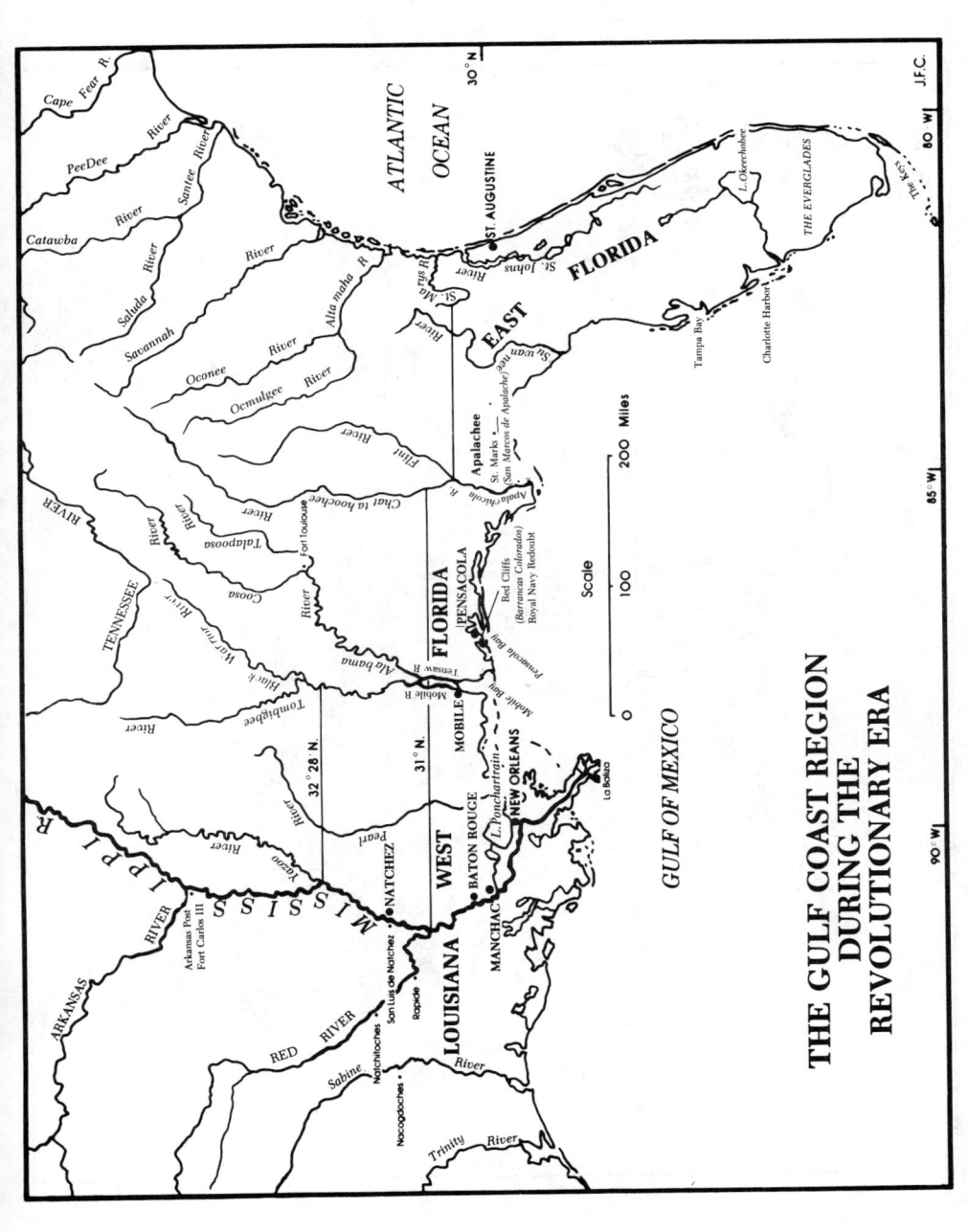

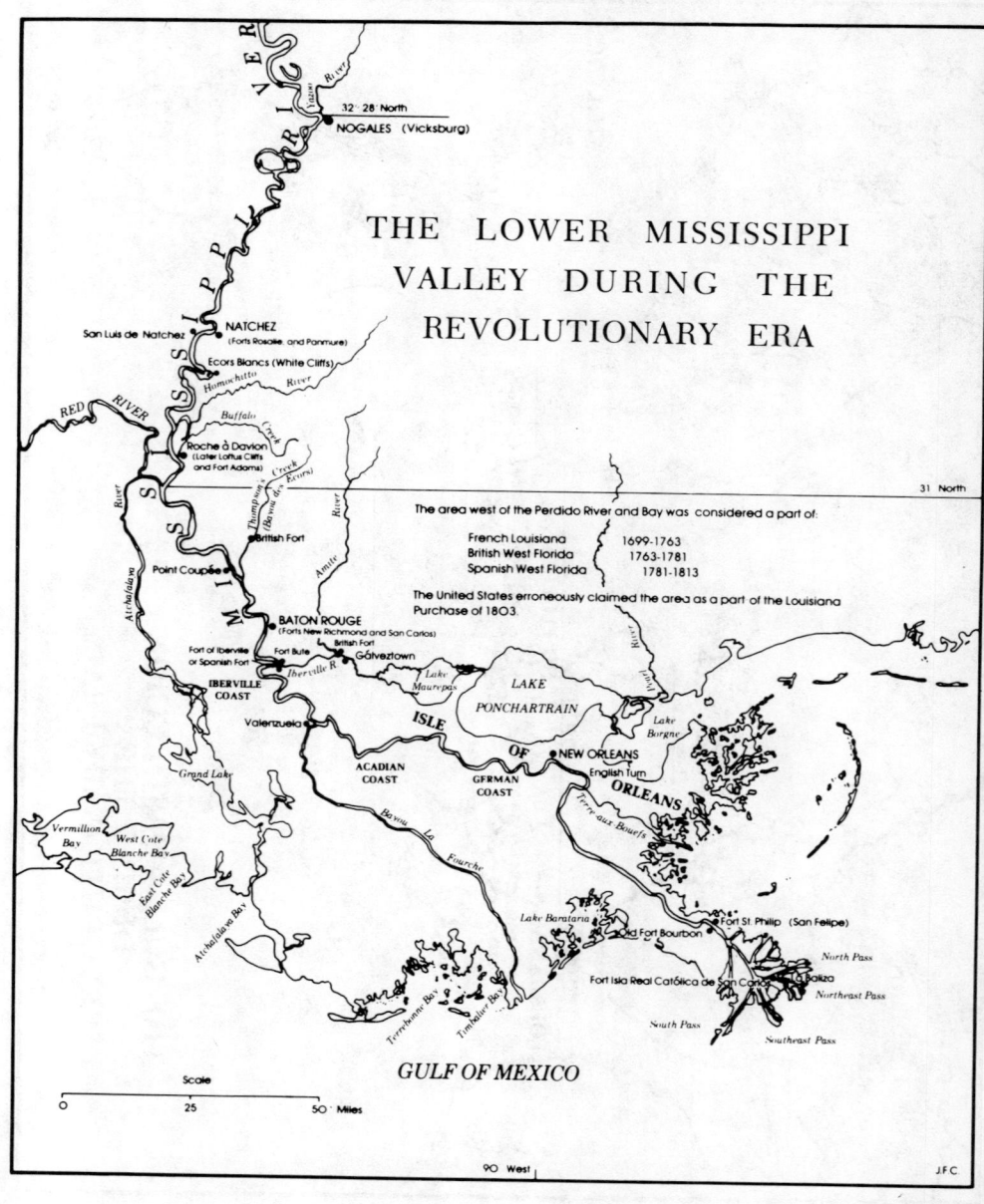

THE LEGACY OF SPAIN

A. P. Nasatir[*]

It has only been in recent times that the part played by Spain in the American Revolution has been researched in depth. No one has yet put the story together in its entirety, for Spain's role did not begin when the Revolution broke out in 1775—it derived from centuries of Spanish history and her struggle for supremacy in both Europe and the colonial world. Nor was the part played by Spain in the Revolution either altruistic or based upon the principles of democratic freedom. Rather, Spain's course of action was an integral part of imperial rivalries in the Americas and elsewhere.

Spain's vaunted monopoly of colonization was shattered in 1763 by the overwhelming victory of England in the Seven Years War. From that era the American Revolution took its beginnings as the defeated European nations licked their wounds and waited for the opportunity to gain revenge upon their enemy. With France eliminated from continental North America, a new border at the Mississippi River was shared by Spain and England.

Spain took its time occupying French Louisiana west of the Mississippi. Suffering a setback under Antonio de Ulloa, Spain sent Alejandro O'Reilly to establish Spanish rule in Louisiana, and over it Luis de Unzaga became governor. Cautious and conservative, Unzaga faced several frontier crises with the English across the Mississippi in West Florida. He survived a critical threat of war (the Falkland Islands affair) in 1771. He had difficulty with English smugglers and Indians. The English on the east bank of the Mississippi, the Natchez and Manchac districts, increased much more rapidly than the population of the Spanish settlements; in them Unzaga saw a menace to Spanish control west of the Mississippi. He recognized that their smuggling might penetrate even to the precious Kingdom of New Spain. With the outbreak of war between some of England's colonies and the mother-country in 1775, the problem which, in Unzaga's mind, had been chronic, became acute.

What then did Spain do? Spain declared its strict neutrality, but in no sense did Spain or her colonies adhere to strict neutrality. It was the policy of the enlightened government of Charles III to assist in keeping England's colonies in a state of disaffection by giving them money secretly through Vergennes and later through the House of Gardoqui. Her task was to encourage resistance on the part of England's colonies, but when colonial grievances led to independence, Spain lost interest in the insurgents, for she feared their influence on her own colonies. Spain's interest was in her own welfare; only for the moment was it bound up with the interests of England's rebellious colonies. Spain announced her neutrality but prepared for any contingency. She opened her ports to American corsairs, and from March, 1777, Spanish and French ships brought provisions to Caribbean ports, thus forcing England to increase its naval forces in American waters.

Spain's neutrality enabled her to get information and mature plans for defense, for they saw that war was coming, but Spain immediately began making military plans, the centers of activity being Havana and New Orleans. The Spanish engaged in espionage and fostered an American expedition to the southwest (which the colonials used to get much needed military supplies). Spain ordered the governor of Louisiana to encourage the Americans to take Pensacola, and Unzaga was asked for trading privileges by Virginia. The governor was sufficiently impressed by the prospects of a western expedition that he requested instructions from Spain.

With the outbreak of the American Revolution, Unzaga had been ordered to investigate, with all discretion and secrecy, not only the success of the English armies and of the rebelling colonies, but also the intentions of both sides. He sent a ship to Philadelphia, under cover of purchasing flour, to discover colonial designs. Reports of British intentions were alarming, and Unzaga was not reassured by a survey of the defenses of Louisiana. There were not sufficient troops to defend the colony, nor could dependence be placed on militiamen; therefore he would pursue a policy he had formulated in 1770: in case of attack he would retreat and fall back to Mexico. Uneasy about Louisiana's defenses and its exposure to attack, and unconvinced that the security of the province could be achieved by aiding the Americans, Unzaga referred the matter to Spain and asked for instructions.

On January 1, 1777, Unzaga relinquished his office to young Bernardo de Gálvez who, with the support of the Spanish court, actively aided the Americans while strengthening provincial defenses. When Patrick Henry and Thomas Jefferson asked that New Orleans be made a free port for western American products, Gálvez balked, but he did assist the American rebels in many ways, seizing English contraband vessels on the Mississippi and ordering all English subjects to leave Louisiana in 1777. With the youthful and forceful Bernardo de Gálvez in charge of Spanish Louisiana, conditions on the frontiers of Louisiana changed both for the better and the worse.

The American Revolution triggered a series of events that intensified British and Spanish rivalry in the Mississippi Valley. Spain fancied that she saw a chance to regain the Floridas, lost to England in the Seven Years War, as well as an opportunity to grasp the entire basin of the great river. The ambitious Spaniards clearly perceived certain economic advantages, for the products of the back-country of an independent neighbor would be shipped to New Orleans, and if Spain regained possession of the Floridas, she would enjoy a monopoly of that trade. On August 15, 1777, the Spanish government informed Bernardo de Gálvez that should the American rebels seize any of the British settlements on the Mississippi and be disposed to deliver them up to the Spanish sovereign, Gálvez was empowered to receive them in trust or deposit, taking care not to provoke any countermeasures from England.

Gálvez favored war. He believed the English were awaiting an opportunity to swoop down on the Spanish. He saw the weaknesses in the defenses of his own colony, and he saw danger in the right of the English to navigate the Mississippi. He also saw in the governorship of Louisiana an opportunity to advance his own professional ambitions, to expand the strength of his colony, to close the lower Mississippi Valley to illegal traffic, and to wrest West Florida from British rule. He changed the policy in Louisiana quickly.

The high point of Gálvez's direct assistance to the Am ericans was his assistance to James Willing. Gálvez also facilitated American shipping by sea and up the Mississippi, and he cooperated with Oliver Pollock in sending supplies to Washington's army and to American forces in the west. Willing raided the loyalist settlements on the lower Mississippi in

February, 1778, and was warmly welcomed in New Orleans. Willing was commissioned to take letters to New Orleans, bring supplies back up the river, and to raid English settlements on the Mississippi; he also seized vessels on the river. Willing's second task, to invade West Florida, met with disaster, for the effect of his initial success persuaded the British to reinforce West Florida and blockade the river. But early in 1778, the British flag was excluded from the Mississippi, and the Spanish were in complete possession of its commerce.

Spain also employed secret agents as an intelligence service; Jacinto Panis, for example, was sent to Mobile and Pensacola. Gálvez thereby learned of the fortifications and defenses of the British possessions in West Florida, of the English attempt to organize Indians against the Americans, and discovered an English spy system in New Orleans.

English officials vigorously protested these actions of Gálvez, particularly Spanish aid to the Americans and Spanish harassment of English merchants. Their protests were more than verbal, for the English fired on boats descending the Mississippi from Illinois and maintained troops and Indians at *Barrancas de Margot*. Spain, on her part, protested the presence of English traders among the Indians west of the Mississippi. In effect, Gálvez approved anything short of war in aid of the Americans.

Gálvez also tried to strengthen Louisiana by means of increased immigration. He authorized Fernando de Leyba at St. Louis to grant inducements to Catholic settlers, especially French and Germans east of the Mississippi, to settle in Spanish territory. He imported Canary Islanders and colonists from Málaga. Many pro-Americans fled to Spanish Louisiana, and one group founded Galveztown.

On March 9, 1778, Fernando de Leyba was appointed lieutenant governor of Spanish Illinois. He arrived in St. Louis on July 10, shortly before George Rogers Clark captured Kaskaskia. Leyba's instructions were ambitious. He was to encourage immigration into Spanish Illinois, to treat all British and American emigrés in Spanish territory with fairness and in accord with the rights of Spanish subjects, and to engage in secret correspondence with the Americans. He was to secure the friendship of the Indians within the dominions of Spain and also those under British jurisdiction. And he was to do all this without implicating the Spanish government and without inviting British complaints and reprisals.

Leyba did aid the Americans, Clark in particular. Twenty-six days after taking office, he engaged in a long and friendly correspondence with Clark. He invited Clark to visit St. Louis, where Leyba welcomed him with great ceremony. An intimate relationship between the two developed, and the Americans benefitted correspondingly. Supplies were obtained from merchants in St. Louis and New Orleans, and the success of Clark's campaign was heavily indebted to Spanish aid and supplies. With his own funds, Leyba backed purchases from St. Louis merchants when the credit of the Americans fell. Anxious for the friendship of the Indians in his territory and the security of Spanish possessions, Leyba naturally spent more on Indian presents than on aid to the Clark campaign across the river. The Spaniards aided in another way: to avoid British destruction of American supplies on the Mississippi, Pollock's shipments were dispatched under the Spanish flag and consigned to Leyba; thus the boats were able to slip past the British post at Natchez. Without this ruse, Clark could hardly have held the country he had conquered. Clark was also aided by Francisco Vigo, a business associate of Leyba; by Gabriel Cerré, a French Canadian by birth, a British subject by virtue of his residence and business in Kaskaskia, but Spanish in sympathy; by Charles Gratiot; and Father Pierre Gibault.

Leyba watched the British movements closely. He told Gálvez of the uselessness of Fort Carlos III, located at the mouth of the Arkansas River, and suggested the establishment of forts at *Aguas Frías* and at the mouth of the Des Moines River, to be garrisoned with a sufficient force to prevent Englishmen from entering that river. Gálvez informed Leyba that he could not authorize such an ambitious program because of the expense, at least not without authorization of the court, but he did instruct the lieutenant governor to prevent incursions by English traders and their enticement of "our Indians."

The British, too, were active. Almost from the outset they were aware of Spanish aid to the Americans. Guy Carleton wrote Lieutenant Governor Henry Hamilton in October, 1776, telling him to intercept correspondence between the Spaniards and the Americans but to take care not to create a breach between England and Spain. "The Spanish side must be respected upon all occasions," Carleton warned. The English intended to drive the rebels out of Illinois in order to cut off their communication with the French and Spanish. They were alarmed when the Spaniards wanted to erect forts in the Illinois country, and they worked to defeat Spanish attempts to win native support. Hamilton wrote Gálvez on January 13, 1779, requesting him to prohibit the New Orleans commerce in gunpowder with the rebels. Hamilton warned Gálvez that if rebels took refuge in Spanish territory to avoid a British force, he would be obliged to attack the Spanish posts. Eleven days later, he informed General Frederick Haldimand of his belief that war existed with both France and Spain, but he had received no word to justify offensive action.

British traders had entered Spanish territory by way of the Des Moines River. They attempted to plant a post at the mouth of the Ohio, and they desired to control the mouth of the Missouri where they could undersell the Spaniards and control the Indians. They hoped that Hamilton's recovery of Vincennes from Clark would permit the realization of these ambitions. When Hamilton accomplished that feat, he communicated to Pensacola his plans for a joint attack upon the Americans in the West. He summed up his view of the combatants: "The Spaniards are feeble and hated by the French, the French are fickle and have no man of capacity to advise or lead them, the Rebels are enterprizing and brave, but want resources, and the Indians can have their resources but from the English if we act without loss of time in the favourable conjuncture." But Vigo gave the British plans to Clark, and he reconquered Vincennes and captured Hamilton. In these decisive events, the creoles in Illinois aided Clark, and Clark relied chiefly on Pollock and Gálvez for essential supplies.

In June, 1779, Spain severed relations with England, and on July 8, declared war, ordering her colonies to attack British possessions. England, on the other hand, interpreted Spain's severance of relations as a virtual declaration of war. Lord George Germain advised General Haldimand on June 17, that Spain had declared war and told him to commence hostilities, to attack New Orleans, and to reduce the Spanish posts in the Illinois.

During the winter and spring of 1780, the British made comprehensive plans to conquer the West. They planned to enlist the Indians to join British troops coming up the Mississippi, surprising the Spanish forts and capturing exposed parties, settlements, and villages. In preparation for this ambitious program and in order to meet similar activities on the part of the Spaniards, the British stationed spies among the Indians of the Illinois. Planning for the capture of upper Louisiana was left to Governor Patrick Sinclair at Michilimackinac, who proceeded with energy and dispatch. Sinclair immediately took steps to win the allegiance and aid of the Sioux Indians, under Wabasha, and the Sac and Fox Indians. No British troops could be spared for the upper Mississippi Valley campaign, and Lieutenant Governor Sinclair was compelled to carry out his instructions by using Indian allies and such white traders as he could persuade to undertake the assignment.

Gálvez intercepted British correspondence, however, and learned of British plans as soon as Sinclair himself. Gálvez favored an immediate attack on the British posts in the lower valley, but his *junta* or council of war rejected his plans in favor of bolstering the defenses of New Orleans.

The British planned five simultaneous movements: Captain Charles Langlade would attack from Chicago via the Illinois River; another party would watch Vincennes; Wabasha and the Sioux who accompanied Emmanuel Hesse and the main party attacking St. Louis would attack the rebels at Kaskaskia and Ste. Geneviève; Bird would "amuse" Clark at the falls of the Ohio; and another expedition under General John Campbell would proceed from Mobile up the Mississippi. The expeditions from the north and from the south would meet at Natchez.

The first objective of this potent scheme was the capture of St. Louis, which the British hoped would guarantee control of the rich fur trade of the Missouri Valley. More importantly, the strategic location of St. Louis made its occupation essential to the defense of the Mississippi Valley. The British assumed that St. Louis was vulnerable because of the carelessness of the inhabitants and the weakness of its defenses in both men and cannon. Since that was the primary objective of the British in the north, the other expeditions, such as Langlade's, were only precautionary flanking attacks. This was the most comprehensive strategy for the conquest of the West that the British undertook during the Revolution, one that appeared to have every prospect of success because of the weakness of the American and Spanish garrisons in the Illinois country.

When Spain entered the war, Gálvez received orders to conquer Pensacola, Mobile, and the British posts on the Mississippi. The Spaniards feared a British attack on New Orleans, but Gálvez had long anticipated that threat and had prepared well.

He had learned of the British plans to attack the Spanish colonies on the Mississippi, to strengthen Natchez, Baton Rouge, and Manchac with an additional fifteen hundred men from Canada, and to dispatch an equally large expedition by sea from Pensacola. Initially, Gálvez kept news of the Spanish declaration of war on England secret. He believed that Louisiana's best defense was to attack the British posts on the Mississippi. He therefore struck at Baton Rouge, Manchac, and Natchez, conquering 480 leagues of fertile lower Mississippi land and driving the English from the banks of the Mississippi River. He then proceeded to conquer Mobile and Pensacola and wrest West Florida from English hands. Meanwhile, Balthazar de Villiers, commandant of the Arkansas Post, crossed the Mississippi River and, on November 22, 1780, took formal possession of the east bank north of Natchez in the name of Spain.

The other part of the British campaign for the conquest of the West fared no better. The Spanish had long feared a British attack on St. Louis, and Leyba probably learned of British preparations in February, 1780, certainly before March 9. He prepared hastily, with much help from New Orleans, throwing up fortifications that were still incomplete when the British attacked. He called in traders to man the walls, and militiamen arrived from Ste. Geneviève. He dispatched scouts to warn him of the British approach. Alarms of the English and Indian advance were received at Vincennes, Kaskaskia, Cahokia, and St. Louis. Various subordinates of Clark had informed him of the impending attack, assuming that it would come against Cahokia whose citizens sent Gratiot to Clark to announce their peril and ask for help. Gratiot presented Clark with a plan to anticipate the attacks on St. Louis and Cahokia with an offensive expedition designed to scatter the enemy and strike terror among the Indians. The Cahokians were eager to join in such an undertaking. On May 11, 1780, John Montgomery left Kaskaskia for Cahokia to prevent the enemy from reaching that village. Montgomery and others also suggested to Leyba a joint expedition to intercept the approaching British force. Leyba promised a hundred armed men, but the counteroffensive did not get underway before the British attacked.

With both Cahokia and St. Louis preparing desperately, and with Leyba's small detachment up-river to give notice of the enemy's approach, the British struck on May 26, 1780. One division of Indians under Jean Ducharme attacked Cahokia, and the other, including Sacs and Foxes under Calvé, attacked St. Louis. St. Louis held, partly because of the timely approach of George Rogers Clark with reinforcements. Once repulsed, the flight of the attackers was headlong. Calvé, Wabasha and the Sioux, and most of the the traders retreated up the Mississippi to Prairie du Chien. Others fled up the Illinois River. Clark was obliged to hasten away to meet the threat of Bird's expedition, but before he left he ordered Montgomery to organize a pursuit with 350 men, of whom Leyba contributed one hundred. This force marched against Rock River and Prairie du Chien, burned a Sac and Fox village, but missed the supplies at Prairie du Chien which were withdrawn by the British before the raiders arrived.

The defeat of the British was of far more than local consequence. Their failure doomed the plan to hem in the rebellious American colonies on the West, and the frontiers of the struggling colonies were thereby protected from assault. In addition, there was demoralization among the British allies, and the delay permitted Clark to send Montgomery against the Sacs and Foxes. Those important Indians were divided in their allegiance and were buffeted by both sides. Despite their British leanings and British pressure, they did not participate actively in the attack on St. Louis. In fact, until the full economic effect of the war was felt through the shortage of supplies at St. Louis, many of them came over to the Spanish side.

The defeat of the British-Indian force did not allay the fears of the inhabitants of Spanish Illinois. They knew the influence of British traders among the Indians, and their own inability to compete with the British in supplies and presents apparently prompted Indian raids against scattered farmers and traders. The Indians, now coming daily to St. Louis for conciliation, gifts, and supplies, brought reports of British activity among the Indians and of future British-Indian attacks. The insecurity of the inhabitants almost led to the abandonment of the Illinois settlements. Yet the Sac Indians proved more faithful to the Spaniards than to the British, even though they had been the only losers in the British attack on St. Louis. Immediately after the Rock River campaign, the majority of the Sacs and Foxes proved to be of great help to the Spaniards in countering British activity.

Leyba had been critically ill during the attack of 1780, and died shortly thereafter. Gálvez appointed Francisco Cruzat his successor as lieutenant governor on July 25, and Cruzat took over the duties from ad-interim commandant Francisco Cartabona on September 24. Gálvez instructed Cruzat to defend the province against both British and Indian raids, to woo Indians from the British to the Spanish side, and to maintain good relations with American commandants. Cruzat immediately set to his tasks. He watched American, British, and Indian movements closely. He stationed Indians and agents, such as Etienne Boucher de Monbrun and Jean Baptiste Malliet, with small detachments, up the Mississippi and Illinois Rivers to observe British movements and provide timely warnings to St. Louis. As a result of rumors of intense British activity among the Indians and preparations for another attack on Spanish Illinois in 1781, Cruzat paid increasing attention to the defenses of St. Louis, constructing, for example, a wooden stockade.

Cruzat also decided to take the offensive, but only after carefully weighing alternatives. Canadian merchants were fraternizing and trading with the Indians, persuading some to join the British in an attack on Spanish Illinois early in 1781. Douget and other traders were stockpiling supplies in St. Joseph and Du Quindre defeated an American party. Cruzat also received pleas from the Milwaukee chiefs, El Heturno and Naquiguén, to send a detachment (which they would join) against St. Joseph in order to check the activities of these traders and their growing influence. All of these facts, said Cruzat, "caused me to send with the above mentioned chiefs, Captain of the militia, Don Eugenio Pouré with a detachment of Spanish and Indians, not withstanding the rigorous winter, to attack St. Joseph." By destroying the supplies and stores at St. Joseph, Cruzat hoped to prevent, or at least make more difficult, a British attack on St. Louis the following spring. It was a shrewd move.

Leaving St. Louis on January 2, 1781, with a detachment of sixty-five soldiers and sixty Indians, Pouré led his expedition up the Mississippi and Illinois Rivers, where the Spanish detachment under Malliet joined them. Ice in the river forced Pouré to abandon his boats and march overland. Surprising Fort St. Joseph, he formally took possession on February 12, and for twenty-four hours the Spanish flag graced that British outpost. After distributing the captured spoils among the Indians, the expedition returned to St. Louis, reaching the city on March 6.

The St. Joseph expedition was a spectacular success even though British reports viewed it as a matter of small consequence, an isolated outrage committed by a band of marauders. It did much to bolster Spanish morale and lower British prestige with the Indians, and those were the objectives incorporated in Cruzat's instructions. The expedition stopped, or at least deterred, enemy attacks — Indian as well as British — and thereby furthered Spain's Indian policy. Cruzat hoped that the attack on St. Joseph would create hostilities between the Milwaukee Indians and those who were pro-British, thereby forcing the former to be loyal to Spain. The safety of the valley required compliance with Indian requests, lest they learn of Spain's weakness and defect to the British. In part, then, Cruzat had yielded to the urgings of the Indian Chiefs Heturno and Naquiguén, because he dared not refuse. Spanish prestige was increased by this offensive act.

Throughout the remainder of the war, the British attempted no other expedition against Spanish Illinois. They did seek to incite the Indians against the Spaniards, but they were generally unsuccessful. Yet the Mississippi Valley continued to have its share of problems. A rebellion of the loyalist settlers at Natchez occurred, and Natchez was briefly lost. James Colbert and his Indians raided Spanish settlements and stopped navigation on the river by capturing boats ascending from New Orleans, thus hurting the economy of the upper valley. Spain took some measures to suppress piracy on the Mississippi, sending troops to Natchez and an expedition to *Barrancas de Margot*. Jacobo Dubreuil also sent an expedition, mainly of Indians, into Chickasaw territory. The Chickasaw Indians asked Cruzat to persuade the northern Indians not to attack, and Cruzat laid down conditions for doing so which the Chickasaws accepted. Colbert and the Chickasaws attacked the Arkansas Post and laid siege, but Dubreuil successfully withstood their efforts. Cruzat's problems remained the same throughout the war: he had to pacify pro-Spanish Indians, convert pro-British Indians, and defend the Spanish possessions.

The St. Joseph expedition was later approved by the governor at New Orleans and by the Spanish court. On the basis of information sent to him by Cruzat, Estevan Miró advised José de Gálvez on November 20, 1782, that the Americans had abandoned the eastern posts of Illinois, and he represented "the utility and convenience that would result to the state and province," if Gálvez would suggest to His Majesty that the cession of those posts to Spain be obtained from the American Congress. Gálvez took no action on the matter. Actually, the territory had not been abandoned, but the troops had been withdrawn from Vincennes and other posts, and civil government had been established. In fact, the preliminary articles of peace had already been drawn up.

Cruzat's chief difficulty was his lack of soldiers and supplies. He bitterly complained of the shortage of presents necessary to retain the friendship of the Indians. He was sent little from headquarters, and some of that little never reached St. Louis because of the pirates and enemies operating on and near the river. This meager aid was always accompanied by the ubiquitous cry to economize "*los inmensos dispendios que sufre el Real Erario.*" But only gifts could keep the Indians in line. Cruzat's resourcefulness was put to the test. He obtained supplies from the merchants of St. Louis, some of which had been brought up from New Orleans, and, in this writer's opinion, he also obtained merchandise from British merchants, usually through local traders and merchants.

Both Cruzat and the British continued their efforts to win over the Indians. Cruzat was tireless in this regard. To win the allegiance of those Indians under English jurisdiction, as well as those uncommitted, he dispatched men to go among them in order to change their affections. This was usually the case where and when British agents were active. For example, Malliet's information of British activities in the upper lakes region — later the Old Northwest — and among the Sioux, was a stimulus to Cruzat's expedition against St. Joseph. To combat evil influences among the Sioux, Cruzat sent Dorion who succeeded in winning over the Sioux, except for Chief Oja's important bands. Cruzat reported large numbers of British traders among the Indians, even in Spanish territory: over one hundred canoes had been licensed by the British to trade in the Mississippi River region in 1780-1781; and in 1782, the British granted licenses to trade in the northwest to 120 canoes and 250 bateaux with goods valued at £184,000, much of which undoubtedly reached the Spanish side. Thus the British matched the Spaniards and succeeded in some instances in winning over bands from among the Sioux, Ottawa, Sacs, and Foxes that had previously been under Spanish influence.

The British were even more successful in penetrating Spanish jurisdiction north of St. Louis. Traders from Michilimackinac and Prairie du Chien poured across the Mississippi River. Without merchandise and supplies, Cruzat and his traders got nowhere with the Indians, for the English were plentifully supplied. Even Indians who were or became attached to the Spanish begged Cruzat for permission to trade with the British, and Cruzat reluctantly agreed. For example, Parent, who had long been trading near Prairie du Chien with a license from Leyba, accompanied a number of Indian chiefs to St. Louis and solicited permission to trade with the British. This may be taken as the beginning of the end of effective Spanish control of the Upper Mississippi-Missouri region. British traders were now allowed to trade with the Indians, and practically no Spanish traders went out in 1781. In 1782, Cruzat stated that there were more British merchants with more supplies than ever before in the Mississippi region. Although Cruzat carefully watched the movements and actions of the British, in his effort to economize he refused to release from service the detachments which he had earlier sent to the Illinois and Mississippi under Monbrun and Malliet.

The southern portion of the British strategy was thwarted at the source. On August 29, 1779, José de Gálvez had advised his nephew that "the King [had] determined the principal object of his forces in America during the war against England shall be to expel them from the Gulf of Mexico and the banks of the Mississippi where their establishments are so prejudicial to our commerce and also to the security of our more valuable possessions." Bernardo de Gálvez struck swiftly to crush Campbell before he could attack. The capture of the lower Mississippi posts was a prelude to the campaigns against Mobile and Pensacola. The fall of Pensacola was a stunning blow to English prestige and a cause of joy to Washington's harassed men. Enormous quantities of supplies fell into Spanish hands with the capture of Pensacola, supplies that would not be used against Americans in South Carolina and Georgia nor be given to the Indians, for Gálvez's campaign against Pensacola pinned down British forces at a moment when affairs in the southern colonies were going badly for the American cause.

Less than six months after the fall of Pensacola, a final disaster for Great Britain occurred with the surrender of Cornwallis at Yorktown. The Spaniards also had a part in that act. The intervention of de Grasse and Rochambeau enabled Washington to force the surrender of Cornwallis; but Spanish aid at Yorktown was also important, for Spanish officials in the Caribbean provided the financial and military support needed by Washington and Rochambeau, both of whom were impoverished for cash. More than silver *pesos* came from the Spanish Caribbean. France and Spain had interests of their own in the war: the French came to the aid of the Spaniards in the Caribbean, and when de Grasse sent an urgent message to Havana for cash, funds were raised by Francisco de Saavedra and others in a very great hurry. It was a remarkable accomplishment for the people of Havana to raise 1,500,000 *pesos* for Rochambeau by public subscription in twenty-four hours;they were later repaid. Rochambeau also relied on de Grasse for supplies which came from the Caribbean.

Although victorious in her drive to acquire England's Florida possessions and successful in Indian diplomacy, Spain failed to win the peace at Paris. Gálvez's campaigns had a great deal of influence, however, on the making of the treaty. England recognized the loss of the Gulf Coast and ceded East as well as West Florida to Spain. Spain's recovery of the Floridas had manifold consequences: (a) the cession of trans-Appalachia to the United States was due more to England's loss of the Gulf Coast than to the power of American forces in the west, (b) renewed Spanish interest in the southeastern Indians produced efforts in the next two decades to enlist the support of those powerful tribes, (c) Spain's subsequent dispute with the United States over the West Florida boundary was in reality an attempt to reap the full rewards of Gálvez's victories. Even the question of the closure of the Mississippi arose only because Spain, by having the Floridas, controlled all other convenient outlets for the American west. Spain's most obvious gain was the removal of the English menace along the Mississippi and Florida frontiers. Later events, however, would prove that in removing the English menace, the Spaniards had jumped into the frying pan of American expansion.

The peace negotiations affected the upper Mississippi Valley but little. The removal of the English threat along the Mississippi consolidated Spanish control over Louisiana, but Spain was still threatened in the upper area by the British in Canada. Economically, however, the war had a tremendous effect upon the upper valley. During the war, Spain had been able to send few supplies to the Spanish Illinois country, thus at the end of the war the British were in complete control of the trade and commerce of the upper Mississippi Valley and held a monopoly of the Indian trade that extended north of St. Louis and as far west as the Missouri. As a result, very few Indians remained loyal to the Spanish cause. These few, especially those who took part in the St. Joseph campaign, urged Spain to take the offensive against the British at *El Estrecho* (Detroit), but Spanish merchants were forced to purchase goods from the British merchants and traders at Michilimackinac who were operating in the Illinois country.

Certainly all that Spain wanted she did not get. Her war aims of expelling the British from the Gulf of Mexico and recovering the Floridas were achieved. Spain fought a war of territorial aggression--but hardly for the independence of the United States. Nevertheless, Americans should be most grateful for the aid of Spain in achieving their independence, and increased attention in both Spain and the United States to making better known the part Spain played in the American Revolution is most appropriate and praiseworthy.

As Lawrence Kinnaird has written:

> Had Spain not entered the war and the Floridas remained British, the United States would have had another Canada on its southern and western borders, with southern and northern Indians controlled by hostile traders and agents. To understand the impact of Spain's conquest on the United States' history it is only necessary to contemplate what might have occurred if the Floridas had remained British and been settled by embittered Loyalist refugees.[1]

---

*Professor Emeritus, San Diego State University, San Diego, California.

[1] Lawrence Kinnaird, "Western Fringe of Revolution," *Western Historical Quarterly* 7 (1976): 253-70.

Bibliographical Note

The bibliography of Spain in the American Revolution is now quite extensive and no attempt will be made to cover the field. The foregoing essay is based largely upon A. P. Nasatir, "Anglo-Spanish Frontier in the Illinois Country during the American Revolution, 1779-1783," *Journal* of the Illinois State Historical Society, 21 (1928): 3-70, and *Borderland in Retreat: From Spanish Louisiana to the Far Southwest* (Albuquerque: University of New Mexico Press, 1976). Naturally a bit more emphasis and space has been devoted to the Upper Mississippi Valley largely because of my half century of research and publications in that area. I have supplemented that material by a wide reading in the literature reflecting the areas involved. A careful review of the documentation in the other papers included in this volume will provide the reader with a good overall bibliography of Spain in the American Revolution.

THE CUBAN FISHING *RANCHOS*: A SPANISH ENCLAVE WITHIN BRITISH FLORIDA

James W. Covington*

With the capture of Havana, Cuba, in 1762, by a British armada, Spain was forced to exchange Florida for the return of that Cuban city in the Treaty of Paris which ended the war known in the thirteen English colonies as the French and Indian War. Article 20 of the Treaty of Paris stipulated that all Spanish territory east and southeast of the Mississippi River would become a possession of His Britannic Majesty.[1] In a proclamation dated October 7, 1763, George III divided Florida and Louisiana east of the Mississippi into two administrative provinces designated East and West Florida and divided by the Apalachicola River.[2] Persons living in both Floridas were allowed by the terms of the treaty to remain there and practice their Roman Catholic religion or, if they chose to leave, they were given eighteen months to settle their affairs and sell their property to British subjects.

Although Spanish settlers might have remained in East Florida, retaining their real estate holdings and leading a good life, between April, 1763 and January, 1764, 3,100 persons, representing the vast majority, were packed into transports and taken either to Havana or Campeche.[3] Sixty-five stayed at *San Marcos de Apalache* (St. Marks) until they were evacuated in February, 1764. Also carried away by the Spaniards were the contents of royal military storehouses (down to the very nails), personal possessions, and even some of the recently dead from the graveyards. Such an exodus took place because the Spanish government promised compensation to the migrants, and Catholic Spaniards did not trust Protestant Englishmen to allow freedom of religion in British Florida. Thus, on the surface, Spain and the Spanish people washed their hands of Florida and would have nothing to do with the peninsula.[4]

The Treaty of Paris had not mentioned the Florida Keys in detailed terms, and, as a result, both nations could claim the chain of coral islands extending to the southwest of the peninsula. Nine months after the Spaniards left Florida, a Spanish representative made a determined effort to keep the Keys. Don Juan Elixio de la Puente was instructed by King Charles III of Spain to dispose of all Spanish properties remaining unsold, and he met with Major Francis Ogilvie, commander of the British military forces in Florida at St. Augustine.[5] Ogilvie, questioning Puente about the Keys, was surprised to find that the Keys were considered to be part of Cuba. Ogilvie warned Puente that the English considered the Keys to be part of Florida, and any ships coming from Cuba or the Bahamas to the Keys for timber, turtles, or fish would be seized. After the conference, Puente wrote to his government restating the need for occupation of the Keys.

The English knew very little about the newly acquired peninsula separating the Gulf of Mexico and the Atlantic Ocean. The one book containing useful information on Florida was *An Account of the First Discovery and Natural History of Florida* by William Roberts, which was published in February, 1763. Since it was the only volume available to settlers and speculators, it went through several editions, and it remained the only pertinent work on the market until 1767.[6] The 102-page work contained accounts of the people, cities, rivers, bays, and coastline, and of the discovery and explorations by the Spanish in Florida. Probably the weakest part of the geographical section was the space devoted to the Gulf Coast of Florida. The author was confused about the extent of present-day Tampa Bay and Charlotte Harbor and knew nothing about the fishing *ranchos* in the region which extended from the Keys to Mobile.[7] More familiar was Pensacola and its harbor, and the English hoped to use it as a base for trading with Central America and the Caribbean.[8] So little was known of the land west of Pensacola that the Lords of Trade had only one source, an inadequate map, for use in setting the boundaries of West Florida in June, 1763.[9] Members of this board complained that much of newly acquired America had not been surveyed at all, and available maps and charts were of no use.[10]

The western coast of peninsular Florida and the panhandle represented a rich terrestrial and aquatic storehouse of treasures for those who wished to endure the harsh elements. Five hundred or more Creek Indians from settlements along the Apalachicola River, and two hundred Creeks from the Oconee River in present-day Georgia, came to hunt for deer so that they could trade the skins for European products.[11] In addition, skins from wild cattle that had escaped during the destruction of the Apalache missions were supplied to the whites.[12] When they had spare time from hunting, these Indians gathered honey which they sold in buckskin bags. Some of these Indian villages had moved from Georgia into Florida so that their inhabitants might trade at *San Marcos de Apalache* or with Spaniards stopping along the coast.[13] Others ventured on hunting trips as far south as Tampa Bay and Charlotte Harbor but carried their deerskins back to Pensacola, St. Augustine, or Georgia to the traders.[14]

When the coastal waters of Cuba showed signs of depletion of their rich supply of fish, Spanish fishing vessels began to explore the resources of the adjacent Florida peninsula. It may have been the Indians of southern Florida who commenced the traffic in aquatic products by catching fish, drying them in the sun, and trading them, together with hats and mats made from grass and bark, with the crews of Cuban vessels that came to exchange European goods for Indian produce.[15] In 1743, the Jesuits established *Santa María de Loreta* at the mouth of the Miami River. The Jesuits found that the Indians supported themselves by fishing and gathering wild fruits; each September they were taken by Cuban fishermen to the Florida Keys and the southwest coast for more fishing.[16] Fish from Florida sold in Cuba and Jamaica for a higher price than cod from Newfoundland because it kept better and had a more delicious flavor.

From Key West, fishing activities expanded northward along the coast and to the west as far as Mobile Bay. Each year some three or four hundred men in thirty or more fishing vessels came from Havana to take part in a task which lasted from the end of August to the final days of March. Before leaving Cuba, ship captains were obliged to go to the King's Warehouse where they paid $1.50 for two bushels of salt gathered at *Cayo Sal*, an island group lying to the northeast of Havana. Each man in the crews of the ships was required to pay his share of the cost of salt, nets, lines and food. When the voyage was concluded and the profits divided, the owner received one-third; the captain received two shares, each member of the twelve-or-more-man crew one share, and young helpers one-half of a share of the remaining two-thirds.[17] In the 1769-70 season, the share of each crew member in one vessel amounted to $180 for an eight week cruise.[18]

A coastal island was usually chosen as a base of operations. When the vessel arrived at the island in September, the fishermen repaired their old huts; in the case of those that could not be repaired, new huts took their place. Nets were prepared for the long season, and lines made from native silk grass were strung along racks so that the cleaned and split fish could be hung to dry in the sun. Roe taken from mullet and drum was placed in a salty solution and dried and pressed between two boards. Finally, the roe was cured by the smoke of burning corn cobs in a smoke hut.[19]

Some provisions for the crew, which ranged from twelve to thirty in number, were brought from Cuba. Such items included corn, rice, sweetmeats, and bread. Meat was supplied by hunting in the nearby forests, and the remainder was a seafood diet consisting of drum, turbot, trout, Spanish mackerel, mangrove snapper, pompano, sheepshead, and oysters.[20] It was said that meat and fish were in scarce supply at both Mobile and Pensacola because of the activities of the Cuban visitors. On some islands Cuban fishermen established permanent bases and sold fresh corn, tomatoes, and squashes to the crews of the boats.[21] Some of these year-round residents married Indian women and sent their children to Cuba for baptism, education, and jobs.[22] Other offspring of such unions, as well as full-blooded Indians, obtained jobs as fishing crew members. At Charlotte Harbor, the Cubans traded with a nearby village of Seminoles for skins and furs which they took to Cuba along with the dried fish.[23] It was said that prices charged by the Cubans for clothes and other items were much more reasonable than those charged at St. Augustine or in Georgia.[24]

Some Indians from northern Florida made their own voyages to Cuba, the Keys, and the Bahamas in large canoes capable of carrying twenty to thirty passengers. These sea-going canoes usually carried deer and bear skins, dried fish, and honey to be exchanged for rum, coffee, sugar, and tobacco.[25] One Seminole presented William Bartram a piece of tobacco that he had received from the Governor of Cuba.[26] Others went as passengers on the fishing vessels, returning with clothes made in Cuba, cigars, and rum.[27]

Probably the first indication that the English had of the great extent of the Cuban fishing operations came when Pierce A. Sinnot, an English trader at *San Marcos de Apalache* wrote to John Stuart, Superintendent of Indian Affairs in the Southern District, on March 1, 1768. Sinnot told about an Indian who had been near the mouth of the Caloosahatchee River observing three fishing vessels in the area.[28] Men from one of the vessels called to him in the Creek tongue, inviting him to come aboard and have a smoke. In a second letter dated the next day, Sinnot informed Stuart that a number of Lower Creeks had gone to Havana and returned home with a rich assortment of Spanish clothes.[29] According to the information Sinnot received, many Indians liked such visits so much that they considered offering land on the Apalachicola to the Spaniards so they would live near the Indian villages.

The information that the Creeks had offered land to the Spanish alarmed English authorities, and countermeasures were planned. Major General Thomas Gage, commander in chief of British troops in North America, wrote to Wills Hill, earl of Hillsborough, Secretary of State for the Colonies, on September 7, 1768, that John Stuart, Superintendent of Indian Affairs for the Southern District, would keep a close watch on the Creeks regarding their contacts with Havana and the offer of land on the Apalachicola River.[30] Gage, repeating the order to Stuart in a letter dated October 12, 1768, stressed that he was commanded by the king to "pay the strictest attention to the correspondence between the Creek Indians and the Spaniards at the Havannah and particularly relative to the tract of land (it is reported) that those Indians offered the Spaniards on the River Appalachie."[31] Finally, Gage informed Hillsborough on January 7, 1769, that John Stuart had told him that the Spaniards were "tampering with the Creek Indians but without success." In fact, the cession of land by the Creeks never took place.[32]

Visits of the Creeks to Havana in 1769, alarmed the British again. It was reported by Gage that six Creeks had returned from a trip to Cuba loaded with valuable presents.[33] The report that both the Upper and Lower Creeks had planned a meeting with the Spaniards at the mouth of the Apalachicola River was circulated by the British. John Stuart promised to have his informants check into the meeting and determine if any threat to the British position might occur.

By 1769, the British were obtaining some excellent information concerning the fishing operations from a top-flight observer, Bernard Romans, and by 1774, from the equally astute William Bartram. While surveying the panhandle coastline during the winter of 1769-70, Romans anchored near a Spanish fishing vessel and observed the number of the crew, their operations, and the size of their catch. In 1774, William Bartram, visiting the Indian villages on the Gulf Coast, talked to Indians who had been to

Cuba. From the observation of these men, and other evidence, British authorities learned that they had little to fear from the fishing operations.[34]

Great Britain did not, in any case, have the manpower or facilities to supervise the trade between Cuba and Florida. In 1763, St. Augustine had been selected as a principal military post in Florida, with a regiment of infantry and a company of artillery stationed there, but due to a high absentee rate, only two hundred men were available for the infantry regiment. Small detachments were maintained at such outposts as Apalache, but because of sickness and shortages of food and water, Apalache was abandoned in 1769.[35] Since Pensacola lacked adequate barracks, was more remote from New York, and had a record of strife between civil and military authorities, it was by-passed in favor of St. Augustine. Although St. Augustine had a poor harbor and inadequate barracks for even one regiment, it was designated as the principal station in the Southern Military District. Consequently there were no available military units in the western sector to police the Spaniards who went ashore from the fishing fleets. Yet, when a dispute concerning the Falkland Islands arose between Spain and England in 1770, the British rushed one thousand men to Pensacola and made plans to seize New Orleans in two drives — one coming down the Mississippi and the other from Pensacola.[36]

James Grant, Governor of East Florida, finally achieved a practical decision concerning the Spanish fishermen. Realizing that if these fishermen were prevented from traveling back and forth between Cuba and Florida it would be more difficult for the British to trade illegally with Cuba, he gave his approval to the continuance of the fishing *ranchos*.[37] When the English had occupied Havana in 1762, they had traded with the city's merchants, and after the peace treaty they continued to trade in an illegal fashion with Cuba and other Spanish colonies. Pensacola had been acquired so that it might become a rival to Jamaica as a source of contraband for Spanish-American ports, and ships from there were soon seen in New Orleans, Vera Cruz, and Central American harbors. Other British traders were smuggling goods into the Texas coastline between the Sabine and Río Grande Rivers and trading with the Indians despite Spanish patrols.[38]

In 1774, possible trouble developed with the Lower Creeks.

Superintendent Stuart was informed that supplies of ammunition were being furnished to the Creeks by the Spanish at the mouth of the Peace River in Charlotte Harbor. In addition, Alligator and Escootehabe, two Creek leaders, were given military commissions by the Spaniards. Besides their dealings with the Creeks, the Spaniards were alleged to be visiting the Choctaws. Actually, Charlotte Harbor, three hundred miles distant from the Creek towns, would have been a poor choice of ports to land ammunition for the Creeks, and this story cannot be verified.[39]

The Cuban fishing *ranchos* survived the English occupation of Florida but slowly shifted operations to a point south of Tampa Bay and centered at Charlotte Harbor. In 1824, there were as many as one hundred and thirty men living at four *ranchos* there. The Second Seminole War (1835-42) would bring an end to the *ranchos*, however, because the Americans believed the Cubans supplied the Indians with guns.[40]

---

*Dana Professor of History, University of Tampa, Tampa, Florida.

[1] Frances Gardiner Davenport and Charles Oscar Paullin, eds., *European Treaties Bearing on the History of the United States and its Dependencies* (Washington, 1917-1937), 4:96.

[2] Verner W. Crane, ed., "Hints Relative to the Division and Government of the Conquered and Newly Acquired Countries in America," *Mississippi Valley Historical Review* 8 (1922): 367-73; C.O. 5/323, fol. 16.

[3] Robert L. Gold, *Borderland Empires in Transition: The Triple-Nation Transfer of Florida* (Carbondale, 1969), 66-117; Wilbur M. Siebert, "How the Spaniards Evacuated Pensacola in 1763," *Florida Historical Quarterly* 10 (1931): 1-23; Siebert, "The Departure of the Spaniards and Other Groups from East Florida, 1763," *Florida Historical Quarterly* 19 (1940): 145-54.

[4] J. Leitch Wright, Jr., *Anglo-Spanish Rivalry in North America* (Athens, 1971), 108-109.

[5] Gold, *Borderland*, 23-26; Charles W. Arnade "Florida Keys: English or Spanish in 1763," *Tequesta* 15 (1955): 41-53.

[6] William Roberts, *An Account of the First Discovery and Natural History of Florida*, intro. Robert L. Gold, Bicentennial Floridiana Facsimile Series (Gainesville, 1976), xvi-xvii.

[7] Ibid., 15-18.

[8] Clinton N. Howard, *The British Development of West Florida 1763-1769* (Berkeley and Los Angeles, 1947), 18.

[8] Clarence W. Alvord, "The Genesis of the Proclamation of 1763," *Michigan Pioneer and Historical Collections* 36 (1908): 20-52.

[10] Robert R. Rea, "British West Florida: Stepchild of Diplomacy," *Eighteenth-Century Florida and its Borderlands*, ed. Samuel Proctor (Gainesville, 1975), 81.

[11] P. Lee Phillips, *Notes on the Life and Works of Bernard Romans*, intro. John Ware, Bicentennial Floridiana Facsimile Series (Gainesville, 1975), 124-25.

[12] Jerald T. Milanich and Charles H. Fairbanks, *Florida Archaeology* (New York, 1980), 256.

[13] John R. Swanton, *Early History of the Creek Indians and their Neighbors*, Bureau of American Ethnology Bulletin 73 (Washington, 1922), 192-225.

[14] Jack D. L. Holmes, "Two Spanish Expeditions to Southwest Florida, 1783-1793," *Tequesta* 25 (1965): 102; *Narrative of a Voyage to the Spanish Main*, intro. John W. Griffin, Bicentennial Floridiana Facsimile Series (Gainesville, 1978), 164.

[15] James W. Covington, "Trade Relations Between Southwestern Florida and Cuba, 1600-1840," *Florida Historical Quarterly* 38 (1959): 114-28.

[16] Milanich and Fairbanks, *Florida Archaeology*, 236.

[17] Covington, "Trade Relations," 117.

[18] James G. Forbes, *Sketches: Historical and Topographical of the Floridas*, intro. James W. Covington, Floridiana Facsimile and Reprint Series (Gainesville, 1964), 118.

[19] Bernard Romans, *A Concise Natural History of East and West Florida* (New York, 1775), 185.

[20] Ibid., 186.

[21] Thelma Peters, ed., "William Adee Whitehead's Reminiscences of Key West," *Tequesta* 25 (1965): 38.

[22] Petitioners to Joel Poinsett, Secretary of War, in "A Petition from some Latin-American Fishermen; 1838," James W. Covington, ed., *Tequesta* 14 (1954): 61-65.

[23] John Lee Williams, *The Territory of Florida*, intro. Herbert J. Doherty, Floridiana Fascimile and Reprint Series (Gainesville, 1962), 26.

[24] Phillips, *Romans*, 124-25.

[25] Augustus Steele to General William Thompson, Jan. 10, 1835, Florida Seminoles, 1835, Records of the Bureau of Indian Affairs, National Archives, Washington, D. C.

[26] Francis Harper, ed., *Travels of William Bartram* (New Haven, 1958), 143.

[27] George Humphreys to John C. Calhoun, March 2, 1825, Florida Seminoles, Records of the Bureau of Indian Affairs.

[28] Sinnot to Stuart, March 1, 1768, Mark F. Boyd, "From a Remote Frontier: Letters and Documents Pertaining to San Marcos de Apalache, 1763-1769, during the British Occupation of Florida," *Florida Historical Quarterly* 19 (1941): 136.

[29] Sinnot to Stuart, March 2, 1768, ibid., 136-37.

[30] Gage to Hillsborough, Sept. 7, 1768, Clarence E. Carter, ed., *The Correspondence of General Thomas Gage with the Secretaries of State 1763-1775* (New York, 1969), I: 191-92.

[31] Gage to Stuart, Oct. 12, 1768, Gage Papers, American Series, vol. 81, William L. Clements Library, Ann Arbor, Michigan.

[32] Gage to Hillsborough, Jan. 7, 1769, *Correspondence*, I: 214.

[33] Gage to Hillsborough, Sept. 9, 1769, ibid., 235.

[34] Helen Hornbeck Tanner, "Pipesmoke and Muskets: Florida Indian Intrigues of the Revolutionary Era," *Eighteenth-Century Florida and its Borderlands*, 19.

[35] Charles Loch Mowat, *East Florida as a British Province, 1763-1784* (Berkeley, 1943), 26-27.

[36] Wright, *Anglo-Spanish Rivalry*, 118.

[37] Gage to Hillsborough, July 7, 1770, *Correspondence*, I: 262.

[38] Wright, *Anglo-Spanish Rivalry*, 118-19.

[39] Stuart to Gage, May 12, 1774, enclosing Stuart to Haldimand, May 13, 1774, Gage Papers, vol. 119.

[40] *Pensacola Gazette*, March 12, June 25, 1836.

ANGLO—SPANISH COMMERCE IN NEW ORLEANS DURING THE AMERICAN REVOLUTIONARY ERA

ROBIN F. A. FABEL*

A frustration of studying the history of the Gulf Coast in the eighteenth century is that the available evidence is fragmentary. The paucity of records left by British merchants trading in New Orleans during the Spanish period of Louisiana history probably explains why they have not received particular attention; otherwise their neglect is surprising because they were extremely important. John G. Clark, the historian of the economy of New Orleans in the eighteenth century, has asserted that from 1764 to 1768 "the English dominated the economic life of the colony." In 1769, Governor Alejandro O'Reilly wrote that nine-tenths of the profits of Louisiana trade found their way into British pockets. In 1776, Francisco Bouligny estimated that they pocketed an even higher percentage. Recently, Gilbert Din judged that foreigners, of whom the British were the most significant, cornered three-quarters of the Louisiana trade.[1] Clearly the British merchants at New Orleans deserve attention even if war, expulsions, and fires have destroyed most of their account books. Fortunately they were a litigious group, and surviving court records throw additional light on their activities, as does governmental correspondence.

Most of the traders were Scots, not English; others had Welsh and Irish names. The prefix "Anglo" is here used to mean any subject of King George III, including some who might have preferred to be called American. In fact, these traders were not chauvinists. In general they were less interested in flags than in Spanish milled dollars, livres, and golden guineas, though usually, despite their preference for coin, they had to accept goods in kind or promissory notes. To stay in business several changed their patriotic allegiance more than once.

Many of them had a connection with the British colony of West Florida. It was natural; even if a British trader's headquarters was in New Orleans, he was eligible, gratis but for legal fees, for land in the British province where he could double as a planter, or, alternatively, improve his commerce through possession of a waterside lot on the English side of the Mississippi.

Even if he owned no land in Florida, there was good reason to develop contacts with the trading houses of Pensacola and Mobile because, in many respects, the economies of Louisiana and West Florida were complementary while the British province had access to the variegated products of the British imperial system.

Britain's acquisition of the Floridas, in 1763, raised extravagant hopes among entrepreneurs who supposed that much of the silver of Mexico could be funneled into the British accounts. Apart from soldiers to garrison them, merchants out to make a quick *peso* rather than genuine settlers first peopled Pensacola and Mobile. Their hopes were not realized. Although British vessels were barred from Spanish harbors, the chief reason for this disappointment was the zeal of the British navy: thanks to new regulations, catching Spanish smugglers was a very profitable pursuit. By February, 1765, it was estimated that some two hundred immigrants to West Florida had left because their ambitions on the Spanish trade had been thwarted. Among them was Robert Law, the Pensacola factor for the famous New York house of Beekman.[2]

If Mérida, Campeche and Vera Cruz were cut off, New Orleans was not, since a clause in the peace treaty of 1763 guaranteed the right of sailing the Mississippi to Britons. Initially, English visitors to New Orleans bought more than they sold, for until October, 1764, West Florida was under a military governor who was ordered to send an expedition to the Mississippi. It was outfitted at a cost of some thousands of pounds by two New Orleans firms, Logan, Terry and Company, and by Isaac Monsanto, a Jew who shortly afterwards became a resident of British West Florida.[3]

At the time, buying was easier than selling in Louisiana because, as its French governor lamented, "There is no longer any money, . . . the debtors no longer pay."[4] Aubry exaggerated. Even as he wrote, Charles Strachan, a Scotish entrepreneur from Mobile, was in New Orleans selling $1,000 worth of textiles, glassware and gunpowder.[5] Traders like Strachan could hoodwink the British authorities and escape payment of duties by shipping goods to Tangipaho on the northern shore of Lake Pontchartrain, which was British territory, and then covertly re-exporting them to New Orleans via Bayou St. John.[6] Even though trade with New Orleans from West Florida was possible, it remained initially stagnant. Antonio de Ulloa, the first Spanish governor of

New Orleans, demanded that British vessels obtain permits at the Balize before proceeding up the Mississippi. Ships' masters had to produce invoices of all cargo; Spanish authorities decided the prices at which it could be sold at New Orleans. It was of no avail to avoid the Balize by using the alternative lake route: without a permit nothing might be sold in New Orleans.[7]

English traders were also discouraged by the yellow fever and fluxes which carried off many of the inhabitants of New Orleans in 1766, and the report, ill-founded though it probably was, that all French traders were emigrating from New Orleans to Hispaniola, although such an exodus undoubtedly took place seven years later.[8]

Complaints continued in 1767, of Ulloa's discouraging British traders. He took to informing his fellow governors of Vera Cruz, Campeche, and Cuba of British vessels frequenting Pensacola so that they might better control attempts at illegal trade. Nevertheless, growing anti-Spanish resentment among the French inhabitants of New Orleans distracted the few Spanish officials from trade regulation, and in December, 1767, it was reported that West Florida merchants were disposing at great advantage large quantities of goods there.[9]

Even New York traders found it worth their while to send cargoes to the port during the period of transition from French to Spanish rule, particularly the years 1766 through 1768. A traveler who left New Orleans on June 11, 1768, reported that Captain John Walker's brig *York* was there, while the brig *Africa*, which was owned and captained by William Moore, was toiling its way upriver towards the city. Both vessels had made repeated visits to New Orleans. Other vessels from New York at that period were the *Belle Savage* and the *Little Bob*, both mastered by Robert Harris, and Captain John Pell's brig *William*.[10]

New York flour was in constant demand in the region and fetched a high price. In 1764, when the British moved onto the Gulf Coast and some French moved out, Jean-Baptiste Grevembert had sold Horn Island to a consortium of British merchants for 625 quarters of flour.[11] Flour was the chief cargo of the *Africa*, the New York vessel which most frequently visited New Orleans in the late 1760s. Her owner, William Moore, first took her there in June, 1766, visited again later in the year, and, in 1767, made three voyages to New Orleans. He filled large orders for the

Spanish authorities, but they were slow to pay. Moore became impatient. Repeatedly he asked to go to Cuba to recover what was owed from Ulloa's superior, Don Antonio Bucarelli. With permission, he finally sailed on June 23, 1768.[12] As passenger he took with him a messenger from Ulloa, Lieutenant Andrés de Balderrama, who prevailed on the Cuban governor to send some chests of coin to Ulloa in *La Hermosa Limeña*. Even so, by August 2, 1768, a year after Moore had delivered the bulk of his flour to New Orleans, he had still been paid only one-third of the $25,000 debt.[13]

Perhaps the combination of late and paltry payment overstrained his finances, for when next encountered, Moore was captain of a different vessel, and the *Africa* had changed hands. In 1769, Moore was captain but not owner of a brigantine of 140 tons, the *St. Peter*, and by 1771, the *Africa* was the property of Thomas and Phillips Comyn, the first of whom was a London merchant.[14] Thereafter, the *Africa* continued to frequent New Orleans but from the British capital rather than New York.

Another common visitor to New Orleans after 1764 was Captain Thomas Hammond whose sloop, the *Live Oak* made voyages to the Mississippi from various American ports, including Savannah, New York, and Pensacola where, in 1768, he unloaded an unusual New Orleans export, mules, probably for the Pensacola merchant, John Stephenson, who ordered 120 mules from Natchitoches through his agent in New Orleans, John Fitzpatrick.[15]

Ulloa could not enforce Spain's commercial policy, although he promulgated regulations. New trade rules for Louisiana were formulated in Spain in March, 1768. Nine ports of Old Spain were opened to imports from Louisiana. Duties on them would be a low 4%. From these nine, goods might be exported to Louisiana duty-free, but only Spanish ships were allowed to carry them, and thenceforth no trade was allowed directly between Louisiana and any French ports. This royal edict failed to cure Louisiana's economic woes. There was almost no market for Louisiana products in Spain, while the European goods which Louisianans preferred were made in countries other than Spain — French wine for example — and importing them by way of Spain made them inordinately expensive.

The regulations matched the needs of Spanish Louisiana as badly as did contemporary British regulations the needs of West

Florida; from 1764, every one of West Florida's natural exports — indigo, hides, skins, lumber, pearl ash, and potash — was theoretically barred from foreign, that is, the most promising, markets.[16] The difference between the provinces was that West Florida had governors who neglected trade rules and encouraged smuggling, while the French merchants of New Orleans had a foreign governor who allowed smuggling only with reluctance and had to publish even more repugnant trade regulations than the British colonists had to endure. The Spanish edict was a dead letter. It turned simmering resentment into blatant defiance, and Ulloa was expelled from his province on October 29, 1768.[17] Retribution soon followed.

The arrival of a military governor, Alejandro O'Reilly, in August, 1769, ended both rebellion in Louisiana and tolerance for English trade. Unlike his predecessor, the general had enough soldiers to enforce Spanish trade regulations. He seemed shocked at British commercial dominance. "I can safely assert that they pocketed nine-tenths of the money spent here," he reported. "I drove off all the English traders and the other individuals of that Nation whom I found in this town, and I shall admit none of their vessels."[18] Since uncompromising exclusion was the official policy of Spain, it was natural that a governor should write in this vein to his superiors, but O'Reilly is more likely to have sincerely intended rigidity than other governors of Louisiana who had to live longer with the economic facts of life in the province.

In the end, only seventeen merchants of all nationalities were ejected from New Orleans by O'Reilly.[19] All the same, September, 1769, was a very bad month for English trade with Louisiana because not only were English residents affected but also the many English traders living elsewhere who did business in the Spanish town through agents. One of them was John Fitzpatrick, and the entries in his letter book, from September 1 until he was compelled to leave on O'Reilly's orders on September 22, are instructive.

Among other things they show what kinds of goods were being supplied by English merchants at Mobile, Pensacola, the Illinois country, and Natchez to New Orleans at that time. They included flour, slaves, strouds, blankets, checked cloth, and bear oil. They show too what goods were in demand at the Illinois, from which a correspondent had floated goods down on a bateau. Fitzpatrick was asked to sell the vessel, remitting the proceeds in taffia and barrels of pitch. Payment in kind was normal. In West Florida skins were more welcome than pitch, which was a product of that colony; but also acceptable were paper debits on account with respected British firms or the government. These letters also demonstrate that O'Reilly's exclusion edict was not as comprehensive as his official report would suggest. Any Britons who were married to Louisianans or who were planters were exempt.

The British firms or individuals whose affairs Fitzpatrick had to wind up in a matter of days numbered eleven. They included McGillivray and Struthers at Mobile; John Ritson, Valens Comyn, John Falconer, and James Amoss, all at Pensacola; Henry Le Fleur, Alexander McIntosh, Robert Barrow and John Bradley at Natchez; and the Illinois branch of the Philadelphia firm of Baynton, Wharton and Morgan. Britons with whom he did not correspond at this time but whom Fitzpatrick mentions and with whom he had dealings numbered another seven, including Evan Jones, Captain Thomas McMin, Charles Stuart, William Marshall, Sylvester Fanning, Hayton and Williams and Co., and John Gradinigo. There were other British merchants in New Orleans who had no dealings with Fitzpatrick, but his letters do confirm the existence of a great many Britons with a commercial stake in the city. By 1769, the scale of their dealings was paltry. The largest outstanding debt mentioned was for $254. The figures would probably have been much larger if a desperate shortage of specie had not throttled a great deal of potential trade. The advent of O'Reilly, presumably with a treasure chest, was not therefore seen as an unmitigated disaster by Fitzpatrick because, prior to the general's arrival, his Spanish debtors had been unable to meet their obligations, and he had lost potential customers because he was compelled to refuse Spanish paper.

He even saw commercial opportunity in the expulsion of all British merchants from New Orleans, since it would increase a demand for goods which Fitzpatrick planned to satisfy. He would operate from the English side of the Mississippi with a stock of $3,000 worth of textiles, mostly cottons. In exchange he was prepared to take items of local produce, deerskins, indigo, tobacco, rice, and raw cotton, but not lumber products, presumably because they posed problems of transportation.[20]

Fitzpatrick was not alone in viewing O'Reilly's arrival optimistically. *The South Carolina and American General Gazette* of September 13, 1769, described it as "good news for West Floridians" because of the half-million dollars that he reputedly brought with him. Another newspaper report contained the opinion that it would be much more beneficial for the West Floridians to have Spanish neighbors than French.[21] Lax Spanish enforcement of their commercial regulations was taken for granted, and many adventurers with merchandise of different kinds at once left Pensacola for New Orleans, hoping to exchange it for dollars. They were lucky because, by October 10, only a few days after the British merchants had been expelled, it was reported from Pensacola that O'Reilly had relaxed his initially rigid exclusion of British goods.[22]

Three months after arrival, O'Reilly handed over the governorship of Louisiana to Colonel Luis de Unzaga who knew well that, though some trade with the English was desirable, the general effect of the large and growing British presence in the region was injurious to Louisiana's economy. Effective British control of the pine forests on the northern shore of Lake Pontchartrain barred Louisianans from the manufacture of pitch and tar. Energetic British hunters reduced the amount of deerskins and furs locally available, while the Indians and habitants of Louisiana usually sold their furs to the ubiquitous British traders. Legal Louisiana exports were thus reduced to indigo, lumber and, in some years, rice, and the governor railed against the "fraud and malversion" of the British traders.[23]

Spaniards elsewhere also had desperate needs which only the British could supply. In August, 1770, two flour-laden English brigantines arrived in the Mississippi. Unzaga diverted their captains to Campeche, on the Yucatan Peninsula, where the colonists were starving. Although Unzaga explained to his superiors that had he done otherwise, the flour would have been covertly sold elsewhere in Louisiana, he was reprimanded. The governor was also frustrated that British vessels had a perfect legal right to sail under his very nose at New Orleans on the pretext that they were going to English Manchac and Natchez, when he knew full well that they intended to dispose of their cargoes to Spanish subjects. Usually he confined himself to warning them against illegal trade.[24]

These warnings may have deterred some merchants from planning voyages since the severe penalties for smuggling were publicized as far away as New York and Rhode Island. Importers of cotton cloth into Louisiana, for instance, were liable not merely to have their cargoes confiscated, but also to pay a fine of twenty bits (over two dollars) for every yard of illegal textile.[25] Despite all threats British trade with Louisiana intensified.

Winking at breaches of the law for a time and then abruptly enforcing it was an infuriating characteristic of contemporary British customs officials in this era. Unzaga did the same. A sufferer was the Rhode Islander John Nash who, with Christopher Whipple, owned a sloop, *The Two Pollies*, which plied between New England and New Orleans. On October 1, 1773, the sloop began such a voyage under Ephraim Carpenter, probably one of a Newport family which settled in West Florida.[26] In November, Nash and Whipple also left Rhode Island, in the sloop *Hope*, for the Mississippi where they found *The Two Pollies* anchored about six miles below New Orleans. To her Nash transferred merchandise from the *Hope*. Then he took *The Two Pollies* past the Spanish city and anchored two leagues above it. The Spaniards doubted Nash's story that his cargo would be sold only at the British settlements upriver. While at anchor on February 17, 1774, a Spanish sergeant and a corporal boarded *The Two Pollies* and asked to buy some codfish for their men in New Orleans. The sergeant borrowed a boat to carry it back to the town. With him Nash sent a sailor, William Proud, who was to bring back the craft but was seized in New Orleans and jailed. When Nash went to New Orleans to protest, the governor would not see him. On February 20, Spanish troops with drawn swords and fixed bayonets tried to board *The Two Pollies*, allegedly on the governor's orders — which Nash thought illegal, since she was moored three thousand feet from the shore. Nevertheless, he let her be taken to New Orleans to be stripped of rigging and cargo which, with confiscated cash amounting to $5,760, were deposited in the royal warehouse. On March 4, the cargo was auctioned for $1622.5 *ryals*, and on March 7, the sloop fetched $482. Meanwhile Nash, Carpenter, his mate Benjamin Pilcher, and crewman William Proud were all in jail.

On May 2, Nash was charged with illegally introducing fish for sale in New Orleans. In reply he petitioned Governor Unzaga for his release and succeeded, perhaps because of strong support from Governor Chester of West Florida, on May 16, 1774. On June 17, Unzaga revoked the proceedings against Nash, except those that concerned fish, and refunded $3,535.4 ½ ryals. The Englishmen were released only after four and a half months in confinement, and Nash estimated his total loss at $9,127.1 ½ ryals, of which he received scarcely a third in compensation. After vainly asking Unzaga for a fairer settlement, he sent complaints to Chester for transmission to Lord Dartmouth, the plantations secretary in Britain.[27]

This case shows Unzaga as perhaps vindictive and certainly negligent in supervising subordinates. Sergeant Hildago and his corporal were both dismissed from the Spanish service for their part in buying English fish. The case also suggests a regular commerce between Spanish Louisiana and Rhode Island and reveals the kind of cargo for which a market existed up the Mississippi: an amazing variety of textiles, many coarse and cheap, and all from Europe, mostly from England. Such would certainly have been the origin of the beaver hats which were part of Nash's cargo, since he would scarcely have declared in a memorial to the British government items that could not legally be exported from the colonies. The money confiscated from *The Two Pollies* was enough to suggest that Nash had probably engaged in some trading before her seizure, perhaps, as Unzaga suspected, with the "country people" of Louisiana.[28] *The Two Pollies* episode illustrates the misfortunes attending entanglement with the Spanish authorities. If an indignant press report is to be believed it was not an isolated instance of Unzaga's rigor: at nearly the same time, dry goods to the value of $12,000 belonging to a merchant named Basset had also been seized in New Orleans.[29] Nash was not so disenchanted by his treatment as to leave the Mississippi forever. By February, 1778, he was an inhabitant at Manchac.[30]

Unzaga's temporary strictness did not deter English traders. Shipping lists for the year 1774 show that well over a dozen voyages took place to the river from mainland colonial ports.[31] Nor did the advent of revolution in 1775, end traffic with the Mississippi, although it introduced several new factors into the trade.

For example, from its founding, guns, ammunition, and powder had been exported from West Florida to the Mississippi. For defense and hunting they were, for white settlers and Indians alike, a necessity of life. That imaginative man, George Johnstone, the province's first governor, had sought without success to stimulate local production of gunpowder.[32] When the quarrel between Britain and her colonies descended into violence, George III curbed the flow of munitions to North America, and provincial governors intervened in what previously had been purely private transactions. In November, the ship *Ann,* William Reid master, arrived from London at Pensacola. The West Florida council ordered that its cargo of 9,000 pounds of powder, 925 Indian guns, and a quantity of bullets ordered by James Mather, an English merchant residing in New Orleans, should be unloaded. Only a thousand pounds of the powder might be sent by way of the lakes and the Iberville, where the risk of rebel interception was slight, to British Manchac where its sale would be supervised by the deputy commissioner for Indian affairs, John Thomas.[33] Similar treatment was accorded the brig *Norton* which, two months later, arrived from London with powder and ball. Captain William Pickles asked for and was denied permission to carry it directly to Manchac, a sensible strictness in the light of Pickles's future pro-American activities.

Unquestionably, the Continental Congress was keen to obtain military supplies from New Orleans. In 1776, a large barge containing nineteen men and a boy left Fort Pitt on the Ohio, sailed into the Mississippi, and arrived, on August 1, at Walnut Hills (Vicksburg) in the northwest corner of West Florida where they raised the American flag. Part of the purpose of Captain George Gibson, who led this expedition, was to carry dispatches from Congress to Governor Unzaga and to his royal master, but also he wanted to trade his cargo (presumably of skins) for gunpowder. The success of this type of trade, about which Unzaga was initially cautious but which was subsequently fully approved, made the British authorities extremely apprehensive.[34] Competition for Spanish customers increased to the detriment of British and Spanish governments. It was implemented by Bernardo de Gálvez, who succeeded Unzaga as Governor of Louisiana on January 1, 1777. Exports to France and the French West Indies became legal on payment of a 5% export duty; direct imports from France were also permitted; thus there was no further need for the French to resort to subterfuges like purchasing vessels of British registry in order to practice commerce with Louisiana.[35] Now slaves could be sent from the French West Indies in payment for the products of the Spanish province. John Fitzpatrick of Manchac saw a gloomy future for British rivals to the French traders. "They certainly undersell us and their goods are better calculated for this province," he wrote.[36]

Nevertheless there was no hint that Spanish regulations against Englishmen trading with Louisianans would be suddenly and vigorously enforced. One writer noted that successive governors had "for years past" connived, in return for a small share of the profits, at such activity.[37] In fact, the word on the river was that Gálvez was even more liberal towards English traders than his predecessors. "The new governor," wrote Fitzpatrick in February, "allows the English liberty to trade or hunt up any of the rivers on the Spanish side they please; further — all the English merchants that kept their stores on board the vessels have now their shops in town."[38] The sense of security into which they had been lulled must have been profound indeed if they had abandoned the sensible practice of maintaining their floating warehouses in favor of buildings in New Orleans — but disillusion was soon to follow.

Governor Gálvez's motives for reversing this tolerant policy included the new instructions opening his colony to French traders and excluding the British. Gálvez also discovered that Louisianans were ready to inform against Britons, and he was piqued at a new British insistence on seizing small Spanish vessels which infringed British trade regulations on Lake Pontchartrain.[39] Lieutenant George Burdon had been legally correct but perhaps a little over-officious in seizing, early in April, 1777, two schooners going from Bayou St. John to the Pearl River. They were smuggling wine and tobacco; one of them had 160 "sticks" or "carrots" of tobacco — something less than three-quarters of a ton.[40] The schooners presumably intended to load tar or staves for the return voyage.

There were, however, two additional factors to be considered. One was economic — the draining effect on the Louisiana economy of the one-sided trading with the British. Louisianans sold very little to the Floridians and bought much from them. Figures are difficult to compile, but one estimate is that the habitants had an annual import bill of $700,000.[41] Exports, according to Francisco Bouligny, were smaller, $100,000 worth of lumber, $180,000 of indigo, and $200,000 of peltries; with the addition of such less important extras as mules and bear oil, a total of perhaps half a million dollars. In 1776, Bouligny estimated that, apart from $15,000 going to the Spanish and a smaller amount to the French, the whole of this trade swelled

British accounts.[42]

The other factor was political—the effect of the Revolution. New Orleans, being inhabited by both loyalists and rebels, was increasingly disturbed by rival English-speaking partisans. There were repeated brawls in the taverns and inns. Spanish citizens complained that there was "no time of the night or day in which they were not alarmed with screams, blows and cuffs besides private challenges." Gálvez decided that he could not permit "this petty civil war" in the heart of his capital. One center of strife was the boarding house of Hannah Ogilby where loyalists only were welcome. Her out-spoken condemnation of rebel politics eventually, according to her analysis, caused confiscation of her property and twenty-four days imprisonment in a Spanish jail; finally Hannah fled to Pensacola with her small daughter.[43] Political consideration apart, the English residents of New Orleans were of low caliber—"vagabonds and bankrupts," wrote Gálvez, who offered as proof that the British prisoners in New Orleans jail outnumbered Louisianans by two to one. All of them were guilty of crimes against society. Transient Englishmen behaved no better than residents. From their vessels they ran amok among the plantations of Louisiana, taking off slaves, killing cattle, and shooting at plantation owners, before retiring to the sanctuary of their boats on the neutral waters of the Mississippi.[44] Naturally Gálvez did not mention American influence on his decision, but he was not the first governor of New Orleans to favor American patriots.

In 1776, Unzaga had shown partiality to George Gibson, who had successfully dispatched a bateau up the Mississippi bearing the Spanish flag, a Spanish pass, and 8,600 pounds of gunpowder which eventually reached the Ohio for use by revolutionary troops in the spring of 1777. Gibson himself had sailed under Spanish colors for Philadelphia and delivered two tons of powder to the firm of Willing and Morris.[45] These invaluable cargoes were obtained from Oliver Pollock, the American agent at New Orleans who, in his turn, had bought them from Unzaga who justified disposal of these Spanish government stores as old and partly spoiled.[46] Gálvez's partiality for Americans was as pronounced as Unzaga's—naturally so since their king repeatedly ordered him to favor them.[47] In April, 1777, a Spanish vessel at New Orleans was allowed to fly at her masthead "a flag in which was a snake and a hand grasping thirteen arrows and the field divided into thirteen stripes of different colours."[48] The corollary to being pro-American was hostility to Britons. On April 17, Gálvez ordered the seizure of all British vessels between the Balize and Manchac and, on the next day, commanded all English merchants to quit his province within fifteen days.

At that time there were fifteen vessels on the river. Two escaped. The Glasgow brig *Jesse* was under sail and could not be stopped; another vessel bound for Britain was moored inaccessibly, weighed anchor, and also got away. Spanish boarding parties took eleven vessels with English-speaking crews. The masters of the two most valuable, Joseph Calvert and William Pickles of the brigs *Steady Friend* and *Norton*, turned out to be Americans. No doubt Gálvez would have left them alone, but distinctions were hard to make when the Americans carried English passports and flew English colors. Pickles claimed, moreover, that in return for services, Unzaga had given him leave to trade with Louisiana. Subsequently, both received their vessels back.[49] Another of the larger vessels seized was the brig *Hannah*, owned by Archibald Dalziel of Jamaica, which was in ballast on her way upriver. Another Jamaican, Captain Collart, owned the sloop *Peggy*. The remaining seven vessels—three brigs, two sloops, and two schooners—were owned by Britons living in New Orleans. Major sufferers were George and Robert Ross who lost the brigs *Hercules* and *Camilla*. John Waugh, a seafarer from London who had made the Mississippi the theater of his commercial operations, lost the brig *Berwick* and a very old and small sloop. John Campbell lost a small sloop worth only $150, and David Ross lost the equally wretched schooner *Sally*. The firm of Patrick Morgan and James Mather lost an ancient schooner in itself worth little but containing a valuable cargo of twenty-two slaves.[50]

All vessels taken were sold by the Spanish authorities at auction or, as the current phrase went, at vendue. The vessels themselves realized a total of $10,475 of which over half, $5,800, came from the two American vessels and was probably refunded in full. The cargoes, of which the most valuable was the boatload of slaves, fetched $43,000, and so the total proceeds of sale were $53,475. Perhaps less was offered than the confiscated property was worth. British authorities put the total loss at $70,000, but they may well have magnified the value of the seizure. Nevertheless it is probable that Gálvez was disappointed.[51] With different timing, he could have obtained much more, since several richly laden vessels had left for Britain shortly before his swoop.

Replying to inevitable protests, Gálvez cited the peace treaty of 1763. Free navigation, which the treaty allowed the British, did not include the right to trade with Spanish subjects. That the British were doing so was attested by the existence of cargoes and storehouses on the Louisiana shore and even bridges built between the shore and vessels permanently moored in the Mississippi. To the charge that he should have arrested only on proof and not upon mere suspicion of smuggling, the governor replied, "I think differently."[52]

He soon relaxed his ban on English residents, offering to let them return and trade, provided that they promised not to disturb the inhabitants of the province. Some firms preferred to stay in West Florida, to which their members had fled. Others, including David Ross and Company, John Campbell, the partnership of George and Robert Ross — all of whom had suffered in the spring of 1777 — accepted the offer. Traditionally, Spanish persecution of the English had been short-lived, and such was the pattern in 1777. As early as the summer, David Ross was involved in a court case following the arrival of his vessel *Polly* from London, and in the fall, George and Robert Ross employed Jean Lombard, the owner of *La Mamie*, to take a cargo of staves from New Orleans to Teste Island.[53]

Following the famous raid of the American, James Willing, on the Mississippi in the early months of 1778, a Royal Navy vessel, the *Sylph*, arrived at New Orleans to evacuate "His Majesty's loyal subjects residing in Louisiana." The response of fourteen of the loyal showed little gratitude for the opportunity, although those with nothing to lose, like Hannah Ogilby, took advantage of it. Trading concerns, wrote the fourteen who had much to lose, could not be wound down overnight, and slaveowners could not abandon their property. Rather than evacuation, dispatch of a hundred redcoats would be a better answer to their problem. Separately, Patrick Morgan and Robert Ross wrote to suggest that the *Sylph* should delay departure for five days so that she could escort to Pensacola their ship, the *Live Oak*, which was to be loaded with indigo and peltry for London.[54]

Since there was some reason to believe that indirectly (by way of the firm of Morgan and Mather and the Spanish Commissioner for Indian Affairs) James Willing had been resupplied with powder from the *Live Oak*, Governor Chester was furious. He suggested that the plantations secretary should ban all British exports to New Orleans.[55]

Gálvez's attitude toward the British was ambivalent. Some sufferers from Willing's depredations had successfully sought his protection; others, however, had been seized, even in New Orleans, put in irons, and placed aboard the *Rebecca*, which the Americans had captured and anchored off the town. Then, on April 15, 1778, Gálvez summoned all British residents of New Orleans, took out his watch, and told them that they had half an hour in which to decide whether or not they would take a stringent oath of loyalty to Spain. Not only would they have to swear neither directly nor indirectly to offend or conspire against the Spanish nation, but they would also have to promise to defend it and to reveal any information they might obtain of schemes against it. Those who refused would have until noon the following day to leave Spanish territory.[56]

Among those Britons who took the oath were Robert Ross, John Campbell, and, it seems, David Ross, who continued in business at New Orleans despite all misfortunes. Ross had suffered comparatively lightly from Gálvez in April, 1777, but endured a much more severe loss from Joseph Calvert, one of Willing's henchmen, in March, 1778. His schooner, *Dispatch*, under its master, James McCrugh, was valued at $3,550, much more than the two small vessels he had lost to Gálvez. Her cargo consisted of fifty picked slaves, each worth an average $300, and a hundred barrels of flour, each valued at $14. McCrugh brought the *Dispatch* from Kingston, Jamaica, and after a stop at Pensacola, was navigating her up the Mississippi when, four leagues above the southwest pass, he was intercepted and taken by Calvert. Ross estimated his loss at $21,450. Although Gálvez restored both vessel and cargo, it is doubtful whether either was in its pristine state.[57]

One must ask how such Britons could continue to make a living, for, quite apart from the fluctuating toleration accorded them by successive governors, business life in the town had become much more competitive. In 1777, the French had obtained the right to supply Louisiana with slaves, the province had been given permission to trade with Yucatan and Cuba, and the export duty had been reduced to 2%, making recourse to illicit British buyers less attractive.[58] Furthermore, Gálvez had let it be known that, in settling claims, creditors who were citizens of

New Orleans were to be satisfied before any foreigners.[59]

Nullifying these disadvantages were the presence of British Navy cruisers and privateers[60] waiting for French prey after 1778, and the continued Louisianan demand for textiles, the most important British export, which neither Yucatan nor Cuba could supply. Moreover, for economic and political reasons, hundreds of families had settled on the English shore of the Mississippi. In 1778, Natchez and Manchac acquired the right to send representatives to the West Florida Assembly. New Orleans was an entrepôt for these settlements: in general it was more cost-effective to offload at New Orleans than to press on hundreds of miles to the scattered upriver communities. Britons there supplied new settlers and supervised a new development in the export trade. Thanks to the Revolution, the British West Indies no longer received the shingles, staves, and lumber formerly imported from New England. Louisiana and the western areas of West Florida could make good the deficiency.

Robert Ross, a Scot with interests on both sides of the Mississippi, was one Briton who continued to thrive at New Orleans. He had come to West Florida soon after it became a British colony, acquired town lots in Pensacola, and paid tax on three slaves. He represented Pensacola in the provincial legislature in 1768 and 1771. Already he had interests on the Mississippi, in that he traded with John Fitzpatrick at Manchac and offered to supply Louisiana with slaves from Jamaica. He had at least one vessel, the sloop *Liberty*, but he would subsequently acquire several more. In 1772, he was granted title to 1,000 acres on the Mississippi below Natchez. On March 9 of that year he delegated the duty of collecting his debts to John Stephenson of Pensacola, probably because of his imminent departure for New Orleans.[61]

At New Orleans, Ross bought tobacco and indigo and sold dry goods and Jamaica rum. Probably he traded in slaves as well. He maintained his connection with Jamaica, acting on behalf of the Kingston merchants, Lewbridge Bright and David Duncomb. He seems to have prospered, although on occasion he was embarrassed. In 1777, he had property seized by the Spanish authorities because he owed the comparatively small sum of $450 to William Furlong, who had cheated his London partner and then sought to escape retribution through residence in Louisiana. Gálvez was sympathetic to complaints against Furlong and seized all his assets. In spite of the outbreak of the American Revolution, Ross also had dealings with the American trader, Joseph Calvert, who brought cargo for him from Jamaica to New Orleans. Ross survived the seizure of a brig by Gálvez in 1777, when his partner, John Campbell, lost a sloop. Both suffered grievously from the Willing raid.[62]

Ross and Campbell took the oath required by Gálvez for continued residence in New Orleans on April 15, 1778. Less than a month later, on May 14, they were arrested and charged with abusing their privileges by conspiring against the inhabitants of Louisiana. Ross denied misbehavior: obedience to the authorities of Spain, with whom the British were not then at war, did not preclude efforts to thwart American revolutionaries with whom they were. He had no qualms about warning the inhabitants of Natchez of an impending shipment of supplies to Americans at Fort Pitt under cover of a Spanish passport. For this, solely, according to Ross, on Willing's complaint, he and his partner were subjected to a "mock trial," imprisoned for fifty-five days, and fined $600, although certain proof of their guilt was lacking.

Their activities landed Ross, Campbell, and their messenger Alexander Grayden in dire trouble—especially Grayden, who was sent to a Cuban prison. At least, though, they attained their purpose of warning the British authorities that Oliver Pollock was sending supplies for the revolutionary cause up the Mississippi. To avoid embarrassment, Gálvez called back the supply vessel. For further discomfiture, Ross and Campbell had not only to give security against a case for $6,000 brought against them by Pollock and James Willing but also to accept permanent banishment from Louisiana. Ross re-established himself in Pensacola where he applied for land on the Pascagoula River to make up for the uncultivable grant which he had formerly been given near Natchez. Before the end of the Revolution he retired to London.[63]

Among British traders who maintained more amicable relations with the Spanish was William Walker, a refugee from St. Vincent who fled to the mainland from the economic blight which descended on the British West Indies with the advent of the Revolution. Initially Walker, who had been a councilor and substantial proprietor on St. Vincent, went to West Florida with some of his family and three dozen slaves. There, aided by a substantial crown grant of land, he began as a planter; but from 1777, he voyaged between New Orleans and the West Indies, selling coffee and sugar to the English settlers of the Natchez district through John Fitzpatrick. Walker retained his island property, being described in 1781, as "late of Pointe Coupée but now of St. Vincent." After the Revolution he was allowed to return to New Orleans to salvage what he could of his property there.[64]

Despite heightened tensions, normal, if illicit, trade between England and New Orleans seems to have endured up to the outbreak of hostilities between Britain and Spain on June 15, 1779. In May, the *Live Oak* arrived once more from London. Her captain, now Robert Nicholson, had a crew of twenty-seven. Eight of them jumped ship as soon as her cargo was unloaded. The rest demanded payment of their wages before loading a fresh cargo. Once paid, they loaded the ship and immediately disappeared into the town. The rumor was that they had signed for service on an American frigate. Nicholson was still recruiting a new crew a mere four days before war broke out.[65]

That it was possible for British traders to survive commercially in wartime New Orleans is shown by the story of the partnership of James Jones and his younger brother Evan which runs from 1765 into the nineteenth century and also demonstrates the economic interdependence of West Florida and Louisiana. The brothers originated in New England, but their strongest connection was with New York where lived a third brother, Dr. John Jones, who propagandized for them and possibly sent the goods which the brothers received from New York. They also had a connection with Jeremiah Terry of Logan, Terry & Co. of New Orleans. Perhaps it was Terry who persuaded the Jones brothers to immigrate to the Gulf Coast. On April 21, 1766, Evan was granted a lot on Bute Street on Pensacola's eastern side. In 1767 and 1768, they paid taxes on their slaves to the West Florida government and from it received, either separately or jointly, five hundred acres on the East River, four hundred acres on the East Lagoon, and some islands in the Middle River.[66]

Subsequently, following a noticeable general trend to move away from the coast to richer soil inland, James acquired twelve hundred acres on the Amite River in 1772, while Evan received six hundred acres on Thompson's Creek. There the climate and soil suited indigo which, thanks to a British government bounty of sixpence a pound, could be a most profitable crop: the brothers produced between fourteen and fifteen hundredweight in 1775. They augmented their plantation income by lending money at 8% to fellow West Floridians, by serving as agents for

Philadelphia and New York merchants, and by trading in New Orleans where both intermittently appeared. In 1769, Edward Mease encountered one of the Jones brothers when he visited the city. As merely occasional residents, they employed John Fitzpatrick to conduct their business, which consisted chiefly of selling flour and cottons and of buying cattle.[67]

Their chief activities lay in West Florida in the 1760s. Evan's career was not apparently hurt by a duel which he fought with an unpopular governor, while James gained the eminence of a seat on the provincial council and entertained Israel Putnam and others of the exploring committee of the New England Company of Military Adventurers in March, 1773. In the 1770s, when Louisiana acquired a new stability, the interests of the Jones brothers shifted westward. James ceased to attend West Florida council meetings after December, 1773; when it was learned that in 1778, he had taken the oath of loyalty to Spain, Governor Chester suspended him from office. James had moved permanently from Pensacola and acquired a house on Bienville Street, New Orleans.[68]

As the possibility of an Anglo-Spanish war heightened, the Jones brothers prepared for any eventuality. While James became a Spanish subject, Evan remained British, at least until the result of the Revolution was determined. When the British cause began to fail, the brothers started to sell their land in Florida: in 1778, Evan sold four hundred acres near Pensacola for $400, and in May, 1779, he and his brother sold a luckless infantry sergeant half of a Pensacola town lot for $150.[69]

Thereafter they prospered in Louisiana, in 1781 winning a suit against William Walker for $2,351. In 1787, James sold his New Orleans house for $2,235. Evan later served on the New Orleans City Council, became acting U.S. vice-consul in the city, and finally, in 1810, became the director of the New Orleans branch of the Bank of the United States.[70]

Another Briton who transferred his allegiance from the British to the Spanish king was Captain John Davis who immigrated to West Florida in February, 1778. He successfully applied for crown land in May, 1779, and earned a precarious living trading between Mobile and Jamaica. Very soon after he received his land grant he moved to New Orleans where he supplied British traders farther up the Mississippi with such goods as rum, French soap, linens, gunpowder, shot, and sugar. Once the war was over, he resumed his voyages to Jamaica.[71]

Yet another British merchant who continued to trade in New Orleans after the outbreak of the Anglo-Spanish war was Stephen Shakespear. Until October, 1775, he was a prosperous Philadelphia merchant. Fleeing from the upheaval of revolution, he arrived at West Florida in December, 1776, with four slaves. Intending permanent settlement, he sent for his wife and six children whom he had dispatched for safety to England. With misplaced optimism he established himself at the trading center at Manchac, thus placing himself directly in the path of the raider, James Willing, whose men seized a loaded bateau of Shakespear's at Manchac. Together with other property taken or damaged, Shakespear calculated his loss at $8.000. Subsequently he was granted thirteen hundred acres of land in West Florida, three hundred on family right and a further thousand as a bounty for loyalism. It was located on the Pascagoula River, far from Manchac but not far enough to escape Spanish conquest in 1779. In the aftermath he moved to New Orleans where he engaged in trade on a small scale.[72]

Of the goods supplied to British merchants in Louisiana, there seems to have been a consistent market for textiles and a fluctuating market for flour and rum, but selling slaves was probably the most profitable business. An aggrieved Francisco Bouligny described the process thus: "An Englishman in Jamaica hires a ship of 150 tons for 500 *pesos* at the most to come to the Mississippi loaded with goods which he obtains there on credit. With twenty or thirty negroes and with the sale of the goods, he repays the capital, pays for the freight and has money left over" even without selling all the blacks.[73]

Bouligny might well have been writing about Samuel Steer who prospered in Georgia until September, 1775, when he refused to join the revolutionary cause. Compelled to abandon his lands and debtors, he fled to Jamaica where he began to practice the type of commerce described by Bouligny. In 1777, he moved his base to West Florida, landing twenty blacks and all the equipment needed for a plantation. All fell to James Willing in 1778, but Steer soon resumed business. In November, 1778, at Kingston, he shipped a cargo for Pensacola, aboard the schooner *Eleanor*, consisting of rum, sugar, and claret. On the eve of the war with Spain in 1779, he was granted five hundred acres in West Florida. He continued to do business even after the Spanish conquest, apparently with residences both in New Orleans and Kingston. In 1781, John Davis brought suit against him for selling a consumptive black. In 1782, Steer sued Colonel Anthony Hutchins of the Natchez district for a considerable sum.[74]

Before the American Revolution, supplying slaves to Louisiana had generally been organized by London entrepreneurs with agents in West Florida. Surviving fragments of the account books of Edward Codrington show him financing regular slave shipments to the Mississippi in 1773 and 1774. Conflict of interest was clearly thought irrelevant, since one of his agents was Jacob Blackwell, His Majesty's Collector of Customs at the port of Mobile. Another was James Rumsey, a Louisiana settler who also acted for the Philadelphia firm of Baynton, Wharton and Morgan.[75] Codrington's blacks were shipped either from Charleston or Kingston and, from the sums for which insurance was paid, probably numbered no more than two dozen on each ship.

More important than Codrington was Thomas Comyn of Love Lane, Aldermanbury, London, who was in partnership with his brother Stephen and with Nicholas Donnithorne. Their agents at Pensacola were Thomas's sons, Valens Stephen Comyn and Phillips Comyn. Valens was the more active merchant. Although Phillips traded a little in textiles and rum, his main concern was his nineteen hundred acre plantation on the Comite River. His brother Valens had an establishment in Pensacola, where he owned five town lots which he used as collateral for loans from his father's firm, and a small plantation at the mouth of the East River. In the late 1760s he repeatedly represented Pensacola in the West Florida legislature; in the 1770s he was on the provincial council. Accepting local products, particularly indigo, in payment, he supplied slaves, textiles, and ironmongery to Louisianans through his agent at New Orleans who, until 1769, was John Fitzpatrick and thereafter one of the Jones brothers. Although the Comyn brothers seem to have discovered how to exploit the commercial potential of the New World, by 1781 both were dead.[76]

Others who trafficked in slaves included the firm of Morgan and Mather and David Ross who apparently ran his business separately from his brothers George and Robert. David Ross was one of many Britons who immigrated to West Florida, acquiring considerable interests and property there before deciding that it would be more profitable to move to the Mississippi. He received two town lots from the West Florida government in 1766, one in Pensacola and one in the abortive township of Campbelltown, in addition to three hundred acres on the East River. In 1768, he was given permission to occupy another Pensacola lot and, jointly with John Weir, applied for fourteen hundred acres on the Mississippi.[77] The desire to move westward was evident in this application, but it was not fulfilled because it was not until April 23, 1771, that he finally obtained a paltry three hundred acres on the Mississippi. Being unsatisfied, he applied, on February 4, 1772, for an additional fifteen hundred acres there, alleging that his family had increased, consisting by then of himself, two children, an indentured servant, and five blacks. The council allowed him to purchase merely another seven hundred acres.

At this time Ross was in partnership with a Pensacola merchant, Arthur Strother; they obtained their merchandise from the New York firm of Hugh and Alexander Wallace. The partnership did not always prosper. When the London merchant, Prideaux Selby, on whom Strother thought he could draw, protested bills of exchange used to pay the Wallaces, a court case resulted.[78]

In the 1770s Ross decided to abandon the Gulf Coast and the honor of intermittently representing Campbelltown in the West Florida assembly in favor of permanent residence on the Mississippi. He continued to work his plantation on the river through an overseer, and he bought houses in Baton Rouge; but his main base was New Orleans, where he bought large quantities of beaver, deerskins, and indigo. In return he supplied settlers up the Mississippi with an enormous variety of items, including textiles of course, shoes, saddles, soap, Chinese tea, crosscut saws, and cutlery. Not all of it was from English sources: coffee, French flour, brandy, cottonade, and some of his sugar was not. His foreign source of supply was Cape François on the French end of the island of Hispaniola. His business survived seizure of his vessels by Gálvez and Willing, and soon after the governor's expulsion order he was trading again in New Orleans. Toward the end of the Revolution, Ross evidently planned retirement to his native Britain, but by 1785, he was back in New Orleans, building up a trade connection with Jamaica.[78]

Another merchant who moved west when the gold of West Florida's promise turned to pinchbeck was Patrick Morgan. He arrived in Pensacola in 1764, and wasted little time in obtaining premises in the town, receiving lots there in February, 1765, and May, 1766. The highest official position he attained was, in 1768, deputy vendue-master at Pensacola. In 1769, he was granted two thousand acres on the Mobile River. During this period he was associated with another Pensacola merchant, David Hodge, and seems to have made small sums by selling goods on commission for others like the New York merchant, James Thompson. Like David Ross, he decided, probably for economic reasons, to shift his base to the Mississippi. On July 23, 1773, he ran up a debt of over £100 with the London firm of Walker and Dawson which had considerable interests in West Florida, and on the following day he borrowed $161 from a fellow Pensacolan, John Miller, whom he promised to pay within the month at New Orleans. He intended to return to Europe "to settle his affairs in England and Ireland," perhaps a euphemism for gathering capital, for he further intended, on his return via the West Indies, to buy twenty slaves, in consideration of which he asked for a grant of a thousand acres of land nine miles above Pointe Coupée, on the English side of the Mississippi.[80]

On his return he worked in partnership with James Mather, an established figure in New Orleans. Although he and Mather lost a vessel to Gálvez in 1777, the scale of their business seems to have been considerable. By April, 1778, Philip Barbour of the Natchez district owed them $10,984, and they were renting cargo room in their 110 ton vessel, the *Julie,* for voyages from New Orleans to the West Indies. In the same year, Morgan authorized the sale of lots he had bought in Pensacola through his former partner, Arthur Strother, a sign that he foresaw an end to commercial prospects there.[81]

James Mather was destined for a long Louisianan career. Originally a merchant in Bochin Lane in the City of London, he emigrated to New Orleans in the 1770s. Like other Louisianans of British citizenship, he acquired free land in Florida, in his case 408 acres on the Mississippi five miles above Bayou Manchac, but being firmly based in New Orleans he often represented absent British merchants in court there. He was an energetic executor of the estate of John Waugh, who died in 1777, bringing an action on his behalf against Oliver Pollock and defending the estate against the dubious claims of John Davis. Two years later he represented John Campbell; in 1793 he represented the estate of the Mobile merchant, William Struthers, who had gone insane, and in 1784 he spoke for Thomas Bowker, the Mississippi planter. That he and Morgan traded heavily in slaves is suggested by the seizure of their vessel with twenty-two slaves aboard in 1777, but another specialty was gunpowder and ammunition for which, on occasion, John Fitzpatrick supplied the lead.[82]

The Spanish conquest of West Florida did not damage Mather's commercial opportunities. On the contrary, it eliminated some of his British competitors, and the Spanish government allowed him, together with Morgan's old partner, Arthur Strother, to supply an annual shipload of merchandise to Pensacola and Mobile. They were too ambitious. In 1785, they had to relinquish to William Panton the right to trade with Pensacola and, in 1788, with Mobile as well. Nevertheless, the Mather family was by then firmly established on the Mississippi. James's son George was loyal to Spain, but his grandson, George Mather, Jr., took the anti-Spanish side in the West Florida revolt of 1810.[83]

The aim of this essay has not been to consider every Briton trading at New Orleans during the revolutionary era, but rather, by considering a sufficient number of them, to derive some understanding of the English trading community, how they were affected by Spanish rule, the kind of trading in which they engaged, and what effect it had. These traders seem to have come from every part of the British Isles and from Britain's American and West Indian colonies. It is hard to find one who did not have a substantial stake in West Florida and difficult to discover any who wanted to stay and trade in New Orleans who were not tolerated, even in time of war between Britain and Spain, provided only that they were prepared to show loyalty to the Spanish authorities and to endure the very occasional enforcement of the not very practical trade regulations for Louisiana devised in Spain. This tolerance would surely not have been accorded to them if they had been mere parasites, but only if they were useful to Louisiana.

In fact, British trade with Spanish Louisiana in the 1760s and 1770s served the interests of the province quite well. It supplied buyers for local products for which there was little market in Spain or in those few Spanish colonies allowed to buy from Louisiana. Unlike mercantile houses based in Spain and France, they would accept those local products in small quantities. It offered Louisianans goods, particularly textiles, slaves, and ammunition, for which there was a consistent demand. Finally, it enabled

Louisianans to obtain these goods on credit or by payment with bills at a time when specie was usually scarce.

Very occasionally, Spanish governors of Louisiana observed their uncompromising instructions to allow no trade with the British. More generally, though, they recognized that the presence of British traders was necessary for Louisiana's economic health and allowed them to do business. Surviving evidence suggests that Louisianans always bought more than they sold. There was a permanent balance-of-payments deficit which was made good with specie from Spain. Therefore, although Louisiana's economic health may have benefited from illicit trade with the British, Spain paid for the medicine; since, in strategic terms, Louisiana formed a valuable buffer between the British empire and New Spain, the Spanish king may have thought the price worthwhile

Economically, English trade with Spanish Louisiana served the purposes of the British empire better than that of the empire of His Catholic Majesty. The province was an outlet for British manufactures like shoes, hats, cutlery, ironmongery and, above all, textiles. Whether the textiles were entirely British, or German textiles re-exported from Britain, they benefited the economy of Great Britain—although French items such as David Ross imported from Saint Domingue did not. In addition, Louisiana supplied items which Britain needed and could not produce herself: deerskins, beaver pelts, tobacco, and indigo. In the case of indigo the British crown was spared the necessity of paying the bounty due if it had been grown in the British colonies.

During the American Revolution, when the traditional trade between New England and the West Indies was disrupted, trade with Louisiana alleviated the distress of West Indians like William Walker and Samuel Steer. The islanders also found in Louisiana an alternative source of lumber and an alternative market for sugar, rum, and slaves. Louisiana also gave opportunities to numerous Britons like Patrick Morgan and Evan Jones who had been disappointed by West Florida's slow development.

Inherent in this economically beneficial trade with Louisiana were strategic disadvantages for Britain. Helping the Louisiana economy to survive strengthened future enemies. Even before Spain formally became a belligerent, the activities of nominal Britons like Oliver Pollock and the partiality of Gálvez resulted in the supply from British sources of war material vital to the revolutionary cause.

In the twentieth century, Marxists describe as victims of neocolonialism those new states, once colonies, which, having obtained political independence from Britain, still retain traditional economic ties and thus a degree of dependence on her. The condition of Louisiana in the 1760s and most of the 1770s was in some ways similar. The Spanish paid for its administration and defense, but the British reaped economic advantage from a province which was to an extent dependent on them. As long as peace endured, it was a happy situation for Britain, but the coming of war turned customers into invaders. British power, not only on the Mississippi but along the entire Gulf Coast, was destroyed, even though a number of Britons of flexible patriotism were not.

*Professor of History, Auburn University, Auburn, Alabama.

[1] John G. Clark, *New Orleans, 1718-1812, an Economic History* (Baton Rouge, 1970), 161. J. W. Caughey, *Bernardo de Gálvez in Louisiana, 1776-1783* (Gretna, 1972), 40. Gilbert C. Din, ed., *Louisiana in 1776, a Memoir of Francisco Bouligny* (New Orleans, 1977), 9, 12.

[2] George Johnstone to John Pownall, Feb. 19, 1765, Public Record Office, T1/437:224. Philip L. White, ed., *The Beekman Mercantile Papers, 1764-1799* (New York, 1956), 1:450, 2:852.

[3] Peter J. Hamilton, *Colonial Mobile* (Boston, 1910), 225. Bertram Wallace Korn, "Jews in Eighteenth-Century West Florida," in Samuel Proctor, ed., *Eighteenth-Century Florida: Life on the Frontier* (Gainesville, 1976), 56.

[4] Aubry to the Minister, Feb. 12, 1765, Clarence W. Alvord and Clarence E. Carter, eds., *Collections of the Illinois State Historical Society* (Springfield, 1915), 10:435.

[5] Strachan to Petit, Feb. 7, 12, 1765, The Letter Book of Charles Strachan, National Library of Scotland, for transcripts of which I am indebted to Dr. Robert R. Rea of Auburn University.

[6] Johnstone to Pownall, Dec. 29, 1765, C.O. 5/574:951, PRO.

[7] *New York Journal*, Nov. 11, 1776.

[8] *New York Journal*, Nov. 27, 1776; Feb. 19, 1767; Albert C. Bates, ed., *The Two Putnams* (Hartford, 1931), 135.

[9] *New York Journal*, Aug. 5, 1767; March 4, 1768.

[10] *New York Journal*, July 28, 1768; Oct. 16, 1766; April 23, 1767; June 20, July 23, Aug. 5, 27, Dec. 10 and 24, 1767; April 28, May 12, Oct. 13, 1768.

[11] *Louisiana Historical Quarterly* 6 (1923):712.

[12] John Fitzpatrick to John Stephenson, June 30, 1768, Margaret Fisher Dalrymple, *The Merchant of Manchac: The Letterbooks of John Fitzpatrick, 1768-1790* (Baton Rouge, 1978), 38.

[13]Antonio de Ulloa to Antonio de Bucarelli, July 20, Aug. 1, 2, 1768, Stanely C. Arthur, ed., *Despatches of the Spanish Governors of Louisiana* (New Orleans, 1937-38), I:52, 58.
[14]*Louisiana Historical Quarterly* 6 (1923):162, 519; C.O. 5/591:351, PRO.
[15]Ulloa to Bucarelli, Nov. 11, 1768, *Governors' Despatches*, I:68. Fitzpatrick to Stephenson, Sep. 28, 1768, *Merchant of Manchac*, 42.
[16]Ian R. Christie and Benjamin W. Labaree, *Empire or Independence, 1760-1776* (New York, 1976), 36.
[17]Clark, *New Orleans*, 167-68.
[18]Caughey, *Gálvez*, 40.
[19]Bertram W. Korn, *The Early Jews of New Orleans* (Waltham, 1969), 33.
[20]*Merchant of Manchac*, 10-76. Fitzpatrick to Le Fleur, Sep. 9, 1769; ibid., 72. Fitzpatrick to Arthur Strother, Nov. 7, 1769, ibid., 77.
[21]*South Carolina Gazette*, Sep. 19, 1769.
[22]*New York Journal*, Nov. 23, 1769.
[23]Unzaga to Bucarelli, July 8, 1770, *Governors' Despatches*, 2:54.
[24]Unzaga to Bucarelli, Aug. 31, Nov. 11, 1770, ibid., 3:3, 13. Unzaga to Bucarelli, Jan. 22, 1771, ibid., 26.
[25]*New York Mercury*, July 13, 1772.
[26]C.O. 5/613:139, C.O. 5/577:71, PRO. Eight years earlier a Richard Carpenter returned from Pensacola to Newport, *Pennsylvania Gazette*, July 11, 1765.
[27]C.O. 5/591:415; C.O. 5/591:371-82, PRO.
[28]Unzaga to Chester, June 17, 1774, C.O. 5/591:423-25, PRO.
[29]I have not been able to confirm this incident reported in the *New York Gazette* of May 16, 1774, from any other source.
[30]C.O. 5/580:311, PRO.
[31]See shipping news in the colonial newspapers in general and for more detailed information on some of these voyages see C.O. 5/613:307-308, PRO.
[32]He offered a reward of $5000 to anybody who would introduce the manufacture of saltpeter into West Florida, *Scots Magazine* 29 (Jan., 1767):51.
[33]C.O. 5/634, Council Minutes for Nov. 28, 1775, PRO.
[34]Chester to Lord George Germain, Nov. 21, 1776, Headquarters Papers of the British Army in America (Sir Guy Carleton Papers), 3:330 (3-6). Cited hereinafter as B.H.P.
[35]C.O. 5/630, Council Minutes for Dec. 15, 1772, PRO.
[36]Fitzpatrick to William Wilton, Jan. 23, 1777, *Merchant of Manchac*, 236.
[37]Anonymous memo, n.d., B.H.P. 5:549 (1-2).
[38]Fitzpatrick to Michael Hoopock, Feb. 14, 1777, *Merchant of Manchac*, 236.
[39]J. W. Caughey, "Bernardo de Gálvez and the English Smugglers on the Mississippi, 1777," *Hispanic American Historical Review* 12 (1932):48-57.
[40]Log, *West Florida*, PRO, ADM 51/4390. I am grateful to Dr. R. R. Rea for this information.
[41]Caughey, "Smugglers," 57.
[42]Bouligny, 62.
[43]C.O. 5/635, Council Minutes for Nov. 17, 1778, PRO.
[44]Gálvez to Alexander Dickson and John Stephenson, Aug., 1777, C.O. 5/631, Council Minutes for Sep. 29, 1777, PRO.
[45]Anonymous, n.d., B.H.P. 5:549 (3).
[46]Dickson and Stephenson to Gálvez, Aug. 17, 1777, C.O. 5/631, Council Minutes for Sep. 29, 1777, PRO.

[47]Gálvez to Diego Joseph Navarro, Nov. 9, 1778, *Governors' Despatches*, 8:64.
[48]Henry Stuart to John Stuart, Aug. 11, 1777, C.O. 5/594:135, PRO.
[49]Gálvez to Thomas Lloyd, May 11, 1777, B.H.P. 5:523 (1-40). Pickles's luck would change soon afterwards. He was turned loose in a small boat by the mutinous crew of his schooner *Bostonian*. He safely reached Cuba and returned to New Orleans. Gálvez to Navarro, April 12, 1778, *Governors' Despatches*, 7:70.
[50]Fitzpatrick to Alexander McIntosh, April 28, 1777, *Merchant of Manchac*, 245.
[51]C.O. 5/631, Council Minutes for Sep. 29, 1777, PRO.
[52]Gálvez to Lloyd, May 11, 1777, B.H.P. 5:523 (1-4).
[53]*Louisiana Historical Quarterly* 8 (1925):731, 734.
[54]C.O. 5/635, Council Minutes of Nov. 17, 1778, PRO. "Loyal subjects residing in Louisiana" to Ferguson, March 27, 1778, C.O. 5/631, Council Minutes for April 25, 1778, PRO. Their names were Richard Bradley, Donald Campbell, John Campbell, John Davies, William Dunbar, William Garden, James Mather, William McIntosh, Philip Moore, Alexander Ross, David Ross, George Ross, William Swanson, David Williams. Morgan and Ross to Ferguson, March 26, 1778, ibid.
[55]Chester to Germain, May 30, 1778, C.O. 5/594:613, PRO.
[56]C.O. 5/635:165-68. Council Minutes of April 25, 1778, PRO.
[57]Ross to Ferguson, April 11, 1778, ibid.
[58]Caughey, *Gálvez*, 76.
[59]*Louisiana Historical Quarterly* 13 (1930):529.
[60]Ibid., 8 (1925):737. *Rivington's Royal Gazette*, March 20, 1779.
[61]Clinton N. Howard, *The British Development of West Florida, 1763-1769* (Berkeley, 1947), 58, 72. Robert R. Rea and Milo B. Howard, Jr., *The Minutes, Journals, and Acts of the General Assembly of British West Florida* (University, Al., 1979), p. xxiii. Fitzpatrick to Robert Ross, Sep. 20, 1768, *Merchant of Manchas*, 41-42. Jack D. L. Holmes, "Robert Ross' Plan for an English Invasion of Louisiana in 1782," *Louisiana History* 5 (1964):171. C.O. 5/612:32, PRO. Chester to Lord Dartmouth, Dec. 20, 1777, C.O. 5/591:183, PRO. C.O. 5/613:80, PRO.
[62]Fitzpatrick to Ross, Jan. 10, 1778, *Merchant of Manchac*, 276. C.O. 5/613:515, PRO. *Louisiana Historical Quarterly* 12 (1929):513-14. Holmes, "Ross' Plan," 162. *Rivington's Royal Gazette*, May 5, 1779.
[63]Robert V. Haynes, *The Natchez District and the American Revolution* (Jackson, Miss., 1976), 91-92. C.O. 5/635, Council Minutes for Sep. 17, 1778, PRO. Fitzpatrick to John Stephenson, Jan. 10, 1782, *Merchant of Manchac*, 391.
[64]C.O. 5/634, Council Minutes for Dec. 26, 1776, PRO. Fitzpatrick to Walker, June 12, 1777, *Merchant of Manchac*, 253. Louisiana State Museum, Louisiana Historical Center, Judicial Records of the Spanish Cabildo, no. 1781011902.
[65]*Louisiana Historical Quarterly* 8 (1925):738-39.
[66]Petition of Bernard Lintot to the General Assembly of Connecticut, Jan. 16, 1784, Connecticut Archives, Manuscript Division, Revolutionary War, 1763-1789, series 1, vol. 27, fol. 64a. Fitzpatrick to Evan and James Jones, May 13, 1772, *Merchant of Manchac*, 121. Hamilton, 225. Howard, 73-74, 84, 93. C.O. 5/577:76, PRO.
[67]C.O. 5/591:183; C.O. 5/613:537; C.O. 5/613:172, 285, PRO. *Louisiana Historical Quarterly* 6 (1923):161. C.O. 5/588:359, PRO. Fitzpatrick to Evan and James Jones, May 13, July 19, Oct. 16, 1772; May 8, 13, July 7, 1773, *Merchant of Manchac*, 121, 124-25, 132, 149, 154, 194.

⁶⁸Cecil Johnson, *British West Florida, 1763-1783* (New Haven, 1941), 72-73. *The Two Putnams*, 155. C.O. 5/613:196, PRO. W.P.A. Calendar of Documents in Louisiana State Archives, no. 1669, Dec. 4, 1787.

⁶⁹C.O. 5/617:406, PRO.

⁷⁰Judicial Records of the Spanish Cabildo, no. 1781021001. W.P.A. Calendar of Documents in Louisiana State Archives, no. 1669. Clark, 165, 215.

⁷¹C.O. 5/635, Council Minutes for May 17, 1779, PRO. Fitzpatrick to Davis, May 16, July 12, 1779; July 4, Sep. 28, Nov. 25, 1780; Jan. 1, 1781; March 28, 1785, *Merchant of Manchac*, 320, 330, 345, 357, 364, 370-71, 373-74, 414.

⁷²C.O. 5/635, Council Minutes for Nov. 16, 1778, PRO. Fitzpatrick to Shakespear, March 2, 1780, *Merchant of Manchac*, 342.

⁷³*Bouligny*, 63.

⁷⁴C.O. 5/613:510; C.O. 5/635, Council Minutes for May 17, 1779, PRO. Judicial Records of the Spanish Cabildo, nos. 1781999901, 1782041501.

⁷⁵Clarence W. Alvord and Clarence E. Carter, *Trade and Politics, 1767-1769* (Springfield, Ill., 1921), 181.

⁷⁶C.O. 5/591:183; C.O. 5/604:294; C.O. 5/612:31, PRO. Howard, *British West Florida*, 85. Rea and Howard, *General Assembly*, pp. xxiii, xiv, 128. Fitzpatrick to Valens Comyn, July 18, Aug. 1, 11, Sep. 1, 1769, *Merchant of Manchac*, 60, 62, 67, 70. W.P.A. Calendar of Documents in the Louisiana State Archives, no. 658.

⁷⁷Howard, *British West Florida*, 64, 74, 79, 90, 92.

⁷⁸Library of Congress, West Florida Papers, Council Minutes for Feb. 4, 1772.

⁷⁹Rea and Howard, *General Assembly*, 174. *Merchant of Manchac*, 41n, 217. Fitzpatrick to David Ross, Dec. 1, 1775; Nov. 25, Dec. 10, 29, 1776; Jan. 23, Feb. 13, 21, May 21, June 7, July 3, Aug. 14, 1777; June 27, Aug. 7, 1778; ibid., pp. 196, 216-17, 221, 224, 229, 235, 237, 250, 252, 255, 259, 297, 301. Fitzpatrick to Ross, April 20, 1782; Oct. 22, 1785, ibid., pp. 402, 491.

⁸⁰Howard, *British West Florida*, 60, 74, 101. C.O. 5/613:34; C.O. 5/614:284; C.O. 5/634:134, PRO.

⁸¹C.O. 5/612:612; C.O. 5/613:454-56, 497, PRO.

⁸²*Louisiana Historical Quarterly* 13 (1930):521-28. Judicial Records, nos. 178309241, 1784080501. Fitzpatrick to Alexander McIntosh, April 28, 1777, *Merchant of Manchac*, 245. Fitzpatrick to Morgan, Feb. 18, 1778, ibid., 286.

⁸³*Louisiana Historical Quarterly* 21 (1938):13n, 688.

THE CREEK CONFEDERACY IN THE AMERICAN
REVOLUTION: CAUTIOUS PARTICIPANTS

MICHAEL D. GREEN*

During the early months of 1781, while the Spanish forces of Don Bernardo de Gálvez laid siege to Pensacola, the British defenders of the town and its forts enjoyed the aid and support of about 500 native allies. Most of these Indian warriors were Choctaws, but perhaps as many as 120 were Creeks. Alexander Cameron, head of the western division of the southern superintendency, thought there would have been many more if Major General John Campbell, British commanding officer in West Florida, had followed his advice. Campbell knew nothing about Indians or Indian affairs, Cameron charged. "He thinks [Indians] are to be used like slaves or a people void of natural sense." With years of experience in the British Indian service, Cameron knew better. The native people of the southeast had a clear understanding of their tribal interests, and they were quite reluctant to subordinate them to the will of others. Students of the history of British/Indian relations in the southeast will never understand the full implications of the events of the eighteenth century if they share with General Campbell the view that native Americans were "void of natural sense."[1]

By the middle of the eighteenth century the fundamental fact of Creek relations with Europeans was their dependence on the manufactured goods, particularly munitions, that they received in trade. The Creeks had irreversibly altered their economy in response to the trade. Becoming commercial hunters, they produced a staggering quantity of deerskins for the European market and, in return, incorporated into their culture a wide range of goods and articles which replaced items of their own manufacture. Creek prosperity and power came to depend on purchased goods and weapons.[2] Indeed, as one scholar has recently suggested, the very lives of the Creek people may have hung on their ability to supply the English with commodities or services valuable enough to render their existence useful and thereby tolerable.[3]

The problem of Creek foreign policy was, therefore, to maximize the trade. This required defending their hunting grounds and acquiring new ones, replenishing their supplies of weapons

CREEK COUNTRY – 1780

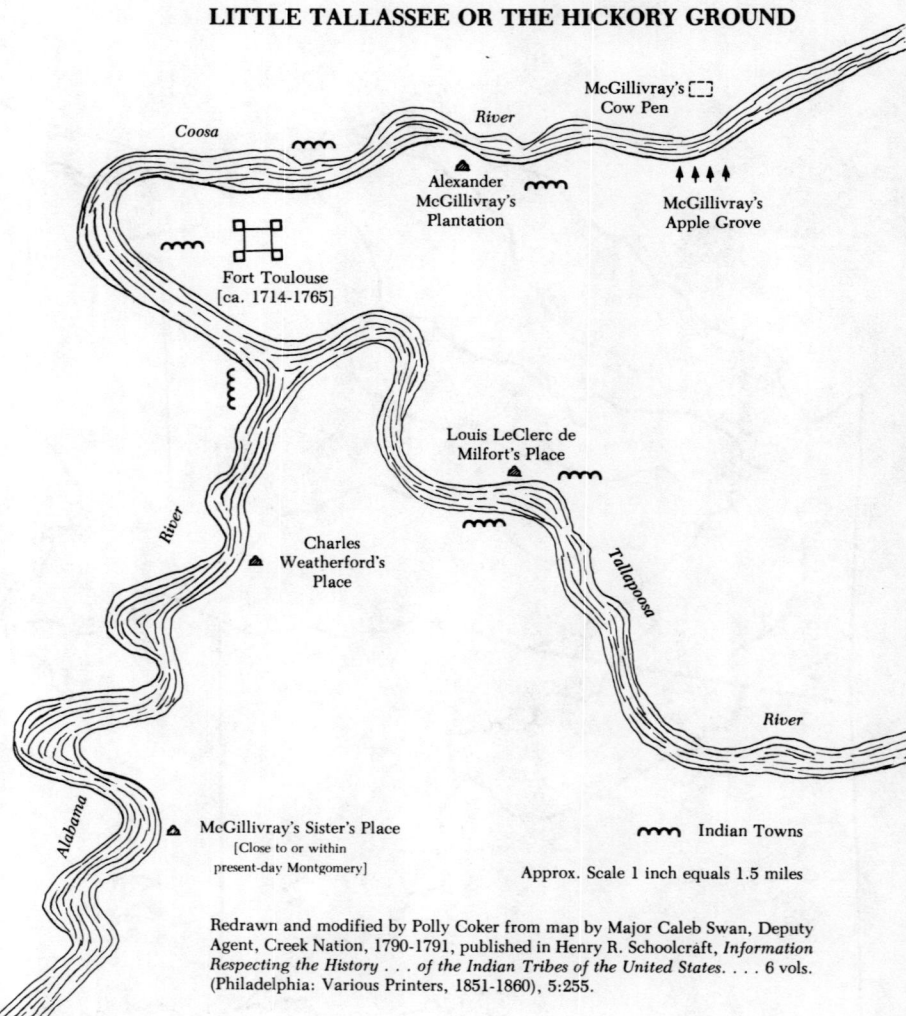

for hunting and war, extending their trade to all comers, maintaining the most favorable exchange rates possible, and weaving a web of political relationships that gave the Creeks the greatest degree of control over their affairs. None of these goals could be met without sacrifice. Creek hunters had to spend more time and travel greater distances to keep the production of deerskins high, and they had to fight more enemies to insure safe access to the herds. Creek towns had to tolerate growing numbers of frequently obnoxious foreign traders. Creek leaders had to accept meddling in their affairs of state, and the nation had to accommodate the attempts of foreign governments to entangle its people in their own incessant conflicts. It was a compromise between absolute autonomy and the necessities of the trade, requiring the utmost care and determination to find and steer the course that produced the greatest gain at the lowest cost.[4]

As the Creeks continually weighed these factors they were influenced by certain strengths and weaknesses. Their most obvious source of power lay in their numbers. With population estimates for the 1770s ranging from 12,000 to 17,000 people, including from 3,500 to 5,800 warriors, the Creeks substantially outnumbered West Florida's puny Anglo-American population, even after it mushroomed to perhaps 8,000 following the influx of loyalist refugees during the late 1770s. And despite more than doubling its population during the 1770s, Georgia's 35,000 whites, in 1780, were barely twice the number of Creeks.[5] Such population comparisons are, of course, misleading. On the one hand, given the hunter-warrior training of Creek men, virtually the whole adult male population could theoretically become an effective fighting force. No comparable settler group could field proportionately so large or well trained a militia. On the other hand, any estimate of Creek military potential based on numbers alone ignores the reality that total mobilization was impossible. Even if the necessary political harmony and agreement prevailed, which never occurred, the men simply had too many other tasks to perform. Creek armies were, in the strictest sense, citizen armies. Their society, unable to support a professional standing army, could not tolerate the absence of large numbers of men for long periods of time. Males had to hunt, prepare the fields, protect their families, and govern as well as fight. Nevertheless, the potential was impressive, and no prospective enemy could afford to ignore it.

Geography improved upon population. Commanding many of the major river systems of the southeast, the Creeks were in control of the best highways from the interior to both Atlantic and Gulf coasts. And during the time before 1763, when European influence in the region was divided among the French, Spanish, and British, the Creeks enjoyed the additional advantage of being located between them. James Adair summarized the benefits of location thus:

> Before the late cession of East and West Florida to Great Britain, the Country of the Muskohge lay between the territories of the English, Spaniards, French, Choktah, Chikkasah, and Cheerake. — And as they had a water carriage, from the two Floridas; to secure their liberties, and a great trade by land from Georgia and South-Carolina, this nation regulated the Indian balance of power in our southern parts of North-America.

Combined with the obvious fact that the Creeks were completely at home in their country, these geographical factors created a clear and significant advantage relative to any European adversary.[6]

Population and location, plus a history of successful dominance of the region, produced an extraordinarily self-confident people. The correspondence of British officials in the 1770s abounds with terms like "proud," "arrogant," "haughty," and "insolent" to describe Creek men. Supremely certain of their abilities, the Creeks could not easily be intimidated.[7]

These strengths were counterbalanced by two substantial weaknesses — economic dependence and lack of centralized political authority. Serious enough when there were three European contenders in the Southeast, after 1763, and the emergence of England as the sole imperial force in the region, they combined to render the Creeks exceedingly vulnerable. Economic dependence was a constant and worsening debility. Large numbers of warriors, regardless of their self-confidence or skill, were only as useful as their supplies of guns and powder permitted. Traditional weapons, effective in certain situations, could never enable the Creeks to defend their country or threaten their enemies. Particularly after 1763, no foreign policy decision could be made without reckoning with the problem that those who posed the greatest threat to Creek autonomy were also those who supplied the weapons necessary for its defense.

Even more grave was the absence of a centralized Creek political authority. As a political institution, the Creek Nation did not exist. Called a confederacy by observers and scholars, the Creek structure was more an alliance of semi-sovereign, semi-autonomous groups scattered throughout the region that has since become Georgia, Alabama, and northern Florida. These groups, called towns in the literature, were united by neither a common language nor a common history. Highly particularistic, they had both the tradition and the will to measure events against their own immediate and localized interests. They often combined in temporary coalitions for defense, and they scrupulously avoided internecine conflict, but except for two loose sectional groupings they rarely united for a common long-range purpose. The Creeks had no central policy-making authority, no national executive structure, no formalized enforcement mechanisms. There was little to bring unity of purpose to a society characterized by intense and bewildering political factionalism. Europeans unable to learn that no town could bind the nation to a course of action were doomed to frustration by what they considered the innate "savage" unpredictability of the Creeks.[8]

Creek town politics were similarly factionalized. The details of local public affairs in the eighteenth century are not well known, but it is possible to catch a glimpse of a struggle for authority between established leaders and interlopers. Many Georgia and South Carolina trading companies set up stores in several towns and hired Indians to manage them. These Creek merchants, by controlling the local trade, were in a position to enhance their personal influence and build a following with which they challenged the authority of the headmen. If these factions reflected just the personal ambitions of fortunately-situated individuals, they were disruptive enough. If, however, they represented attempts by colonial merchants to meddle in Creek political affairs, they seriously jeopardized the autonomy of the nation. Whatever the purpose, the result was that the "influence [of the principal chiefs] and all subordination among [the Creeks] is destroyed [by the native storekeepers, who] are enabled to counteract the chiefs and to prejudice the people against them."[9]

This local factionalism was hard to see: the sources tell us little and its effect on Creek political history can only be surmised. On the national level, however, political factionalism is part of the key to understanding Creek relations with the three contending European powers prior to 1763. Scholars have emphasized the importance of the "play-off" diplomacy of Brims, the so-called "emperor" of the Creeks, and his descendants who maintained Creek power between the 1720s and 1763, with a strict policy of friendship and trade with all sides and alliances with none. An early French visitor wrote that "no one has ever been able to make [Brims] take sides with one of the three European nations who know him, he alleging that he wishes to see everyone, to be neutral, and not to espouse any of the quarrels which [they] have with one another."[10] Some decades later James Adair described the same policy:

> the old men, being long informed by the opposite parties, of the different views, and intrigues of those European powers, who paid them annual tribute under the vague appellation of presents, were become suprisingly crafty in every turn of low politics. They held it as an invariable maxim, that their security and welfare required a perpetual friendly intercourse with us and the French; as our political state of war with each other, would always secure their liberties: whereas, if they joined either party, and enabled it to prevail over the other, their state, they said, would then become as unhappy as that of a poor fellow, who had only one perverse wife, and yet must bear with her froward temper.[11]

Whatever mastery of "low politics" demonstrated by Brims and other Creek headmen in their handling of the contending Europeans, it was nothing when compared to their juggling of the many Creek factions. Each European power had a nucleus of Indians, often of towns, who looked to them for trade and presents. Representatives of each faction attempted to gain adherents by arguing the cause of their suppliers in council. When persuasion failed, pro-French Creeks harassed English officials, or pro-English Creeks tried to expel Spanish representatives. Factional conflict continually threatened the rough equilibrium of the region and prevented any domestic agreement that might have led to a Creek alliance with one of the Europeans. Such a connection would have resulted in a Creek civil war. The only solution that promised internal peace and stability was the kind of neutral policy that Brims pursued. His genius lay not so much in his ability to play off the Europeans as it did in his balancing the many Creek factions and averting civil war.

The end of European competition in the southeast came in 1763. With the French and Spanish out of the way, the English had a freer hand to pursue their interests, and the Creeks had to make a major adjustment in their diplomacy. "Play-off" was no longer possible. At the same time, however, much of the cause of Creek factionalism was also gone. Trade and presents now came only from English sources. The Creek Nation did not unify after 1763, but much of the earlier political conflict did recede, and a rough kind of sectional coalescing occurred.

There had always been two sectional congregations of Creek towns. One, called the Lower Towns by the English, and the Cowetas by the Spanish and French, was a grouping of towns primarily on the Chattahoochee and Flint rivers and their tributaries. The other, farther to the west and called the Upper Towns by the English and the Tallapoosas by the Spanish and French, was composed of towns on the systems of the Coosa, Tallapoosa, and Alabama rivers. Geographical propinquity encouraged common interest within each section, just as the distance between the two inhibited the growth of a national perspective. In the absence of conflicting imperial pressures, the tendency after 1763, was toward the development of two sectional unities.

The future looked brighter for the Creeks in 1763, than it did for many native tribes facing the same problems of adjusting their policies to the new situation of one European presence rather than two or three. Not only was their bitter political factionalism beginning to dwindle, their economic prospects seemed brighter. This was particularly true for the Upper Creeks. They controlled the river and trail networks that led to Mobile and Pensacola. Neither the French nor the Spanish had the resources to develop those port towns into important trade centers. The British, on the other hand, did, and the Creeks encouraged them to do so. At the first congress at Pensacola between the English and the Creeks, in late May and early June, 1765, questions of opening trade, regulating traders and rates of exchange were of prime importance. After much debate, details were formalized in a treaty signed June 4, by a distinguished corps of leading Upper Creek headmen and a handful of Lower Creek observers.[12] The rapid growth in the prosperity and population of Georgia also insured continuing trade relations with that colony.

Improved economic opportunities after 1763, were balanced by increasing encroachments on Creek lands. This was not a particularly serious problem for the Upper Creeks, during the two decades prior to the British loss of West Florida, because the English population on that border was too small and innocuous to cause much trouble. Upper Town leaders successfully rebuffed Governor Peter Chester's rather half-hearted efforts in the early 1770s to extend West Florida's line up the Escambia valley, and the number of squatters above Tensa proved little threat to Creek use of the area. Their greatest concern was for the damage cattle drovers did to their deer grounds when they leisurely drove their herds through to western markets. The Lower Creeks, on the other hand, had a serious problem with the rapidly expanding Georgians. Pressure on their northeastern hunting lands affected the Upper Towns also, but Georgia's demands for additional land, temporarily sated with the so-called "New Purchase" of 1773, of the tract between the Oconee and Ogeechee rivers, had a far more direct impact on the Lower Creeks. Border conflicts were continuous after the 1773 cession, leading to an antagonism between the Lower Towns and Georgia that threatened vital trade links, making the prospective Florida trade even more important and contributing to the strong desire of the Creeks to destroy Georgia's frontier settlements during the Revolution.

From the Creek perspective, the situation was fairly clear after 1763. The Upper Towns could encourage the development of a convenient trade with West Florida without much harmful population pressure from settlers. The Lower Towns, less well situated, could try to encourage a similar trade with either West or East Florida — a less hopeful possibility, however, because they lacked easy access to Pensacola or St. Augustine, and the Apalache trade never got off the ground. Both groups could continue the large and lucrative overland trade with Georgia, although that was becoming increasingly hard to maintain in the face of escalating boundary violations by squatters, herders, and poachers. In the continuing process of weighing autonomy against dependence, the problems with Georgia raised the price the Creeks had to pay to keep the trade protected and flourishing. By the middle of the 1770s, indeed, Creek leaders were forced to execute warriors charged with the murder of Georgia settlers in order to lift an embargo on trade imposed by Governor James Wright. It was in the best interests of the Creeks to nurture the Florida trade and thereby reduce the political costs of their dependence on Georgia.[13]

But the Creeks lived in a world influenced by factors they could little control. Between 1765 and 1776, they were enmeshed in a protracted war with the Choctaws. If the English were not responsible for its beginning, they certainly were not unwilling to see it continue. Indeed, during a lull in the fighting in 1770, Georgia Governor Wright predicted that a peace between the two tribes would cause the Creeks to "pick a quarrel with us, and in the weak and defenceless condition we are at present this very nursling province may be ruined." Wright knew the Creeks had plenty of provocation to attack—he had just finished cooling them off after having been "ill-treated by some of our lawless bad people." West Florida's Peter Chester made the same argument four years later. It would be "fatal" to his back settlements, he believed, if the Creeks and Choctaws made peace.[14]

The war was draining the human and economic resources of both tribes. Uneasy over the costs, several Creek headmen approached John Stuart to help them end it. The second, and by far the most distinguished, superintendent of Britain's Southern Indian Department, Stuart played a pivotal role in the relations between England and the native nations of the southeast. Although Stuart was generally well-liked by the Southern Indians, he was pre-eminently a crown official whose first loyalty was never to them or their interests. His response to the request to mediate their conflict illustrates his technique of Indian management. "Both nations with good reason considered us as the incindiaries who kindled the war," Stuart explained, "both appeared to be heartily tired of it and expressed a strong desire of peace, and both earnestly solicited my mediation to obtain their wishes." Believing that the Creeks and Choctaws were bound to make peace on their own, and thinking that their talks could be stopped only "by our intrigues, the suspicion of which I wished to avoid," Stuart leaped to the forefront and brought the negotiations to a successful conclusion.

> Our refusing to mediate would justify and confirm their suspicions, would of course tend to unite them, and draw their resentment upon us, when on the other hand by complying, I hoped to efface the bad impressions they had conceived of us and give them a proof of sincere disinterested friendship by our becoming the instrument of bringing about what would have taken place without us.

But the Superintendent was insincere. Before the month was out, Charles Stuart, deputy superintendent, successfully blocked the confirmation of the Creek-Choctaw peace planned for Mobile. "I had the good luck to defeat their intentions and to send each party away well satisfied with my endeavours to bring them together," he bragged to his cousin. Some months later, the superintendent blandly assured Lord Hillsborough in London that there had been no bad consequences from his "interference" to conclude the war. It raged on as violently as ever.[15]

For seventeen years John Stuart was the king's diplomatic representative to the Southern tribes. The king, he assured them, was their friend, their "father," a man with great power who wanted only justice and happiness for his native "Children." These were good words, and those Creeks who had long been loyal to the British found them easy to accept. Others, now looking to British Florida for trade, found Stuart's assurances heartening. But it seemed strange that the man who spoke for the great king had so little power himself. Stuart could not force Georgians to respect the boundary; he could not require traders to conduct their business honestly; he could not stanch the river of rum, mostly from Pensacola, that flooded the Creek country. His double dealing was suspicious, and he was not above strong arm tactics.[16] But his words were good; he seemed fair; it looked like he tried, and he was certainly better than the settlers and traders and colonial governments that constantly demanded more land or the heads of the warriors who protected their country from interlopers. It was never that Stuart was such a good friend, but that the colonists were such bad neighbors. After 1775, when Stuart became chief recruiter of Indian allies for the royal army, this latter fact was his best argument.

The Creeks never forgot Stuart's flaws and failures, and their performance in the British service during the Revolution demonstrated their continued distrust. Their interest lay in protecting their country, guarding their autonomy, and preserving their trade. This had been their interest from their first contact with Europeans, and it remained their interest long after the Revolution ended. Stuart offered the Creeks one formula, but there were others to be considered. Caution reigned.

When the Revolutionary conflict began, Stuart received orders from General Thomas Gage, commander of British forces in America, "to hold a correspondence with the Indians . . . and even, when opportunity offers, to make them take arms against His Majesty's enemies and to distress them all in their power." The Creeks, still bogged down in their war with the Choctaws and suffering from a severe shortage of supplies, especially gunpowder, were in no mood to commit themselves. The rebels' nonimportation agreements had cut the flow of trade goods to America to a trickle, and during the summer of 1775, rebels at Savannah seized several shipments of presents and powder consigned to Stuart. Much of this booty found its way to the rebel militias, but the newly-appointed rebel Indian commissioners delivered a portion to the Creeks with the careful explanation that it was the "people of Georgia" who sent their best wishes, not the king's superintendent or the royal governor. Two representatives of the Continental Congress, George Galphin and Robert Rae, were among the best established and most respected traders in the nation. Galphin had traded at the Lower Town of Coweta for years, had an influential Coweta family, and could command the loyalty of a large share of the population. Rae had roughly comparable influence at Okfuskee, an Upper Town. These gentlemen, with connections and powder, were tough competitors for Stuart.[17]

Stuart had to demonstrate that he could do more for the Creeks than could the rebels. Many Upper Creek leaders were anxious to end the war with the Choctaws, and Stuart, knowing that he could get no help from the Creeks while their war raged on, now sincerely worked to bring it to a close. To fill the need for goods, the superintendent opened depots at St. Augustine and Pensacola which funneled powder and other supplies to all the Southern tribes.[18] The impact of this policy can be measured by the value of Stuart's presents, which rose dramatically from about £7,500 in 1775, to £14,500 in 1776, £33,000 in 1777, to £50,000 in 1778.[19] These goods, added to the private trade that developed from loyal East and West Florida, were never enough to compensate the Creeks fully for the disrupted Georgia trade. They helped, however, particularly during 1777 and 1778, when crop failures and poor hunting due to powder shortages caused a "near famine" in the nation. Indeed, to the degree that the British approached their goal of winning loyal Creek allies for their war effort, these presents were the key.[20]

Stuart interpreted Gage's order conservatively. If the Creeks were to provide manpower for the British military, it should be only as auxiliaries commanded by whites and fighting in conjunction with an organized loyalist or royal army. He would have no scalping war directed without discrimination at Carolina and Georgia frontier settlers. Stuart's concern for the safety of innocent women and children may have been sincere, but political questions were uppermost in his mind. The British southern strategy rested, in large part, on the mobilization of the large number of loyalists believed to reside in the backcountry. All Georgia frontierspeople were enemies of the Creeks and candidates for attack, but to Stuart it was imperative that the Creeks recognize the political distinction between loyalist and rebel. He also feared that raids by British Indians would subordinate their political differences and cause loyal and rebel settlers to unite against a common enemy. So, while the superintendent preached alliance with the king in one breath, he argued patience and restraint in the next. Creek warriors found it hard to accept both messages simultaneously.[21]

Galphin, Rae, and the other rebel commissioners to the Indians had an easier task. Momentarily well supplied with seized powder, they gave it freely to the needy Creeks, along with promises of more and better presents and a revitalized trade. All they asked in return was neutrality, a request many Creeks were happy to honor.[22]

The Cherokees were more seriously pressed by illegal settlements. Encouraged by the Shawnees early in 1776, they rejected Stuart's request to await patiently a British army and attacked the Virginia and Carolina frontier. The states responded with devastating counterattacks and Stuart could do nothing to help. Exposed and alone, the Cherokees were badly defeated, much of their country was laid waste, and they were forced to cede a large portion of their territory.[23]

The experience of the Cherokees was sobering. Galphin met with several Creek headmen at Augusta, in May, to repeat his advice that neutrality was the best policy for the Creeks. In August he added to this advice the warning that the Creeks would be "served as the Cherokees have been served" if they embraced the British cause. Galphin's threats, coupled with the stories of hundreds of displaced Cherokees, "dampened the spirits" of the Creeks. In November, Emistisiguo, Stuart's best friend among the Upper Creeks and the spokesman of the loyal majority, wrote to the superintendent that he was

> not out of heart for I have got a strong and able friend, the Great King, and I hope he will not involve me in trouble and then desert me and leave me when I cannot help myself. I know that St. Augustine, Pensacola and Mobile are the places from which we may expect assistance, and should the Virginians get possession of these places we are ruined. We have always assisted the Great King but we never pointed a gun against the Virginians; but now they are the cause of all the troubles in this country and we are ready for them.

The point was clear. The Creeks would not take on the Georgia and Carolina rebels alone and expose themselves to the punishment forced on the Cherokees.[24]

This is not to suggest that prior to 1779, when British troops finally brought the war to the South, the Creeks were totally useless to the British. The defense of both East and West Florida depended in large part on them and the other Southern tribes. Sir William Howe did not worry about a land attack on West Florida while the Upper Creeks were friendly, and Governor Patrick Tonyn successfully defended St. Augustine from more than one rebel invasion from Georgia with the aid of Creek and Seminole warriors.[25] The Creeks simply saw no need to engage in offensive warfare—the presents and supplies came to them from both sides without it. The defense of their prime sources of supply was another matter, however, and knowing full well that a rebel conquest of the British Floridas would bring serious economic hardship they were quite willing to provide the assistance necessary to keep them afloat. As partners in an alliance, the Creeks considered their interests first.

Alexander McGillivray played a central role in the Creek/British alliance. Born probably in 1750, to a Koasati woman of the Wind clan, McGillivray had been raised in a culturally-mixed setting at his father's trading post at Little Tallassee, an Upper Town on the Coosa River near present Montgomery. In his youth, the elder McGillivray sent his son to Charleston for schooling, but by 1777, he was back in the Creek nation working as an assistant to his brother-in-law David Taitt, Stuart's commissary in the Upper Towns. Stuart had "great hopes and expectations" that the young man's "powerful connections," along with his "activity and good sense," would not only "keep him safe" but would yield good results for the British cause.[26]

Stuart had good reason to be hopeful. The Wind clan was the largest and most prestigious in the nation. Many of the high-ranking members of the town councils were Winds; clan kin lived throughout the nation, and no one dared insult or injure a Wind for fear of their certain revenge. Coupled with his education and his articulate literacy in English, his influential clan assured McGillivray a voice in Creek affairs.

McGillivray's appointment began to pay dividends almost immediately. In September, 1777, following a meeting with rebel commissioner Galphin, about 120 headmen and warriors, primarily from Okfuskee, set out to Hickory Ground to kill David Taitt, Alexander Cameron, Jacob Moniac, Taitt's interpreter, and plunder the presents and powder stored there. McGillivray stopped the party and "after a good deal of Talk sometimes Wrangling with them, Prevailed on the Chiefs to return to their home with the young People." A similar band from some of the towns on the Tallapoosa got by unnoticed and stole part of the goods, but McGillivray frustrated Galphin's plan and saved the lives of his colleagues in the British service. After they cooled down, the leaders from Okfuskee began "to show some signs of repentance" and agreed to attend a meeting of the Upper Towns, most of which were loyal to the British. The Upper Creek headmen insisted that McGillivray do the talking, however. Afraid to lecture the belligerent Okfuskees, they reassured McGillivray that "my Powerful Clan will support me."[27]

Stuart's agents fled to Pensacola, leaving McGillivray to handle things. McGillivray's "strong talk" and a temporary suspension of the Pensacola trade brought the Okfuskees and the other rebel sympathizers around. Several hundred delegates from both the Upper and Lower Towns, including pro-rebel leaders from Okfuskee and Cusseta, journeyed to Pensacola during the winter of 1777/78 to mend their fences, invite Taitt and the others to return, and pledge the safety of the traders and their goods.[28]

McGillivray had been instrumental in overcoming the most serious crisis in British/Creek relations during the Revolutionary period. Okfuskee, Cusseta, Tallassee, and a few other towns continued to harbor a rebel faction, but Stuart's men were never again driven out of the nation.

On March 21, 1779, John Stuart died. He left behind a legacy of hard work and loyalty to the Crown that was hard to challenge, but the ministry had grown increasingly disgusted with his policies. The huge sums of money he had spent to furnish supplies and powder to the Indians seemed, in London, to have been wasted. In early 1778, the Choctaws had not noticed James Willing's rebel raiders descending the Mississippi, and in early 1779, the Creeks, who had received more of Stuart's largesse than any other tribe, had not sent warriors to participate in the British capture of Augusta. There were good explanations for these failures, but to English officials the performance of the Indians did not seem to be worth the £100,000 Stuart had invested to secure their loyalty.[29]

Taking advantage of the opportunity presented by Stuart's death, the ministry devised a new system for dealing with the Southern Indians. Lord George Germain divided the old Southern Department into two districts, appointed an agent for each, and placed both officers under the orders of the military. Thomas Brown, based at St. Augustine, had charge of Creek affairs; Alexander Cameron located at Pensacola, conducted relations with the Choctaws and Chickasaws. The money available to both was strictly limited. Two themes were apparent in this administrative overhaul: economy and military control. No longer would the Southern tribes, notably the Creeks, draw supplies and powder without military service defined by British generals as useful.[30]

From the Creek perspective there were several things wrong with this new system. Primarily, they did not consider that they had given nothing in return for the supplies Stuart provided. In their view, they had preserved East and West Florida intact. Had they joined the rebels, they could have obliterated Pensacola and Mobile, and with Georgia's help they probably could have taken St. Augustine. Instead, they had blocked the path to the west, had helped defend St. Augustine, and had periodically raided the Georgia frontier to divert the rebels' attention from East Florida. Creek warriors had died in these skirmishes, and large numbers of men, to the detriment of their families, had stood by their arms when they might have been hunting. Compensation for these services was not only necessary, the Creeks believed, it was just. To add insult to injury, the sharply reduced supplies were in Thomas Brown's custody at St. Augustine. Pensacola, in Cameron's district, was much closer, more convenient, and a far better depot for Creek goods.[31]

Shortly after Stuart's death, Spain entered the war. West Florida and Spanish Louisiana had been uneasy neighbors, and at least since 1777, when Don Bernardo de Gálvez became governor, the neutrality of Louisiana had had a decidedly pro-American tinge. The Spanish threat, hitherto a matter of potential concern, became a real and present danger.

While West Florida's political and military leaders had long seen the Indians as their first line of defense against land attack, the rebel enemy in Georgia was distant. Louisiana, however, was close. British strategists assumed that the real vulnerability of Pensacola and Mobile was from the sea and repeatedly cited the value of a large native defense force to help repulse a seaborne invasion. Therefore, as Pensacola prepared for the inevitable Spanish attack, defense measures included renewed efforts to cement relations between West Florida and the Creeks. But with Stuart dead, a sharply curtailed budget for presents and supplies, a new and divided administrative authority that placed the Creeks under the direction of Thomas Brown at St. Augustine, a stuffy military officer who neither liked nor respected Indians in command of the forces in West Florida, the British defenders of the province had no easy task. To compound their problem, the British army in Georgia and South Carolina competed with West

Florida for Creek help. Most Creek warriors preferred to fight the settlers on their eastern border, against whom they had old and bitter grudges.[32]

Smallpox cut short the Creeks' fighting season in Georgia. By the fall of 1779, after several weeks of action, both with and independent of British troops, the dread disease drove the warriors home. Therefore, McGillivray was in the nation and able to respond quickly when General John Campbell called for help to repulse the Spaniards who were already in Mobile Bay and expected momentarily at Pensacola. Before the end of March, 1780, McGillivray had dispatched a large force from the Upper Towns, notified William McIntosh, commissary in the Lower Towns, to do the same, and was on the road to Pensacola.[33]

Mobile fell too quickly to be saved by the amassing of Creek warriors in West Florida, although about one hundred accompanied General Campbell in mid-March on an abortive relief mission. Pensacola's security, however, was much improved. The eleven to twelve hundred warriors from the Upper Towns had, McGillivray reported, "a very good effect, I believe a very sensible one on Don Gálvez." "Our department," he bragged, "cut a pretty good figure." Alexander Cameron agreed. "The safety and protection of this place . . . was entirely owing to the great number of Indians that speedily repaired to our assistance."[34]

McGillivray and Cameron may be forgiven for overestimating the effect of the Creek auxiliaries, but there is no doubt that they played a valuable role in delaying Gálvez's planned attack on Pensacola. Gálvez wrote to Campbell in April, 1780, asking that both sides agree not to use Indian allies. He couched his suggestion in humanitarian rhetoric, but it is clear that if the Spanish force had had an equal or larger number of native allies, he would have been far less worried about the supposed excesses committed by Indian warriors in battle. Campbell saw through Gálvez's veil and rejected the proposal out of hand. Indeed, Campbell suggested that one explanation for the delay of Gálvez's attack was an attempt to "weary out" his allies, of whom the Spanish were much afraid.[35]

The Creeks remained at Pensacola from late March to late May, 1780. There was nothing to do but wait for the Spanish invaders, who did not come, and they became bored. Campbell refused to let small parties of warriors scout between Pensacola and Mobile for fear the enemy would come while they were gone.

Some of the Creeks traded their supplies for rum and became "disorderly"; others drifted out of camp to visit Gálvez at Mobile and see what sort of presents he had; and many, subsisting on salted provisions and bad water, got sick. By the end of May, McGillivray was anxious to get his people out of Pensacola. Campbell, reassured that they would be replaced by "fresh" reinforcements, recognized their contribution with a "handsome" payment and discharged them.[36]

During the summer of 1780, the Creeks went about their affairs quietly and normally. The several hundred men who had answered Campbell's call to Pensacola had missed much of their winter hunt, but perhaps the payment they had received compensated for that loss. Summer was the agricultural season, and men had little to do beyond governing, local hunting, preparing for the long winter hunt, and conducting religious ceremonies.

With the approach of winter the Creek towns emptied as hunting parties traveled deep into the forests to harvest deerskins. When General Campbell notified McGillivray, in November, that Spanish invasion seemed imminent and a "powerful Reinforcement and aid from our faithful Friends and allies" was desperately needed, there were few warriors to be found. Hardly had McGillivray begun to scour the woods and call in the hunters when Campbell sent another letter saying that the Spanish invasion fleet had been destroyed by a hurricane and the "Services [of the Creeks] will not now be required for the defense of Pensacola." A month later, in mid-January, 1781, Campbell again sent an urgent request for help: "No time is . . . to be lost in your collecting and bringing as many Indians as you possibly can to our aid and assistance." The general promised pay as high as "Pensacola can afford," which could not have been very enticing when he went on to beg that the Creeks bring their own weapons, "there not being one hundred guns in all Pensacola." It was perhaps with some relief that McGillivray received still another dispatch from Campbell. Written in mid-February, the general again cancelled his call for Creek warriors, this time because he had heard a naval reinforcement from Jamaica was on the way. Between November, 1780, and February, 1781, at Campbell's orders, McGillivray had twice sent out messengers to recall the widely scattered hunters, only to cancel the call each time. Campbell's indecision could not inspire trust and confidence among the Creeks.[37]

About forty Creeks preferred hanging around Pensacola to hunting and answered one of Campbell's calls. Pretending they had not heard they were not needed, they arrived in January, with their families, and were on hand when the Spanish finally arrived March 9. Along with six Chickasaws and four hundred Choctaws, they constituted the native presence at Pensacola at the outset of the siege. One month later, on April 8, McGillivray arrived with forty Creeks. Forty more arrived in a few days. If they all remained to the end, and there is no evidence to show that they did, these 120 warriors were the sum of the Creek contingent. Added to the Choctaws, Alexander Cameron commanded about five hundred Indians during the siege.[38]

During the protracted siege of Pensacola, which lasted from March 9 to May 10, the Indians served as snipers, guerrillas, scouts, and messengers; they spied on Spanish positions, picked off careless soldiers, participated in organized sorties with British troops, and kept the invading soldiers in a high state of anxiety. One scholar has suggested that their value was essentially psychological,[39] but their achievements were also very real. The Indians considerably retarded the progress of Spanish entrenchments and accounted for perhaps one-third of the Spanish casualties.[40] Contemporary accounts of the siege, prepared by participants on both sides, continually refer to Indian actions, though rarely by tribal name.[41] On the other hand, it seems unlikely that a much larger number of native auxiliaries would have significantly altered the outcome. The Spanish army was too large, and Campbell's defensive tactics were too conservative. Responsibility for British defeat does not fall on the Creeks.

Still, given the turnout of the year before, the question has arisen — why were there so few Creeks to help defend Pensacola in 1781? The standard explanation has been that they were scattered in the woods hunting and could not be mustered. They were also confused and irritated by Campbell's vacillation. Cameron blamed Campbell's parsimony: "Had my advice been regarded by General Campbell in time," he complained, "instead of 500, I should have had 2000 Indians to oppose the Spaniards at the siege of Pensacola."[42] Campbell had been given authority over Cameron and had refused to provide supplies and powder to his Indian allies except for actual services rendered. Not only a radical reversal of Stuart's openhanded policy that caused economic hardship for the Creeks, it was an insult the British could ill afford. "When [the Creeks] are courted (by as they imagine a powerful nation) we cannot reasonably suppose that they will listen to our talks and risk their lives and country to serve us for nothing," Cameron explained.[43] Stuart's advice to Governor Tonyn of East Florida, given four years before, would have been well directed to Campbell: "We court Indian help, we do not command it."[44]

Campbell's haughty and disrespectful treatment of the Creeks was all the more serious because, in the spring of 1781, West Florida was no longer very important to them. Mobile was already lost, and the Spaniards, old neighbors who posed no threat, were making attractive overtures to Creek representatives, both there and at New Orleans. Pensacola was no more than an alternative to Augusta that had never fulfilled its potential. With Georgia firmly in royal control and Charleston a British city, the Creeks reached the same conclusion as the ministry in London — saving what remained of West Florida was not worth the cost. Why fight and die for a man they did not like, to protect a city they did not need, to retain a trade that was not very good? It made more sense for the Creeks to look once more to Georgia, where the king's men were winning, and to Augusta from whence their supplies had always come. The personality and policies of General Campbell no doubt made it easier for the Creeks to abandon Pensacola, but as always self-interest was the fundamental issue, and in the spring of 1781, the best interests of the Creeks lay elsewhere.

*Assistant Professor of History, Dartmouth College, Hanover, New Hampshire.

[1] Cameron to Germain, Oct. 31, 1780, May 27, 1781, K. G. Davies, ed., *Documents of the American Revolution, 1770-1783* (Shannon, 1972-79), 18:221-22, 20:150 (hereafter cited as *DAR*).

[2] Verner W. Crane, *The Southern Frontier, 1670-1732* (Ann Arbor, 1956); Peter A. Brannon, *The Southern Indian Trade* (Montgomery, 1935); and Brannon, "Pensacola Indian Trade," *Florida Historical Quarterly* 31 (1952):1-15.

[3] Charles Hudson, "Why the Southeastern Indians Slaughtered Deer," paper presented at the meeting of the American Society for Ethnohistory, 1979.

[4] David H. Corkran, *The Creek Frontier, 1540-1783* (Norman, 1967).

[5] John R. Swanton, *Early History of the Creek Indians and their Neighbors*, U.S. Bureau of American Ethnology Bulletin 73 (Washington, 1922), 422; J. Barton Starr, *Tories, Dons, and Rebels: The American Revolution in British West Florida* (Gainesville, 1976), 231; *Historical Statistics of the United States: Colonial Times to 1957* (Washington, 1960), 756.

[6] James Adair, *The History of the American Indians*, reprint ed. (Johnson City, 1930), 277.

[7] David Taitt to Germain, Aug. 6, 1779; Charles Shaw to Germain, Aug. 7, 1779, *DAR*, 17:182, 184.
[8] James Wright to Lord Dartmouth, Apr. 24, 1775, *DAR*, 9:106.
[9] John Stuart to Dartmouth, May 6, 1774, *DAR*, 8:110.
[10] Swanton, *Early History*, 226; Corkran, *Creek Frontier*, ch. 3; Crane, *Southern Frontier*, 259-61.
[11] Adair, *American Indians*, 277.
[12] Dunbar Rowland, ed., *Mississippi Provincial Archives, English Dominion, 1763-1766* (Nashville, 1911), 1:184-215. West Florida was not able to take over the trade. Nine years later, Upper Creek headmen were still expressing desire for a trade from Pensacola or Mobile to offset that with Augusta. Opaya Thlucco Mico to Stuart, Feb. 4, 1774, *DAR*, 7:69.
[13] Wright to Dartmouth, June 28, Oct. 21, 1774, *DAR*, 7:130, 193.
[14] Wright to Hillsborough, July 20, 1770, *DAR*, 2:151; Chester to Dartmouth, March 7, 1774, ibid., 7:55-56.
[15] Stuart to Hillsborough, Dec. 2, 1770, *DAR*, 2:281; Charles Stuart to John Stuart, Dec. 26, 1770, ibid., 2:302-303; Stuart to Hillsborough, Sept. 24, 1771, ibid., 1:401; Alden, *Stuart*, 224-29, 314-15.
[16] Stuart to Dartmouth, Aug. 2, 1774, *DAR*, 8:156-57.
[17] Gage to Stuart, Sept. 12, 1775, *DAR*, 11:105; Wright to Dartmouth, July 10, 18, 1775, ibid., 11:44, 49; Stuart to Gage, Oct. 24, 1775, ibid., 11:164.
[18] John Stuart to Henry Stuart, Oct. 24, 1775, *DAR*, 11:162-63; Stuart to Dartmouth, Oct. 25, 1775, ibid., 11:167; Stuart to Chester, Aug. 15, 1775, ibid., 10:130-31.
[19] William Knox to Grey Cooper, Apr. 27, 1779, *DAR*, 17:112-13; Helen L. Shaw, *British Administration of the Southern Indians, 1756-1783* (Lancaster, 1931), 175-77. I have subtracted about £4,500 from Knox's figures for salaries and contingencies.
[20] Stuart to Germain, Jan. 24, June 14, 1777, Apr. 13, Aug. 10, 1778, *DAR*, 13:27, 14:112-15, 15:94-97, 184.
[21] John Stuart to Henry Stuart, Oct. 24, 1775, *DAR*, 11:162-64; Stuart to Clinton, March 15, 1776, ibid., 12:78-79.
[22] Members of the Tiger clan particularly hated Stuart and the royal government. It was their kin who had been sacrificed in 1774 to lift the trade embargo imposed by the superintendent and Governor Wright. Throughout the Revolution, Tigers were the most constant neutralist, if not outright pro-rebel, faction in the nation. Corkran, *Creek Frontier*, 275, 282-85, 296.
[23] Stuart to Germain, June 14, 1777, *DAR*, 14:114-15; James H. O'Donnell, III, *Southern Indians in the American Revolution* (Nashville, 1973), ch. 2.
[24] Taitt to Stuart, July 7, 1776, *DAR*, 12:159-62; Galphin to Timothy Barnard, Aug. 18, 1776, ibid., 10:395; Galphin to James Burges, Aug. 28, 1776, ibid., 10:399; Stuart to Germain, Jan. 23, 1777, ibid., 14:34; Emistisiguo to Stuart, Nov. 19, 1776, ibid., 12:251.
[25] Howe to Stuart, Jan. 13, 1777, *DAR*, 14:28; Howe to Chester, Jan. 20, 1777, Historical Manuscripts Commission, *Report on American Manuscripts in the Royal Institution of Great Britain* (Dublin, 1906), 1:84; Howe to Dickson, May 6, 1777, ibid., 1:108; Tonyn to Howe, Apr. 6, 1778, ibid., 1:225.
[26] Stuart to Germain, Oct. 6, 1777, *DAR*, 14:194; James H. O'Donnell, III, "Alexander McGillivray: Training for Leadership, 1777-1783," *Georgia Historical*

Quarterly 49 (1965):172-86, and see my *The Creeks: A Critical Bibliography* (Bloomington, 1979), 28-33. McGillivray's birthyear is the subject of some confusion. In my "Alexander McGillivray," R. David Edmunds, ed., *American Indian Leaders: Studies in Diversity* (Lincoln, 1980), 41-63, I cited the generally accepted date of 1759. More recent evidence suggests that 1750 is the proper date. I am grateful to Professor William S. Coker, University of West Florida, for help in this matter.

[27] McGillivray to Stuart, Sept. 21, 1777, C.O. 5/79:33-34.

[28] Stuart to Howe, Feb. 4, 1778, H.M.C., *American MSS.* 1:189-90.

[29] Cameron and Charles Stuart to Germain, March 26, 1779, *DAR*, 17:89; Germain to Stuart, June 2, 1779, ibid., 17:138-39; Taitt to Germain, Aug. 6, 1779, ibid., 17:178-83; Starr, *Tories, Dons, and Rebels*, ch. 3.

[30] Germain to Cameron and Brown, June 25, 1779, *DAR*, 17:154-55.

[31] Stuart to Germain, Apr. 13, 1778, *DAR*, 15:96; Cameron to Germain, Dec. 20, 1779, Feb. 19, 1780, ibid., 16:238, 266.

[32] Germain to Campbell, Apr. 4, 1780, *DAR*, 18:72-75; Campbell to Germain, Apr. 27, 1780, C.O. 5/81:216; Jacob Moniac to West Florida Indian commissioners, May 1, 1779, C.O. 5/80:207-208.

[33] Cameron to Prevost, Oct. 15, 1779, *DAR*, 17:233; Prevost to Clinton, March 2, 1780, H.M.C., *American MSS*, 2:96; McIntosh to Brown, March 20, 1780, McGillivray to Brown, March 25, 1780, C.O. 5/81:167-70. In this instance the Georgia front suffered from Creek attention elsewhere. McIntosh's and McGillivray's reports were explanations why they could not come to Augusta with "1000 Indians at least" to prepare a joint action with British troops.

[34] Campbell to Germain, March 24, 1780, *DAR*, 18:64-67; McGillivray to Brown, May 13, 1780, C.O. 5/81:242; Cameron to Germain, July 18, 1780, *DAR*, 18:120. The official count of native allies compiled in April, 1780, was 1,235 Creeks, 236 Choctaws, 31 Chickasaws. Campbell to Germain, Aug. 6, 1780, *DAR*, 16:377.

[35] Gálvez to Campbell, Apr. 9, 1780; Campbell to Gálvez, Apr. 20, 1780, *DAR*, 16:326; Campbell to Clinton, May 13, 1780, H.M.C., *American MSS*, 2:121-22; Campbell to Germain, May 15, 1780, *DAR*, 18:92-94.

[36] Major James Campbell to Cameron, Apr. 27, 1780, C.O. 5/81:216; McGillivray to Brown, May 13, 1780, C.O. 5/81:242; Charles Shaw to Germain, June 18, 1780, Historical Manuscripts Commission, *Report on the Manuscripts of Mrs. Stopford-Sackville* (Hereford, 1910), 2:286; Cameron to Germain, July 18, 1780, *DAR*, 18:120-25.

[37] Campbell to McGillivray, Nov. 15, 1780, C.O. 5/82:450; Campbell to McGillivray, Nov. 22, 1780, C.O. 5/82:451; Campbell to McGillivray, Dec. 8, 1780, Jan. 12, Feb. 10, 1781, C.O. 5/82:451-52; Cameron to Germain, Feb. 10, 1781, *DAR*, 2:58-60.

[38] Cameron, Return of Indians, Feb. 1, 1781, *DAR*, 19:39; Cameron to Germain, May 27, 1781, *DAR*, 20:150; James A. Padgett, ed., "Bernardo de Gálvez's Siege of Pensacola in 1781 (As Related in Robert Farmar's Journal)," *Louisiana Historical Quarterly* 26 (1943):319, says McGillivray arrived April 9 with 70 Creeks.

[39] Robert R. Rea, "Pensacola Under the British (1763-1781)," James R. McGovern, ed., *Colonial Pensacola* (Pensacola, 1974), 68.

[40] Donald E. Worcester, trans., "Miranda's Diary of the Siege of Pensacola,

1781," *Florida Historical Quarterly* 29 (1951):183; Albert W. Haarmann, "The Siege of Pensacola: An Order of Battle," *Florida Historical Quarterly* 44 (1966):198.

[41]N. Orwin Rush, *The Battle of Pensacola* (Tallahassee, 1966), 41-108.

[42]Cameron to Germain, May 27, 1781, *DAR*, 20:150.

[43]Cameron to Germain, Oct. 31, 1780, *DAR*, 18:222; O'Donnell, *Southern Indians*, 95-100.

[44]Stuart to Tonyn, July 21, 1777, *DAR*, 13:173.

HAMSTRUNG BY PENURY: ALEXANDER CAMERON'S FAILURE AT PENSACOLA

JAMES H. O'DONNELL III[*]

This occasion celebrates the success of Bernardo de Gálvez and the Spanish in capturing Pensacola. For every winner there must be a loser, and it is with the losers that this paper is concerned. In rather typical post-mortem fashion we may ask, what went wrong for the British? That chance shot into the Queen's Redoubt powder magazine shortened the siege, but the battle was lost before then. If we assume that the defense of Pensacola was a matter of interest to the British military establishment, to the civil authority and the citizens, and to the southern Indians who came here for trade and supplies, we have at least three areas for investigation. My purpose is to examine the functions carried out (or not carried out) in the office of the Indian superintendent, and this paper will concentrate on Alexander Cameron, the chief official of the British Indian department in residence in the year before the city fell. Victim of his own insecurities and the particular circumstances of wartime, Cameron failed to exercise the kind of leadership necessary in a moment of crisis. Was the cause of his failure to be found in Cameron's lack of ability, in his personality, or in prevailing circumstances which prevented him from acting?

At the time Pensacola fell, Alexander Cameron held the office of Superintendent of Indian Affairs for the Mississippi District in the Southern Department.[1] This rather awkwardly titled position had gradually evolved from modifications undertaken in the British imperial establishment during and after the Seven Years War. At that time, officials in London reacted to frontier instability by creating two Indian superintendencies. All tribes living north of the Ohio River were placed within the jurisdiction of William Johnson of New York; responsibility for native peoples living south of the Ohio was assigned to Edmond Atkin of South Carolina. Because Atkin died in 1762, the long-term superintendent before the American Revolution was John Stuart of Charleston. Johnson and Stuart had the responsibility of being the king's representatives to the native peoples. Matters of land and boundaries, trade, and warfare were to be negotiated between the superintendents and the tribes involved. Both Johnson and Stuart were given wide latitude in the years between 1763 and 1775. Each man considered himself an independent member of the imperial establishment, answerable only to the secretary of state or the commander in chief. Johnson and Stuart both envisioned themselves as somewhat more important and grander than they were, attitudes especially apparent if one visits Stuart's Tradd Street house in Charleston or Johnson's baronial home in the Mohawk valley. Each depended on a substantial retinue of deputies, commissaries, interpreters, and loyal native peoples to keep their systems operational. Money was spent rather freely, each superintendent drawing directly on the treasury or the commander in chief's office to cover expenditures. Over a period of more than a decade their subordinates grew accustomed both to the independent decision-making of the superintendents and the great freedom with which money was spent.

It is important to consider these aspects of the Indian department because members of a bureaucracy tend to become accustomed to the status quo and resistant to change. This is particularly true of those who find security and preferment in a particular system. The generalization applies to Alexander Cameron and to Guy Johnson, who succeeded William Johnson as head of the northern department in 1774.[2]

Alexander Cameron was one of many Scots who sought refuge in British North America during the middle of the eighteenth century. He was in South Carolina in 1761, in which year he was made an ensign in the Independent Regulars. During the next two years he was stationed at Fort Prince George on the edge of the Cherokee country. In 1763, his fellow Scotsman, John Stuart, offered him a position as deputy in the Indian department, with particular responsibilities for the Cherokees. Much of his time thereafter was spent in the Cherokee country, where the Cherokees called him Scotchie.[3] Because of John Stuart's close affinity with the Cherokees and the easy communication between the two Scots, it is not surprising that Stuart came to regard Cameron as his chief deputy in the department, a post officially awarded him in 1768. Whether Cameron had his eye on Stuart's job at some future date is unclear, but certainly he relished the power of his own role and the prosperity which the superintendent enjoyed and no doubt shared with his chief deputy.

At the outbreak of the American Revolution, Alexander Cameron's ordered world began to fall apart. The South Carolinians pursued him relentlessly out of the Ninety-Six District.[4] He took refuge in the Cherokee country and was there in the spring of 1776, when the chiefs and warriors chose to assault the frontiers. Indeed, he may have participated in some of the raids, since the punitive expeditions sent out by the southern states eagerly sought to capture him. By the fall of 1776, he fled for his life. Virginia troops swept into the Cherokee country; Cameron slipped away to the Upper Creek villages to escape the wrath of the Americans who blamed him for unleashing the Cherokee attacks on the southern frontiers.[5]

Early in January, 1777, Cameron left his temporary headquarters at Little Tallassee and traveled to Pensacola.[6] There he was to meet John Stuart and assist him in the preparation of a major conference with the Choctaws and Chickasaws at Mobile. Once this meeting was carried out in May, 1777, Alexander Cameron returned to his headquarters-in-exile among the Upper Creeks. He and David Taitt were responsible for keeping the Creeks and Cherokees ready in case the British military called on the Indian department for assistance.

Unfortunately for British plans, George Galphin, of South Carolina, was intriguing with the pro-American faction among the Lower Creeks for the assassination of Taitt and Cameron. Galphin's machinations bore fruit in the summer of 1777, when Lower Creek raiders looted Taitt's storehouse and chased the two Englishmen out of the Creek country. Only the timely intervention of Alexander McGillivray prevented worse damage and perhaps the death of the two British officials.[7]

After this incident, Cameron spent less and less time in the Indian country and more and more time in Pensacola. The two major reasons for this were probably Stuart's need for assistance and Alexander Cameron's fear for his life. The superintendent was frequently incapacitated by attacks of gout, a situation which left opportunity for Cameron to oversee the day to day activities of the department. Cameron's fear of capture or assassination did not diminish. He had stayed in the Cherokee country through the summer of 1776, because he knew the Cherokees were loyal and would warn him of efforts to capture him. Among the Creeks, however, he had no network of friends; the activities of the pro-American Creeks in the summer of 1777, had demonstrated that even Taitt's life was in danger among his so-called friends. During this period in Pensacola, Cameron concluded that he would only be safe in the Indian country if he organized a company of loyalist refugee partisans to accompany him and act as his bodyguard. By Cameron's logic, they would also be indispensable in acting with the natives against the rebel frontiers.

On March 21, 1779, "after a tedious and painful illness, which he bore with resignation for several months," John Stuart died.[8] Cameron could not know it, but with the death of Stuart the old order had passed. Alexander Cameron and another of John Stuart's deputies, Charles Stuart, tried to maintain the superintendent's office until appointments could be made in England, but nothing was to be the same.[9]

Given the communications of the day, none of the Indian officials in Pensacola could know that the staggering expenses for Indian affairs were being debated sharply in Parliament. In December, 1778, when the list of extraordinary expenses for the army was presented, exception was taken to the bills presented under the name of John Stuart.[10] Charges were circulated that Stuart and his deputies had engaged in all kinds of financial chicanery for personal profit at the king's expense. The list was not struck and the charges never amounted to more than rumor, but the damage was done. Add to these accusations against the Indian department the increasing unpopularity of the American war, and officials in London had to take steps to make some changes in America. Germain had already sent out a severe rebuke to John Stuart which was en route when the superintendent died. Germain announced that the Indian department would have to stay within budget or its bills would be disallowed and the superintendent or his agents held personally responsible for them.[11] When Germain learned of John Stuart's death, he resolved to take the opportunity to make substantive changes in the department.

In America, on the other hand, Alexander Cameron assumed after John Stuart's death that he would automatically succeed to the superintendency.[12] He should have sensed the winds of change, however, when Governor Peter Chestér appointed a Board of Indian Commissioners to function until word of a new appointee arrived from London. Even Brigadier General Campbell urged Cameron and the other Indian officials to lay aside their "ambition and Pecuniary views for the sake of Peace Concord and Harmony."[13]

If Cameron was unhappy with the temporary arrangements for Indian affairs in Pensacola, he was even less happy with the new arrangements Germain forged for the Indian departments. London had become skeptical about the effectiveness of superintendents who maintained "seats" and conducted business through intermediaries in the several tribes. In the mind of George Germain and other British officials, this practice produced greater and greater expenses with less and less return. The Southern Indian Department was therefore to be divided. Alexander Cameron learned in October, 1779, that he was to superintend the Mississippi District in the Southern Indian Department with responsibility for the Choctaws and Chickasaws. His annual budget was not to exceed £1,955. Any extraordinary monies would have to be approved and disbursed by the military department.[14]

The radical nature of the new situation seemed to terrify Alexander Cameron. He was now placed in an impossible situation (or so he perceived it). Worst of all, Cameron was expected to spend most of the year traveling in the Indian country, visiting the tribes for whom he was responsible, and cultivating their loyalty to the crown. Alexander Cameron was plunged into an identity crisis of the first order.

Faced with what seemed a totally new situation, Cameron lapsed into indecision and quarrelsomeness. Unfortunately, he directed his frustrations toward the British military establishment in general and General Campbell in particular. While Campbell was no model of cooperation, Alexander Cameron's inability to get along with the general was costly to both of them. At least on the surface, their disagreements were primarily fiscal. Part of the legacy bequeathed to Cameron by Stuart was a residue of debt. Cameron was now faced with a number of irate creditors who found that Stuart's drafts were not being paid.[15]

Indeed, the greatest burdens falling on Cameron came to him in part from his predecessor's affluent life style and, perhaps axiomatically, the mountain of debts piled up through the unchecked spending of Superintendent Stuart and his deputies between 1775 and 1779. The superintendent had interpreted General Thomas Gage's instructions about maintaining the loyalty of the tribes in rather broad fashion. In tandem with the extraordinary demands of war, Stuart's understanding of orders from his commander in chief led him to spend money freely. As Stuart's chief deputy, Cameron accepted the rationale that the emergency situation of wartime justified the expenditure of every penny. It was, therefore, extremely difficult for him to follow a different procedure in both style of life and spending, especially when the war continued unabated and the British defense of the Gulf coast appeared to need the help of every forest warrior available.

Another of Alexander Cameron's perceptual boundaries was his own self-esteem; Cameron regarded himself as a "gentleman," a position in society he claims to have sustained throughout his seventeen years of service to the king.[16] Wandering about the country on horseback as a roving ambassador to the Indians was not his idea of a role befitting his situation. It is appropriate to add that not everyone shared Cameron's view of himself. General Campbell, for example, believed that Alexander Cameron was neither well-educated nor was he trained in business.[17]

As General Campbell's judgment of Cameron indicates, the disagreement between the two was more than monetary. Money was, however, the crucial issue, since most of the funds that John Stuart had spent, and those which Cameron wanted to spend, were disbursed on supplies for visiting parties of Creeks, Choctaws, Chickasaws, and other tribesmen who trekked into Pensacola. Stuart and Cameron reasoned that if the parties were treated well they would respond when called upon to aid in the defense of the city against invasion. An "ill-timed parsimony," on the other hand, might save money, but it was likely to cost the Pensacola garrison assistance in time of need. The availability of forest soldiers as auxiliaries was no trifling matter, since the Pensacola garrison was relatively small.

The exchanges between Alexander Cameron and General Campbell were lengthy and at times acrimonious. At the end of one letter, the general's aide wrote: "I perfitly [sic] agree with the conclusion of your letter. That your narration is truly disagreeable to me especially when it contins [sic] invective and accusations that I consider injurious."[18]

Whatever the level of the invective, the real issue was the joint defense of Pensacola, which was not going well. The Cameron-Campbell imbroglio was intensified by the administrative decision in London to place the Creeks (whose warriors should have been of most assistance to Pensacola) within the jurisdiction of Thomas Brown, whose headquarters on the South Carolina-Georgia frontier was too far away to assist the British in West Florida.[19] To make matters still worse, parties of Creeks continued to visit Pensacola, expecting the largess which had been dispensed in the days of the late superintendent. Alexander Cameron could not obtain permission from Campbell to supply the Creek visitors, but he did so anyway, and then issued bills of credit against Thomas Brown, the British superintendent for the Atlantic District.

As if Cameron and Campbell did not have enough problems with Indian affairs, they were further exasperated by the policies being carried out by Governor Peter Chester. The royal governor's annual budget carried a line item entry for £1,000 for the entertainment of Indians; yet neither the general nor the superintendent could persuade Chester to disburse those funds or to entertain the Indians. Using some of the creative accounting so dear to the hearts of institutional budget-balancers, Governor Chester had his entry for £1,000 for Indian expenses transferred "to extraordinary charges as contingent provincial disbursements for which the provincial fund was not equal."[20] By refusing to receive the Creeks, the governor was alienating tribesmen who were accustomed to visiting Pensacola. Worse yet for the tranquility of Indian affairs and the protection of the colony, the governor had frustrated the Creeks by granting "to himself and others, his favorites and dependants, during the course of last month, large tracts of land within the Indian boundary."[21] In the midst of all this administrative and fiscal turmoil, real danger loomed on the horizon. Early in 1780, Gálvez and his forces had succeeded in taking Mobile before either Campbell or the Indians could sufficiently reinforce it. Aware that Pensacola was the Spaniard's next objective, General Campbell requested and received the assistance of numbers of Creek, Choctaw, and Chickasaw warriors in the spring of 1780. On April 16, for example, there were 1,235 Creeks, 236 Choctaws, and 31 Chickasaw present in Pensacola. The number was sufficient for the approaching Spanish commander to request an agreement to "avoid reciprocal hostilities by allied Indians."[22] Before Gálvez could outwait the Indians' patience, additional help arrived for the British, and the Spanish withdrew for the time being.

Once the clear and present danger was gone, Alexander Cameron and General Campbell resumed their bickering. The Indian superintendent wanted the general to maintain at least one hundred warriors at all times to serve as scouts and as messengers to bring in aid when needed. Campbell refused to take such a step, although he did dispense some supplies to visiting parties on a limited basis.

Furthermore, the general declined Cameron's persistent pleas for a paid body of irregulars to act as Cameron's bodyguard and as partisans in time of war. Campbell also pressed Cameron to fulfill Germain's expectations that the Indian superintendency should become itinerant. Germain had explained to General Campbell the orders which had been given to Cameron:

> I have therefore, signified to Mr. Cameron the King's Commands to visit the Indian Nations within his district; and he is not to be allowed any establishment at either Pensacola or Mobile, unless he defrays the Expence out of his Estimate. I know there will be Parties coming to visit you, tho' the Superintendent be absent, which must be entertained & gratified; on which account it will be necessary for you to appoint a person to act as an Interpreter, and to take care of them. The Reception, Care & Delivery of the Indian Presents, sent out by orders of the Lords of the Treasury, will require a Storekeeper, which you will be pleased also to appoint; and a warehouse must be hired to keep them in.

Clearly, explained Germain, there was to be a difference in the Indian department:

> You will perceive, by what I have said upon this Subject, that the present Superintendents of Indian Affairs are not to be considered on the same Foot with the late Colonel Stuart: but are intended to be made subservient to the Military Commanders in their districts . . . . In the event that the office should be vacated it is the King's Command that the officer comman-

ding in the district should appoint someone to fill the place until the King's pleasure should be known.[23]

This change in job-description by Germain did not alter the basic fact that General Campbell needed Cameron's expertise in late 1780 and early 1781. Alexander Cameron, unfortunately, was victimized by his own fears. He did not really accept the limitations placed on him, or so it would appear, since he frequently badgered the general about funds for the parties of Indians who visited Pensacola and support for the troop of irregulars which he insisted was necessary to accompany him into the Choctaw and Chickasaw country.[24] Cameron's behavior characteristics (fear, insecurity, inability to act, and insistence on specific orders with absolute backing) were almost identical to those displayed by Guy Johnson after he returned to New York from England in 1777.

If Alexander Cameron did not have enough difficulty in attempting to fulfill his job and to cooperate with the British military department, he added to his list of woes by discussing partisan politics with citizens of Pensacola who were critical of Campbell. Early in 1781, Cameron alleged that several private gentlemen in Pensacola had urged him to spare no expense in securing the support of the Indians. If the general would not pay the expenses, they would. Cameron's better judgment prevailed in this instance, and he did not accept the offer, but the mere fact that he mentioned it to the secretary of state for the colonies indicates the degree to which fear had risen in Pensacola. Indeed, if we may believe Cameron, some of the citizens of Pensacola and officers from the garrison had protested to Campbell about his refusal to maintain a watch of Indians. They had threatened to send home a representation against the general "as his conduct intimated to them that he meant to give up the Province." When Captain William Johnson, of the Royal Artillery, told the general of this unrest, he added that he would join the protest if some Indians were not kept in service until the plans of the Spanish were known.[25] Cameron believed the general was a good officer, but he "takes the wrong steps to make them [the Indians] useful to government."[26]

The threatened protest by the citizens and perhaps some officers stemmed from Campbell's inconsistent policy with regard to the Indian auxiliaries. The general urgently called for every warrior available, when there was rumor of invasion, but when there was any hope of relief, he immediately sent all the people home, sometimes with less than a pound of powder as a parting present. Such a policy would backfire on the general in the long run.

Indeed, one is somewhat puzzled by Campbell's approach to Indian affairs. Given his experience at Detroit, after the French and Indian War, it may be argued that he appreciated (or at least he should have) the value of forest soldiers.[27] Such an assumption is logical, but I would raise the negative from the same experience, i.e., the attitude shared by many officers in the British army that the warriors were basically untrustworthy beggars, not worth the price of their rations. Another point to consider is that Campbell was a career officer who shared many of his fellow officers' prejudices toward America. Amherst was notorious for his low opinion of America and Americans, a bias which he passed on, not only to his fellow officers in America, but also to his political friends in England and even to the king when he was called upon by the monarch for military advice.[28] At Detroit, furthermore, Campbell should have become aware that part of the background for Pontiac's Rebellion was the penury imposed by Amherst on the flow of supplies for the Indians. Whatever John Campbell learned about forest soldiers while stationed at Detroit, he did not appear to have learned much about forest diplomacy.

Because of criticisms raised at home about the increasing expenditures of the military, General Campbell was pressed to hold down expenses, but his economy ("an ill-timed penury" Cameron would have called it) had negative effects. Like accountants who buy short-run gains with long-run losses, the general's tightfistedness, combined with his "wolf, wolf!" approach, helped in the making of a British loss at Pensacola.

In Campbell's defense it might be argued that he had no choice because he did not have, nor could he obtain, supplies sufficient to support large numbers of warriors on an instant alert basis. His experience of the year before, when Mobile was besieged, likewise should have told him that there was a limit to the length of time the warriors would stay at Pensacola, since they suffered from bad water and poor rations, as did any other soldiers. In other words, the stay of the Indian auxiliaries was often self-limiting.

Alexander Cameron was not the only one of John Stuart's former deputies suffering frustration because of imperial economies and military myopia. Cameron had been joined in Pensacola by David Taitt after he arranged a parole with his Spanish captors on July 29, 1780. Under the terms of his parole, Taitt was not to inform the British about conditions at Mobile, nor was he to use his influence with the Indians *"contra el Dominio Español,"* either in the forests or elsewhere. Limited by the conditions of his parole, Taitt spent his time in frustration from the financial problems left over from the inflated expenses of Stuart's last years in office. When Superintendent Stuart died, Taitt had presented bills to Alexander Cameron for expenses connected with leading a number of Creeks toward the Georgia frontier early in 1779. When Cameron refused to honor them, Taitt went to General Campbell, who responded that he had written to Cameron on the matter. Back to Cameron went David Taitt, to be told by Cameron that he would draw for them only if Taitt would give him a bond of indemnification which would make Taitt liable for the principal and interest if the bills were refused. Since Taitt was unwilling to do that, he sent his bills to General Prevost in Savannah, but Prevost had sailed. Thus, by early 1781, Taitt's creditors in Pensacola were threatening to sue him. Since Cameron had already had a judgment brought against him for the same reason, David Taitt was worried; he explained to Lord George Germain that such a lawsuit would be extremely hard on him, since he had not a penny. He had received no salary from July 1, 1778 to July 1, 1779, and if that was insufficient burden, his bills for 1778 had been protested. This was all too much to take, he lamented to Knox, since he had been "the least expensive and most faithful servant under Colonel Stuart which will appear by every account of mine ever since my being employed."[29]

If officials of the British Indian department, both past and present, were frustrated early in 1781, so were the native American leaders. Alexander McGillivray had received word from Campbell to bring as many warriors as possible. This was in a letter of January 12, 1781, which also requested that each forest soldier bring his own weapon, "there not being one hundred Guns in all Pensacola and not many spare muskets by reason of the immense number of the different Nations who receive Presents since the arrival of the last supply."[30] As the native Americans might have expected, it was not long before General Campbell did a turnabout. The general cancelled his request for reinforcements in mid-February when he understood that assistance was coming. Furthermore, one-half of the seven hundred Choctaw were sent home with little in the way of supplies or gifts.

Hardly had General Campbell dismissed the Choctaw when, as in the proverbial tale of the wolf, the wolf actually appeared. Both Cameron and McGillivray were frantically approached with pleas for help. Try as they might, the British agents could not undo the months of vacillation by the general. When the Spanish fleet arrived, the army of Gálvez was opposed by only fifteen hundred British soldiers and some four hundred Choctaw who were joined late in the siege by another one hundred Creeks. Sent to harass the Spanish while the British strengthened their lines, the warriors were pulled back as the Dons inched closer. On March 30, a Choctaw sally broke the Spanish lines at one point. British failure to follow this lead brought Frenchumastabie back to the British lines in a fury. In his view, every major effort against the Spanish had been undertaken by the Indians without support or reward.[31]

Time and numbers were on the side of Gálvez and his army. On May 10, 1781, General John Campbell capitulated. Campbell's surrender was not only the end of British Pensacola, but also the effective termination of the British Southern Indian Department.[32] Without a Gulf Coast base, Alexander Cameron would be forced to move to Georgia or East Florida if he intended to carry on his office. Consequently, as the Union Jack came down, Cameron, McGillivray, and other departmental officials took refuge once again in the Creek country. From there he intended to take up residence in Georgia, but the upcountry post of Augusta was soon taken by the Americans, and Cameron was forced to locate in Savannah. There Alexander Cameron died on December 27, 1781, to the end believing that his view of the public service was the correct one.[33] He never accepted the alterations forced into effect by Germain, insisting that he and Thomas Brown could deal with the native peoples more effectively if they were permitted to do so in the old way. His failure at Pensacola had been wrought of time, circumstances, and his own insecurities. We may hope that Cameron never realized all this; he died, as he had lived, an officer and a gentleman.

*Professor of History, Marietta College, Marietta, Ohio.

[1] See John Richard Alden, *John Stuart and the Southern Colonial Frontier, 1754-1775* (New York, 1966); James H. O'Donnell III, *Southern Indians and the American Revolution, 1775-1783* (Knoxville, 1973).

[2] James H. O'Donnell III, "The Iroquois in the American Revolution: Suggestions for Investigation," Cherokee-Iroquois Symposium, Cherokee, N.C., April, 1978.

[3] James H. O'Donnell III, "Alexander Cameron," *Dictionary of North Carolina Biography*, ed. William S. Powell (Chapel Hill, 1979).

[4] Cameron to Andrew McLean, Aug. 16, 1775, R. W. Gibbes, *Documentary History of the American Revolution, 1774-1782* (New York, 1853-57), 3:143; James H. O'Donnell III, "A Loyalist View of the Drayton-Tennent-Hart Mission to the Upcountry," *South Carolina Historical Magazine* 67 (1966):15-28.

[5] Cameron to Stuart, Aug. 31, 1776, C.O. 5/78:72-73.

[6] Stuart to Germain, March 10, 1777, C.O. 5/78:105.

[7] McGillivray to Stuart, Sept. 21, 1777, C.O. 5/79:33.

[8] Cameron and Charles Stuart to Germain, March 26, 1779, C.O. 5/80:109.

[9] O'Donnell, *Southern Indians*, 82ff.

[10] John Almon, ed., *The Parliamentary Register* (London, 1775-80), 12:255ff.

[11] Germain to Cameron and Thomas Brown, June 25, 1779, C.O. 5/81:123.

[12] Cameron to Germain, Dec. 18, 1779, C.O. 5/81:37.

[13] Campbell to Cameron and Charles Stuart, March 27, 1779, C.O. 5/80:151.

[14] Germain to Cameron and Thomas Brown, June 25, 1779, C.O. 5/81:123; Germain to Campbell, Aug. 5, 1779, C.O. 5/597, pt. 1:224.

[15] Taitt to William Knox, Feb. 18, 1781, C.O. 5/82:155.

[16] Cameron to Germain, Oct. 31, 1780, C.O. 5/82:111.

[17] Campbell to Henry Clinton, Feb. 10, 1780, C.O. 5/597, pt. 1:315ff. "I must observe to Your Excellency that I believe the Superintendant Mr. Cameron an honest well disposed Man, but indolent in his Disposition of an infirm and Sickly Constitution and no wise qualified from Natural or acquired parts to act but in a Subordinate Degree. In short I take him to have been a very fit and proper Person for a Deputy Superintendant; But he is lost bewildered, and Without Authority at the Head of the Department and unequal to the Task of Correction and keeping under a Spirit of Extortion and Extravagance that I'm afraid was forwarded and encouraged by the Lenity and Indulgence of the late Superintendant."

[18] James Campbell to Cameron, Jan. 30, 1781, C.O. 5/82:141.

[19] Gary D. Olson, "Thomas Brown, Loyalist Partisan, and the Revolutionary War in Georgia, 1777-1782," *Georgia Historical Quarterly* 54 (1970):1-19, 183-208.

[20] Christopher Newsham to Richard Cumberland, April 4, 1780, C.O. 5/595, pt. 3:919.

[21] Campbell to Clinton, Feb. 10, 1780, C.O. 5/99:116.

[22] Gálvez to Campbell, April 9, 1780, C.O. 5/597, pt. 1:413-15.

[23] Germain to Campbell, April 4, 1780, C.O. 5/597, pt. 1:295-307.

[24] O'Donnell, "Iroquois"; Campbell to Clinton, Feb. 10, 1780, C.O. 5/597, pt. 1:315ff.

[25] Cameron to Germain, Feb. 10, 1781, C.O. 5/82:130.

[66] Cameron to Germain, Nov. 30, 1780, C.O. 5/82:117.

[27] J. Leitch Wright, Jr., *Florida in the American Revolution* (Gainesville, 1975), 87.

[28] O'Donnell, "British Leadership and Strategy in the South," Kentucky Symposium on the Bicentennial, Lexington, Oct., 1974.

[29]Taitt's parole is included in Taitt to William Knox, Feb. 18, 1781, C.O. 5/82:155.
[30]Campbell to McGillivray, Jan. 12, 1781, C.O. 5/82:452.
[31]Talk of Frenchumastabie to Cameron, April 1, 1781, C.O. 5/82:210.
[32]O'Donnell, *Southern Indians*, 114ff.
[33]*Royal Georgia Gazette*, Jan. 3, 1782.

THE ANGLO-SPANISH CONTEST FOR THE GULF COAST AS VIEWED FROM THE TOWNSQUARE

KATHRYN HOLLAND*

Writing Indian history has never been an easy task for the non-Indian — differences in culture and outlook invariably combine to make it difficult. Constant diligence must be maintained to avoid unintentionally belittling Indian culture and misunderstanding the Indians' true intent. What we know of the Indians, we know through European records, for the Southeastern Indians were not sufficiently impressed with the written word to learn its use. Indian "talks," so carefully gleaned for information by eager historians, are the products of translators, tinged with European values and concepts.

How then, can we accurately discern the beliefs and views which led chiefs and their followers to take certain actions? There being no choice, we must rely on what we have: reports of Indian agents, soldiers, and traders and what "talks" we can find. We can only infer what the view from the square was—and there were as many views as there were inhabitants of the southern backcountry. No one view prevailed. In each nation there were pro-English, pro-American, pro-Spanish, and neutralist factions. For though there were perhaps seven thousand gunmen in the three nations, only about seven per cent of them came to Pensacola in 1781. Our concern here is to examine the motives of those who remained loyal to their British masters and came to defend Pensacola at the behest of their allies.[1]

Seventeen hundred sixty-three was a momentous year for the Indian tribes along the Gulf Coast, for in that year the Spanish and French were deprived of their holdings in Florida by the victorious British following the Great War for Empire. Spain, soon after, became the owner of New Orleans and the land to the west of the Mississippi. For the new owners of Florida, one of the most pressing concerns was that of Indian relations, and, from the beginning, efforts were made to secure the friendship of the tribes. The Choctaws, whose domain lay to the west of the Tombigbee River, classified themselves in three geographic divisions: the East Party; the West Party; and the Six Villages, a group of southern towns lying between the Pearl and Pascagoula rivers, which had been especially French-dominated prior to 1763. The Chickasaw villages, lying north of Choctaw territory, were remote from West Florida, but their inhabitants were much concerned with establishing peaceful relations and trade with the colony. The Creek nation, consisting of two geographic divisions, the Upper and Lower towns, was actually a loosely organized confederacy of a number of tribes. The confederacy claimed land extending eastward from the Tombigbee-Alabama river system to the Atlantic, as well as most of the Florida peninsula.

Numerous congresses were held in West Florida with all three tribes, between 1763 and 1776, to solve boundary disputes, trade irregularities, and other matters of concern. All such meetings necessitated the giving of presents by the English: as common diplomatic practice and as payment for land and Indian loyalty. British medals, distributed to leading chiefs, were a distinction sought by many. Once accepted, medals bound their wearers to remain friends and servants to the Great King. Naturally, the chiefs also expected to be rewarded with presents of clothing, guns, provisions, and rum in return for their loyalty.[2] As one deputy observed, "Reason and Rhetoric will fall to the ground unless supported by strouds and duffels [heavy woolen cloth and blankets]."[3] For the Indian, loyalty depended on the ability of the European to supply his needs. Consequently, the British, even before 1763, had always found large numbers of adherents in the Southeast.

One of the most important aspects of Indian relations was trade. The Indians, since their first contact with white civilization, had benefited from, and pursued, a steady trade in animal pelts in return for European manufactures and rum. Increasingly, their way of life turned on the collection of furs and skins. By the late eighteenth century, they had become almost totally dependent on European tools, weapons, and clothing. As the capital and leading city of a struggling wilderness colony, Pensacola became the focus of Creek relations. Although citizens and officials of the colony wished for a profitable trade with the confederacy, none of any consequence developed during the first twelve years of the colony's existence. Instead, the Creeks preferred to continue their relationships with traders from Augusta, Georgia. Mobile, on the other hand, opened a fairly profitable trade with the Choctaw and Chickasaw tribes to the north and west of the city. Although the trade was hindered by rival

Georgia traders and angry Creek warriors who actually undertook a war to prevent the commerce, it served to draw the once irascible pro-French Choctaws into the English camp. The Chickasaws, for years the victims of French assaults, rejoiced at the transfer of the area to British control and remained loyal to the new owners of West Florida.[4] Despite much confusion, West Florida Indian relations remained peaceful between the years 1763 to 1776.

The American Revolution brought new problems for West Florida. Remote from the revolutionary turbulence to the northward, the colony became a refuge for loyal Americans and such British public servants as Superintendent of Indian Affairs John Stuart. For the Indians, the colony became the chief source of British presents and trade as the old paths were disrupted by war.[5] The entry of Spain into the war in 1779, drastically changed the circumstances of West Florida, for it became the immediate target of Spanish aggression. Short on supplies, manpower, and funds, and isolated from other areas of imperial control, Indian loyalty and aid became of paramount importance to the defenders of the colony.

At the very time when Indian relations were most important, the Southern Indian Department was subjected to radical reorganization. The death of John Stuart, in 1779, provided the occasion. For a time after his death, Indian affairs were supervised by a five-man commission appointed by West Florida Governor Peter Chester. By October, however, word arrived in America of the department's new structure. No longer to be administered by one man, the department was divided into two districts: the Mississippi District, to oversee Chickasaw and Choctaw relations; and the Atlantic District, to supervise Cherokee and Creek relations. Alexander Cameron was appointed Superintendent for the Mississippi District and was ordered to Pensacola to assume control of Indian affairs there. Cameron was surprised by the appointment. Long the commissary to the Cherokees under Stuart, he had numerous connections with that tribe as well as with the Upper and Lower Creeks and was not acquainted with the more western tribes.[6] Colonel Thomas Brown was given control of the Atlantic District. Even though the Creek tribes were to be supervised and entertained from St. Augustine, they still continued to call upon the more convenient office at Pensacola and proved a heavy burden on Cameron's newly tightened budget.[7]

Cameron's task was not easy. His finances were limited; his health was poor; the area under his supervision was immense and plagued by poor communication with the interior; and the new superintendents were placed under the direction of the ranking military officer for each district.[8] In Cameron's case, this was Major General John Campbell, who, according to the superintendent, was not only stingy with funds but did "not understand anything of Indians or their affairs; he thinks they are to be used like slaves or a people void of natural sense."[9]

Cameron faced more serious problems than these, however, for the Spanish were forwarding "many flattering and inviting talks" to his red charges.[10] Cameron's objectives therefore became to prevent the defection of disgruntled tribesmen, to gain the assistance of loyal Indians for the defense of British territory, and to use the Indians offensively against the Spanish.[11]

West Florida had weathered the Willing raid in 1778, but the next year the western portion of the colony had succumbed to Spanish attack.[12] With the fall of Mobile in March, 1780, Pensacola became the "arrogant guardian" of Britain's remaining Gulf Coast empire.[13] Now, more than ever before, the loyalty of the estimated seven thousand Indians who lived within striking distance of the colony "became a matter of greatest importance."[14] Yet the astounding rate at which the Spanish had "so easily and speedily subdued" the western portion of the colony alarmed many Indians. Indeed, lack of preparedness and failure to relieve Mobile had led many to believe Louisiana Governor Bernardo de Gálvez when he boasted that he would not leave the British "a foot of land in West Florida in a few months."[15]

Choctaw disaffection was feared, as the Six Villages had been courted by the Spanish since early 1779. These unhappy braves, once the favorites of the French, had turned towards Gálvez for "medals, gorgets, and red coats."[16] Invited to Mobile shortly after its fall, some Choctaws had turned in their English medals for new Spanish ones and were entertained and presented with captured British goods.[17]

Some Lower Creeks, as well as nearly twenty Upper Creeks from Tallapoosa, who had cooperated with rebel Georgians earlier, descended on Mobile near the end of April, 1780. The Spanish, low on supplies, could do little more than promise peace and distribute what liquor and goods were available. The Creeks returned in mid-June, some four hundred strong, demanding fifteen hundred barrels of rum, food, tobacco, clothing, guns, and ammunition. José de Ezpeleta, the desperate governor of Mobile, began to suspect that the English had sent them to consume his food supply. Unable to satisfy the redmen, he sent them on to Gálvez at New Orleans. Gálvez furnished the natives with an elaborate reception but could not satisfy them. Cameron rightly believed that if the Spaniard had presents enough, he could do "much mischief." Ceremony, however, would not satisfy the Creeks.[18]

Indeed, the Creeks were in sore need of provisions. Trade disruption, combined with generally poor harvests from 1777 to 1780, forced them to rely on Europeans.[19] For a number of years, the absence of warriors during the planting season had contributed to the famine. When the two Creek deputies, Alexander McGillivray and William McIntosh, received orders to gather their Indians and march to defend Pensacola from impending attack, soon after the fall of Mobile, they managed to collect nearly two thousand Creeks.[20] But the Spaniards did not materialize. The Indians, restless, tired of bad water, salt provisions, the hot Gulf Coast sun, and eager to return to their cornfields, drifted away before the end of June.[21] Gálvez, impressed by such large bodies of warriors, asked General Campbell to refrain from using Indians as combatants. Campbell speedily rejected the offer as "insulting and injurious to reason and common sense."[22]

Anxious to ingratiate themselves with the apparent conquerors, some Choctaws reported to Spanish agents that only trade goods, not genuine sentiment, bound many of their fellows to the English. Later, realizing the inability of the Spanish to furnish them with necessities, some of the Indians returned their medals. Ezpeleta became convinced that only a sound trade would bind the redmen to Spain.[23] Meanwhile, the Spanish encouraged the tribesmen to plunder English civilians and traders in order to satisfy their seemingly insatiable wants.[24]

Cameron and his deputies among the tribes worked valiantly to overcome Spanish temptation. The were aided in their quest by Opaymataha, a great medal Chickasaw who had influence in the Choctaw nation as well as his own.[25] The chief had received an invitation from Gálvez, but instead of making the usual courtesy call for presents and medals, he and his warriors had killed one Spaniard and captured three others when they brushed by Mobile on their way home from Pensacola. While passing through the Choctaw nation, Opaymataha had learned of their disaffection. He warned them to give up their Spanish medals and to restore English property they had taken at the urging of the Spanish lest he unite with loyal Cherokee and Shawnee braves and "march into . . . [their nation] and talk to them with powder and ball." After that, more of the Choctaw chiefs began delivering their Spanish trinkets to Cameron.[26]

Cameron attempted to stop British traders from visiting the disaffected towns until the Choctaw returned the stolen goods and apologized.[27] Combined with the Chickasaw threat, the leaky embargo forced many dissident chiefs to reconsider their position. Farquhar Bethune, Cameron's Choctaw agent, attempted to end the Spanish connection by calling the wayward chiefs to meet with him in August. His arguments proved successful with chiefs from the East and West Villages, and many took to the warpath against the Spanish. Six Village warriors, however, proved more difficult. On August 21, the two factions there debated from eight in the morning until six in the evening. The English partisans cajoled, threatened, and begged their Spanish-minded counterparts to denounce their new benefactors. Poushauma, who realized the advantage of British supply early, had already returned his Spanish medal and warned recalcitrant chiefs that the Spanish were "liker [sic] dogs than men. I know nothing they have but body lice. You who love them go and partake their lice and palmetto matts with them."[28]

The day's speeches convinced many braves to return to the English fold. Those who chose to remain faithful to their new masters, according to Bethune, did so only because of the prestige that came with Spanish attention and medals. The deputy urged Cameron to distribute English tokens "freely" among the Indians to keep them friendly. It is apparent that concern over a continuous supply of goods led many to support the British. The women, who enjoyed the laces, ribbons, mirrors, cloth, and utensils of the British traders, were "violent partisans" of the English. A desire to retain their positions as recognized leaders of the British faction also contributed to the loyalty of many chiefs. Many were genuinely partial to the British and recalled their role in mediating past intertribal disputes, especially the bloody Creek-Choctaw war of 1763-76. This sentiment, of course, was reinforced by the knowledge that the Chickasaws, Cherokees, and Creeks could be turned against them by the British.

In late August, Choctaw villages hummed with rumors of a forthcoming attack on Pensacola. Bethune reported that the Indians, so lately regained to the British interest, were "staggered and alarmed" by the news. Fearing a Spanish victory, they foresaw an end to their source of European goods and munitions and believed they would be left defenseless against irate Spaniards. Their trade still hampered by Cameron's embargo, they begged Bethune for ammunition with which to fight the Spaniards.[29] Even unsupplied by their allies, many Choctaws returned to the warpath. By the end of October, Cameron could happily report that "they are daily out in small parties about Mobile and not a Spaniard can venture out of sight of the fort but they knock up and carry off his scalp. . . . The Spanish are in greatest distress being cooped up by the Indians."[30]

The superintendent was convinced that lack of white, bilingual leadership was hindering the Indians' usefulness. It was his view that had they been properly directed, the Indians would already have dislodged the Spanish from Mobile and The Village, a settlement on the eastern side of Mobile Bay from which the Spanish received their drinking water. Cameron also pointed out that civilians were endangered by the lack of effective leadership. On one occasion, a war party attacked the homes of French-speaking settlers on the path toward Mobile. The warriors killed three and captured fourteen, whom they delivered to Cameron. On being reprimanded for the attack, the wily tribesmen blamed their mistake on lack of leadership. Claiming they mistook the non-English speech of the settlers for Spanish, they said they did not realize their mistake until "after knocking one or two of them on the head"—a misfortune, reported the superintendent, for which the Indians were "ashamed and sorry."[31]

The Choctaws, disappointed at their failure to drive the Spanish from The Village near the end of October, sent word to Campbell to call for Creek aid. They also informed the general of their displeasure at the small amount of powder and shot given them as a reward for their service. They noted that there was no shortage of those items in Pensacola. Claiming they did not desire ammunition for personal use, they said they only "wanted to throw away some of it on the Spaniards, and perhaps throw away some of their lives . . . in support of the English."[32] With that, most of them returned home, as the general had requested.

Cameron rightly informed his superior that these loyal Indians would not long remain faithful with such shoddy treatment, for they had witnessed British generosity to Six Village warriors who had only lately returned to the British interest. Campbell himself noted that only lack of sufficient Spanish presents had convinced many of them to abandon their new friends.[33] The defenders of Mobile, in an effort to halt the Choctaw menace, sent Six Village chiefs still in their interest into the nation with instructions to have Bethune and others who urged attacks on Mobile put to death.[34]

Since the hunting season was near, Bethune was alarmed by reports that trade goods were on their way into the nation. He warned Cameron that as soon as they arrived, the majority of the friendly Indians would be well-supplied for the hunt and would be off to the woods where it would be impossible to collect them and bring them down to Pensacola should the Spanish appear: "The nation [would] be left to the mercy and at the discretion of the disaffected Indians, a base rabble who are always at home."[35] The British Indian department harbored another motive for wishing a complete cessation of trade: if not hunting, the Indians would become "so deep in war . . . they would not be able to treat for peace or commerce" with the Spaniards.[36]

To prevent pro-British Indians from dispersing throughout the hunting grounds, Bethune urged that ammunition and presents of all kinds be sent to him at once.[37] Campbell, however, while willing to part with some ammunition, could not spare horses to transport it into the nation. Only the Chickasaw, "a rich people . . . [with] a great number of horses," would consent to the general's plan to use their horses for the public service—a plan, thought Cameron, which was foolish in any case. The Choctaws found it necessary to visit Pensacola on their way to battle in order to receive their share of powder and ball.[38]

In mid-November, alarming reports of imminent attack led General Campbell to call for Indian reinforcements.[39] So desperate was the general that he instructed Alexander McGillivray to send Creek warriors from each town as soon as they could be assembled and not to delay by trying to march them all down in one large body.[40]

The Spanish invasion fleet was scattered by a hurricane. Campbell was joyous on two counts: no Dons and no need to provision the Indians. He observed, however, that few of the latter had come to his rescue. Bethune and Cameron had been correct. McGillivray's Creeks were all hunting, and the agent had experienced difficulty "procuring Indians."[41] The Chickasaws also were scattered through the woods and could not be collected before the danger was over.[42]

Choctaws, too, were scarce. Having been dismissed from Pensacola on November 7, after their attack on The Village, with only one pound of ammunition per man instead of the two pounds they were promised, most took to the hunt upon their return home. Few answered the general's summons.[43] Cameron aptly observed, "General Campbell is very generous to Indians when he thinks there is danger near but they ought also to be well treated while we apprehend danger at a greater distance."[44]

By the end of December, Campbell felt sufficiently secure to dismiss the few Choctaws and other Indians who had come to defend Pensacola. The Choctaws, however, still smarting from their failure to reduce The Village in October, signified to Campbell their desire to try again. Campbell at first refused to agree to the tribesmen's design. Upon being persuaded that Spanish troops still occupied the site, he dispatched one hundred white troops, including some loyalists and Waldeckers under Colonel Hanxleden, on January 3, 1781, along with 420 Indians, mostly Choctaws, under the command of Farquhar Bethune and John McIntosh, the Chickasaw deputy. The Indians fought valiantly, "firing at every Spaniard that they could see." The Spaniards rushed from their blockhouse and attempted to reach a boat at the water's edge, "but the Indians shot them all down and followed them chin-deep in the water to get their scalps." The Indians returned with forty to fifty scalps from the two hundred soldiers who had been posted at the site.[45] Despite such losses, the Spaniards retained The Village.

On January 12, Campbell received word that another invasion force had set out for Pensacola. He promptly called for Indian aid, asking the Creeks to bring their own guns with them due to the short supply on hand in Pensacola. At the same time, he promised that "no expense shall be grudged in procuring for [the Indians] every reward that Pensacola can afford."[46] By early February, nearly 800 Indians, 744 of whom were Choctaws, were in Pensacola.[47] Cameron was convinced that more Choctaws would have arrived had not the rivers been swollen by winter floods. Chickasaws and Creeks were hunting, and few could be found. Cameron blamed the trade for their absence: "They must purchase clothing and must also turn out to hunt in order to pay for it."[48]

On February 10, Campbell retracted his request, since he had received news he was to be reinforced from Jamaica.[49] The following day, Campbell received definite word of a Spanish invasion fleet and more promises of reinforcements. He recalled the Indians. Cameron was forced to follow them into the woods to solicit their return. On March 7, he overtook Bethune and his party of braves, who were busily dividing up the rum they had received before they left Pensacola. Cameron asked the Indians to return to Pensacola with him and assured them that British ships loaded with more troops and supplies were en route to the town. Their leader, Frenchumastabe, a great medal chief, noted that the British had feared attacks for the past year, but none had occurred. The chief refused to force his warriors to return, "for we received but little provisions and the presents the great warrior [Campbell] made us were nothing." Nonetheless, Cameron was allowed to plead his case, and about one hundred and fifty Indians, including Frenchumastabe, returned with the superintendent.[50] By the time the Spanish actually arrived, March 9, Cameron had stationed nearly four hundred Choctaws at the British fort on the cliffs at the entrance of the harbor. They were quartered with nearly one hundred English troops who were to "support and encourage them."[51]

Campbell was upset with the Indians' performance and claimed that the troops who marched under Ezpeleta from Mobile were "unopposed" by the Indians.[52] The Indians, seeing the huge naval force and nearly four thousand Spanish troops, feared Pensacola must surely fall. Many deserted but were recalled by their chiefs. When castigated by Cameron for their unmanly behavior, they pointed out that should the Spanish take Pensacola, they would be caught without ammunition to defend themselves, since the English had not sent any to their nation. There was also distress over the fact that the presents Cameron had promised them earlier were locked away in the fort "which by all appearance," according to the observant redmen, "must fall into the hands of the Spaniards" who would distribute the goods to their friends upon the British surrender. The chiefs warned that unless the presents were "lodged in some remote place of safety," they could not compel their young warriors to remain much longer in

Pensacola. The small number of Creeks present complained that their families, left in the town, were in need of food. They also expressed their fear that their relatives might soon become Spanish captives.[53]

To the Indian, warfare consisted of participating in raids, ambushes, and surprise attacks against small bodies of enemy warriors. Scalps taken from the enemy gave proof of a warrior's bravery in battle. It was this method which Cameron's red auxiliaries employed against the Spanish. During the siege, the Indians, "enemies whose true advantage consisted in never coming out of the thicket of the forest,"[54] harassed the Spaniards from afar, rarely taking on a sizable body of troops. Indian warriors captured Spanish horses, muskets, drums; killed, scalped, or wounded a fair number of Spaniards; and occasionally presented Campbell with prisoners for ransom. Among the wounded was Gálvez, who suffered a shot through the finger which grazed his abdomen.[55]

On March 30, the Indians, supported by some of Campbell's troops, participated in a three-hour assault against a large Spanish detachment. Although Campbell reported that they made no "perceptible impression that could be taken advantage of,"[56] Cameron chimerically believed that had more Indians been present, the English forces "would have driven the whole Spanish army into the sea."[57]

The next day, in front of his warriors, Frenchumastabe delivered a harangue to Cameron, Bethune, John McIntosh, and James Colbert, the Chickasaw deputy. He claimed that the Indians had not been properly supported since the siege began. He accused British troops of retreating too soon the previous day, leaving the Indians no choice but to follow. "We do not miss those [Spaniards] we kill," he continued, "or it looks as if they came to life again. We have done everything in our power. We find it in vain to make any further attempt." He reminded the superintendent of earlier unkept promises of presents and British reinforcements. He closed, noting, "The talks must have been made here and never come from the Great King." Only after Campbell promised that British troops would support them in the future did Frenchumastabe and his chiefs promise not to "leave Pensacola before its fate was determined."[58]

Indians continued to trickle in as the siege wore on. By April 8, McGillivray and eighty Creeks had arrived. On April 15, Benjamin James and Alexander Frazer, half-breed traders, arrived with ninety more Choctaws. James Colbert's half-breed son arrived with fifty-four Chickasaws on April 27. For the Creeks and Chickasaws, the West Florida theater was not the only area of interest. Many Chickasaws were already engaged along the Mississippi, harassing American troops at Fort Jefferson, while some Creeks were busy supporting the British effort in Georgia.[59]

In early April, Gálvez, in an attempt to end the Indian raids, sent word to Mobile for the Choctaws in his interest to come to Pensacola. He intended they should persuade their fellow tribesmen to cease their forays against his camp. Nearly seventy Choctaws arrived on April 15, but they could not persuade the English Choctaws to end their warfare. Frenchumastabe, true to his word, did not abandon Pensacola until the British surrendered. Two Tallapoosa chiefs of the Creek confederacy also presented themselves to Gálvez during the month of April and were employed in the same manner as the Choctaws.[60]

On May 8, "an unfortunate shell" from Spanish guns "precipitated [Pensacola's] destiny and occasioned its falling under the dominion of Spain."[61] The Indians, who had pitched camp five miles from Fort George "on the path leading directly to their nation," beat a hasty retreat home.[62] Credited with inflicting about one-third of Spain's casualties, the warriors were undoubtedly a nuisance to Gálvez during the siege and hindered his construction of batteries. Cameron, who escaped with the Indians, reported that had Campbell listened to his advice, there would have been two thousand instead of five hundred Indians to defend Pensacola.[63] More warriors, however, would have been able to do no more than prolong the inevitable.

The nature of Indian warfare necessitated planning on the part of the superintendent and Campbell if the redmen were to provide any substantial help. Unfortunately, such foresight was entirely lacking in Pensacola. Campbell's primary objective concerning Indians was to have hordes of them descend on Pensacola at the first sight of Spaniards to act as reinforcements for his understaffed garrison. Such a course would require either that expresses be sent into the Indian nations at the first hint of attack or that Indian armies be maintained near Pensacola. The former, a less costly proposition, was preferred by Campbell. Cameron insisted that that policy would leave Pensacola undefended when the attackers arrived. Preparedness demanded that the warrior, who was also a "breadwinner," abandon his hunt. Unless supplied by the British, he and his family would suffer from the consequent loss of deerskin income. Such a policy would raise considerably the expenditures of both the Indian Department and the military establishment. Cameron was correct. Indians spread through the backcountry were difficult to collect and bring down to Pensacola when the Spanish finally appeared.[64]

The Indians expected to be rewarded at the end of their service. This, of course, is understandable in view of the fact that most soldiers are provided with necessities during their enlistments and receive pay for their services. The West Florida establishment found it very difficult to meet native expectations. In fact, complaints from the Indians and Cameron regularly passed over the desk of Major General Campbell. Lack of adequate compensation on earlier occasions kept many Indians from Pensacola during the spring of 1781.[65] It should also be pointed out that the size of Gálvez's force undoubtedly convinced many Indians to pay more careful attention to their cornfields.

Many Indians had supported Britain because of the superiority of her trade. Pensacola's fall and the dispersal of her merchants and traders disrupted the irregular commerce which had existed prior to 1781. From his hideout in the Creek nation, Cameron reported that the Indians were in great need of provisions and ammunition. Gálvez, realizing the importance of trade, made plans at once to re-establish the Florida Indian trade.[66] Spanish ideas concerning trade were reinforced in 1784, when Alexander McGillivray told the new governor of Pensacola what the British had known all along: "Indians will attach themselves to and serve them best who supply their necessities."[67]

Urged on by British agents, Indians continued their support of the British after Pensacola fell. Bethune and Colbert remained among their charges and directed attacks against both Spanish and American targets. Loyal chiefs extended protection to British settlers who fled the Spanish. Indians and their agents alike urged British authorities to send them reinforcements and munitions with which to expel the Spaniards.[68] Creek warriors set out to support the British cause in Georgia and South Carolina. Back in the Creek nation, staunch British allies accosted itinerant Tories fleeing their unlucky rebellion at Natchez and nearly executed them before they were convinced that they were indeed friends of the Great King.[69] Numerous warriors from all nations, confused and distressed by the British surrender, flocked to Cameron's temporary abode in the Creek nation to question him. Undecided as to the proper course to follow, some said they were inclined to visit the Spanish in order to inspect their presents. Many did visit Gálvez to pledge friendship and receive captured British goods. Others looked to Superintendent Brown at Augusta. Cameron, in poor health and bitter over his misfortune, could only conclude, "They are really an insolvent wavering set, most of them"[70] — too harsh a judgment perhaps, in view of the great risks, eased by few rewards, the southern Indians took in assisting their allies.

Ms. Holland is presently teaching at Opelika, Alabama.

[1] See David H. Corkran, *The Creek Frontier, 1540-1783* (Norman, 1967), ch. 17-18; James H. O'Donnell III, *The Southern Indians in the American Revolution* (Knoxville, 1973).

[2] See John R. Alden, *John Stuart and the Southern Colonial Frontier* (Ann Arbor, 1944); Kathryn E. Holland, "The Path Between the Wars: Creek Indian Relations with the British Colonies, 1763-1774" (M.A. thesis, Auburn University, 1980).

[3] Bethune to Cameron, Aug. 27, 1780, C.O. 5/82, fol. 92.

[4] Holland, "Creek Relations," 53-57, 126, 223, 243-45; Alden, *John Stuart*, 192-261.

[5] Stuart to Germain, Nov. 24, 1766, C.O. 5/78, fol. 72; Kenneth Coleman, *The American Revolution in Georgia, 1763-1789* (Athens, 1958), 169-70; R. S. Cotterill, *The Southern Indians: The Story of the Civilized Tribes Before Removal* (Norman, 1954), 41.

[6] Alden, *John Stuart*, 139-40; Cameron to Germain, Aug., 1780, C.O. 5/81, fol. 320.

[7] O'Donnell, *Southern Indians*, 88-92.

[8] Ibid., 88-89; Germain to Campbell, April 4, 1778, Kenneth G. Davies, ed., *Documents of the American Revolution, 1770-1783* (Shannon, Ireland, 1972), 18:74; Cameron to Germain, Oct. 31, 1780, C.O. 5/82, fol. 171; Cameron to James Campbell, Feb. 27, 1781, C.O. 5/82, fol. 135.

[9] Cameron to Germain, Oct. 31, 1780, C.O. 5/82, fol. 111.

[10] Cameron to Germain, July 18, 1780, C.O. 5/81, fol. 206.

[11] Germain to Campbell, April 4, 1781, Davies, *Documents*, 18:72-75.

[12] J. Leitch Wright Jr., *Florida in the American Revolution* (Gainesville, 1975); J. Barton Starr, *Tories, Dons, and Rebels: The American Revolution in British West Florida* (Gainesville, 1976); Robert V. Haynes, *The Natchez District and the American Revolution* (Jackson, 1976).

[13] Jacinto Panis to Gálvez, April 29, 1779, Lawrence Kinnaird, ed., *Spain in the Mississippi Valley, 1765-1794*, Annual Report of the American Historical Association for the Year 1945, vol. 2, part 1, 337.

[14] Germain to Campbell, April 4, 1780, Davies, *Documents*, 18:73, see O'Donnell, *Southern Indians*, 8-9 for population estimates.

[15]Cameron to Germain, July 18, 1780, C.O. 5/81, fol. 206.
[16]Colbert to Cameron, Nov. 19, 1779, C.O. 5/82, fol. 69.
[17]Wright, *Florida*, 81; Cameron to Germain, July 18, 1780, C.O. 5/81, fol. 206.
[18]Cameron to Germain, Aug., 1780, C.O. 5/81, fol. 320; Francisco de Borja Medina, *José de Ezpeleta, Gobernador de la Mobila, 1780-1781* (Seville, 1980), 302-33.
[19]Corkran, *Creek Frontier*, 314; Brown to Clinton, May 29, 1780, Historical Manuscripts Commission, *Report on American Manuscripts in the Royal Institution of Great Britain* (London, 1904), 2:130.
[20]McIntosh to Brown, May 5, 1780, C.O. 5/81, fol. 240; McGillivray to Brown, May 13, 1780, C.O. 5/81, fol. 242.
[21]McGillivray to Brown, May 13, 1780, C.O. 5/81, fol. 242; James H. O'Donnell III, "Alexander McGillivray: Training for Leadership, 1777-1783," *Georgia Historical Quarterly* 49 (1965):178-79; McIntosh to Brown, May 5, 1780, C.O. 5/81, fol. 240.
[22]George C. Osborn, "Major General John Campbell in British West Florida," *Florida Historical Quarterly* 27 (1949):353.
[23]Borja Medina, *Ezpeleta* 315-22; Juzan to Gálvez, July 11, 1780, Kinnaird, *Spain*, 382-83.
[24]Cameron to Germain, July 18, 1780, C.O. 5/81, fol. 206.
[25]Charles Stuart to Cameron, Dec. 20, 1778, C.O. 5/81, fol. 47.
[26]Cameron to Germain, July 18, 1780, C.O. 5/81, fol. 206.
[27]Ibid.
[28]Bethune to Cameron, Aug. 27, 1780, C.O. 5/82, fol. 92.
[29]Ibid.
[30]Cameron to Germain, Oct. 31, 1780, C.O. 5/82, fol. 111.
[31]Ibid.
[32]Cameron to Campbell, Nov. 8, 1780, C.O. 5/82, fol. 126.
[33]Ibid., fol. 128; Campbell to Clinton, Oct. 31, 1780, H.M.C., *American MSS*, 2:201.
[34]Bethune to Cameron, Sept. 4, 1780, C.O. 5/82, fol. 97.
[35]Ibid.
[36]Cameron to Germain, Nov. 30, 1780, C.O. 5/82, fol. 117.
[37]Bethune to Cameron, Sept. 4, 1780, C.O. 5/82, fol. 97.
[38]Cameron to Campbell, Sept. 18, 1780; Campbell to Cameron, Sept. 18, 1780; Cameron to Campbell, Sept. 19, 1780; Cameron to Germain, Nov. 30, 1780, C.O. 5/82, fols. 102, 105, 107, 117.
[39]Campbell to McGillivray, Nov. 15, 1780, C.O. 5/82, fol. 450; Campbell to Brown, Nov. 15, 1780, H.M.C., *American MSS*, 2:209.
[40]Campbell to McGillivray, Nov. 22, 1780, C.O. 5/82, fol. 451.
[41]Campbell to McGillivray, Dec. 8, 1780, C.O. 5/82, fol. 452.
[42]Cameron to Germain, Nov. 30, 1780, C.O. 5/82, fol. 117.
[43]Ibid.; Campbell to Cameron, Nov. 7, 1780, C.O. 5/82, fol. 124.
[44]Cameron to Germain, Nov. 30, 1780, C.O. 5/82, fol. 117.
[45]Cameron to Germain, Feb. 10, 1781, C.O. 5/82, fol. 130; Wright, *Florida*, 85-86.
[46]Campbell to McGillivray, Jan. 12, 1781, C.O. 5/82, fol. 451.
[47]Return of Choctaw, Chickasaw, Alabamas, and Creek Indians remaining at Pensacola, Feb. 1, 1781, C.O. 5/82, fol. 143.

[48] Cameron to Germain, Feb. 10, 1781, C.O. 5/82, fol. 130.
[49] Campbell to McGillivray, Feb. 10, 1781, C.O. 5/82, fol. 452.
[50] Cameron to Germain, May 27, 1781, C.O. 5/82, fol. 204.
[51] Campbell to Germain, May 7, 1781, Davies, *Documents*, 19:136.
[52] Ibid.
[53] Cameron to Campbell, March 20, 1781, C.O. 5/82, fol. 208.
[54] Gálvez diary, Orwin N. Rush, *The Battle of Pensacola, March 9, to May 8, 1781: Spain's Final Triumph Over Great Britain in the Gulf of Mexico* (Tallahassee, 1966), 67.
[55] Rush, *Battle*, 35-92; James A. Padgett, "Bernardo de Gálvez's Siege of Pensacola as related in Robert Farmar's Journal," *Louisiana Historical Quarterly* 26 (1943):311-29; Donald E. Worcester, "Miranda's Diary of the Siege of Pensacola, 1781," *Florida Historical Quarterly* 29 (1951):163-96.
[56] Campbell to Germain, May 7, 1781, Davies, *Documents*, 19:137.
[57] Cameron to Germain, May 27, 1781, C.O. 5/82, fol. 204; Padgett, "Farmar's Journal," 318; Rush, *Battle*, 67.
[58] Talk by Frenchumastabe to Cameron, April 1, 1781, C.O. 5/82, fol. 210.
[59] Cameron to Germain, May 27, 1781, C.O. 5/82, fol. 204; Padgett, "Farmar's Journal," 320, 323; Corkran, *Creek Frontier*, 320-21; O'Donnell, *Southern Indians*, 92-93; Arrell M. Gibson, *The Chickasaws* (Norman, 1971), 72-73.
[60] Gálvez diary, Rush, *Battle*, 69-70.
[61] Campbell to Germain, May 12, 1781, Davies, *Documents*, 20:138.
[62] Campbell to Clinton, April 9, 1781, Rush, *Battle*, 95-96.
[63] Cameron to Germain, May 27, 1781, C.O. 5/82, fol. 204.
[64] Cameron to Germain, Nov. 30, 1780; Oct. 31, 1780, C.O. 5/82, fols. 117, 111; July 18, 1780, C.O. 5/81, fol. 206; Feb. 10, 1781, C.O. 5/82, fol. 130.
[65] Cameron to Campbell, Nov. 8, 1780, C.O. 5/82, fol. 126; Cameron to Germain, Oct. 31, 1780, C.O. 5/82, fol. 111; Talk of Frenchumastabe, April 1, 1781, C.O. 5/82, fol. 210.
[66] Wright, *Florida*, 92-94; J. Leitch Wright Jr., "British East Florida: Loyalist Bastion," *Eighteenth-Century Florida: The Impact of the American Revolution*, ed. Samuel Proctor (Gainesville, 1978), 12-13; Helen H. Tanner, "Pipesmoke and Muskets: Florida Indian Intrigues of the Revolutionary Era," *Eighteenth-Century Florida and Its Borderlands*, ed. Samuel Proctor (Gainesville, 1975), 27; Corkran, *Creek Frontier*, 321-22.
[67] McGillivray to O'Neill, Jan. 1, 1784, John W. Caughey, *McGillivray of the Creeks* (Norman, 1938), 64.
[68] Bethune to Germain, Jan. 19, 1782; Graham to Shelburne, Sept. 28, 1782, Davies, *Documents*, 19:249, 332; John W. Caughey, "The Natchez Rebellion of 1781 and Its Aftermath," *Louisiana Historical Quarterly* 16 (1937):65; Haynes, *Natchez District*, 131-57; O'Donnell, *Southern Indians*, 54-55; Wright, *Florida*, 149.
[69] Timothy Dwight, *Travels in New England and New York* (Cambridge, Mass., 1969), 1:222-30.
[70] Cameron to Germain, May 27, 1781, C.O. 5/82, fol. 204.

JOSÉ DE EZPELETA AND THE SIEGE OF PENSACOLA

Francisco de Borja Medina Rojas, S. J.*

Two centuries ago an explosion was heard in Pensacola which eventually changed the balance of European power in this part of the world and gave new hope to the cause of liberty and the cause of the first independent American nation that was coming into existence a few hundred miles to the north.

I refer to the explosion of the powder magazine in the Queen's Redoubt. Forty-eight Pennsylvania Loyalists, twenty-seven British sailors, and a negro slave lost their lives. Another twenty-four soldiers and sailors were wounded.[1]

Shortly after the explosion took place, the colonel of the Spanish Regiment of Navarre, José de Ezpeleta, major general of the besieging army, rushed in with sword in hand, at the head of his soldiers to storm the smoldering ruins of the advanced redoubt which was defended by the remaining handful of brave Loyalists and sailors still on their feet. At about ten o'clock, under the pressure of the attack, the defenders gave way. Notwithstanding the British fire, the Spaniards had mounted—or, as an eyewitness put it, "clambered up"—the ruins.[2] Another observer described Ezpeleta as a "bloodthirsty lion," such was his fierce resolution as he pushed through the debris into the redoubt a minute or so ahead of his troops, winning thereby the admiration of a British officer who had deserted a few days earlier to the Spanish camp. The turncoat knew well the disposition of the defenses and the danger to which Ezpeleta was exposing himself by his daring action, but the Spaniard's determination to occupy the redoubt prevented the British from retaking it, for they were already advancing with field cannon for a counterattack. Had Ezpeleta arrived two or three minutes later, the British would have blocked the Spaniards from taking possession of the redoubt, and then the capture of Pensacola would have cost more time and heavy losses. Instead, Ezpeleta hoisted the Spanish flag over the conquered post.[3] For four more hours the battle ensued until General John Campbell, well aware of the futility of defense, with anticipated heavy casualties, and with no hope of relief, beat the chamade. He displayed a flag of truce on Fort George and proposed a suspension of hostilities until next day at noon. The siege of Pensacola was virtually over. It was 2:30 P.M., May 8, 1781.[4]

Pensacola was the final step in the Anglo-Spanish conflict in West Florida. The hero of the campaign was the Spanish Governor of Louisiana, Bernardo de Gálvez, but we should not ignore the role played by José de Ezpeleta. Gálvez had entrusted to Ezpeleta the defense of the Mobile District, of vital strategic importance for the Gulf Coast, and I have dedicated a complete study, recently published in Spain, to Ezpeleta's government in Mobile, May, 1780, to March, 1781. This paper will focus on Ezpeleta's participation in the Pensacola campaign: his strategy with regard to operations intended to open the entrance of Pensacola Bay to Spanish forces, the difficulties he encountered as delays in the Spanish expedition favored the British, his state of mind, and his reactions to the campaign. Finally, we will see Ezpeleta in action and some features of his personality as reflected in contemporary evidence.

José de Ezpeleta, an unmarried nobleman of Navarrese stock, was at that time thirty-eight years old and enjoyed good health. He was a senior officer who displayed exemplary conduct, was credited with bravery, was particularly industrious and very competent. He had deservedly gained for himself a good reputation. So read an official report. A British Royal Navy officer who met Ezpeleta in Havana three years later described him as "a very gentlemanly man."[5]

The West Florida campaign began for Ezpeleta when, at the end of January, 1780, he was appointed to command the veteran troops from the garrison of Havana that were to join the forces from Louisiana operating against Mobile under Bernardo de Gálvez. Gálvez wanted Ezpeleta at his side both because of their old and close friendship and because of his knowledge of Ezpeleta's talents and ability.[6]

The expedition from Havana under Ezpeleta arrived at Mobile Bay after Fort Charlotte had surrendered to Gálvez. For more than a month they waited to proceed against Pensacola. But at the beginning of May, because of divergent opinions between the commanders of the land and sea forces, among other reasons, the expedition was postponed until fall. Juan Bautista Bonet, *General de Marina* and commander of the Havana naval base, returned there with the fleet and the bulk of the expeditionary army. After appointing Ezpeleta governor of Fort *Carlota* (old British Fort Charlotte), and commander of the Mobile District, Gálvez sailed for New Orleans. He left a garrison eight hundred men strong.[7] Besides his duties as governor and the defense of Mobile, Ezpeleta was entrusted with the mission of making preparations for the expedition against Pensacola. This included gathering information about the state of the British post and planning the first operations to facilitate access to Pensacola Bay for the Spanish convoy.

The stragetic position of Mobile in the geopolitics of the Gulf of Mexico — its proximity to Pensacola, only twenty-five leagues distant (about sixty-two miles) — had been the main reason for launching an attack upon Mobile as a preliminary step towards Pensacola, the capital of West Florida. Circumstances made Mobile the ideal base from which to attack Pensacola. In the Spanish plans, Mobile was, therefore, the assembly point for all sea and land forces that were to take part in the expedition.[8]

By the end of July, 1780, Gálvez had left New Orleans for Havana. A powerful Spanish fleet with ten thousand men on board had just arrived there from Cádiz, and Gálvez wanted to move preparations forward and get ready for an autumn campaign. He authorized Ezpeleta to take over the command of Louisiana in his absence, should Ezpeleta think it necessary for its defense. At the same time, Gálvez insisted on the necessity of having everything ready in Mobile for a march over land to Pensacola. Ezpeleta did not judge it expedient to take command of Louisiana. Rather, he left it in the hands of the lieutenant colonel of the Regiment of Louisiana, Pedro Piernas, as provided by Gálvez. However, the Governor of Mobile became virtually commander in chief of the defense of the whole region.[9] In the course of events, after the British attack on the District of Mobile had been repelled at the beginning of January, 1781, Piernas exalted the role played by Ezpeleta and acknowledged him "the Defender of this Province" and "the worthy Protector of this Colony."[10]

At the outset, Ezpeleta gathered information about Pensacola. Gálvez used this information in his plans and in the conferences of the *junta* of generals in Havana. By the beginning of September, 1780, the generals had examined intelligence furnished to Ezpeleta by not less than fifteen deserters from the British side. The information transmitted to Havana covered all aspects necessary for a complete review of the situation at Pensacola: defenses, artillery, troops, magazines, men-of-war and other vessels there. In the light of this intelligence, the generals discussed projects and planned operations.

While Ezpeleta rendered this service to the *junta* of generals in Havana, he also let Gálvez know his plans.

The project of marching the army by land from Mobile to Pensacola had been included in the general planning of operations against the British post; it was later discarded, however, because the nature of the terrain, with its woods and swampy and sandy ground, made it almost impossible to move the artillery, stores, and ammunition overland. Instead, they decided to transport the men, ordnance and stores on ships into Pensacola Bay. But, first, this operation required the elimination of the obstacles at the entrance to the bay: a battery mounted on *Barrancas Coloradas* (Red Cliffs) and naval forces at the bar. Both battery and ships had to be taken into account.

After the expedition was again postponed, the Spaniards decided to readopt the plan to march forces from Mobile overland, while the rest of the army went by sea to Pensacola Bay. Ezpeleta strongly supported the plan, and he was entrusted with finding practicable routes and organizing the march.[11]

In the preparation of the expedition in Mobile, there were three distinct periods.

During the first period, July—September, 1780, Ezpeleta considered the reduction of the post at *Barrancas* an easy objective. It was defenseless, so deserters reported. The first step would be to occupy the post in order to open the bay to the Spanish convoy. Ezpeleta would be responsible for the land operations. Taking advantage of the reported scarcity of food in the town, he intended to set up a land blockade of Pensacola before the bulk of the Spanish expeditionary army arrived. For that operation he considered one battalion of soldiers and two field cannon sufficient. But he would need some small craft to ferry his army across the *Perdido*.

By the beginning of September, the situation had changed some, but optimism still dominated the planning. News had come in early August that the post at *Barrancas* mounted four eighteen-pounders. As Ezpeleta lacked the necessary artillery to reduce such a battery, and as an attempt to storm the site would attract the British from Pensacola, he planned to attack it at the moment the Spanish convoy appeared on the scene. To insure the success of the operation, Ezpeleta wanted the help of the navy. The first step would consist in a blockade of Pensacola by sea. Warships should be sent ahead of the convoy. They could help protect Ezpeleta during his attack on *Barrancas*. After the Spaniards possessed the battery there, the entrance of the bay would be closed to the British. Ezpeleta commented cheerfully in a private letter to Gálvez, "So then, let me know it [the sending of the ships] in time and I shall shut the cage up so that the bird cannot escape."[13]

Once the entrance of the bay had been closed to the British and opened to the Spaniards, the rest seemed quite simple to Ezpeleta. With two thousand veteran troops — Ezpeleta did not trust the militia — with the needed laborers, and with sufficient artillery, Fort George would be reduced to ashes eight hours after the cannon opened fire. Ezpeleta reasoned that the British could only oppose him with six cannon mounted in the two small redoubts adjacent to and north of the fort. With these and with mortars they could do some damage, but as soon as the Spanish artillery opened fire, the British batteries would be silenced.[14]

As time passed, this period of great optimism gave way to a second rather grim one. In mid-October, trusting perhaps too much in the intelligence supplied by deserters from Pensacola, Ezpeleta still believed the entrance of the bay defenseless. They now reported that the post at *Barrancas* had no cannon and the vessels at the bar could offer little resistance.[15] By the end of the month, however, further intelligence produced additional changes.

News reached Mobile that a battery of twelve cannon had been erected at *Barrancas*. Now all previous plans were at stake. It became imperative to attack the battery by land, because it would be most difficult for the ships to aim at a well-covered battery on top of a cliff. A march by land seemed to be the right solution, but the situation around Mobile at the time made that almost impossible. The Indians, who had declared a general war against the Spaniards the first of October, had stolen the horses rounded up for the expedition. The available troops were engaged in the defense of vital posts and settlements in the Mobile area. Ezpeleta could only take with him some five hundred regulars, sixty militiamen from New Orleans, and a few sappers, roughly six hundred men in all, a number by no means adequate for a march of twenty leagues on bad roads through woods full of hostile Indians. It might be possible for this detachment to push its way through as far as the *Perdido*, but beyond that point

Ezpeleta would need reinforcements. He could not risk crossing the *Perdido* in sight of the British, who had built a blockhouse on the east bank, nor could he proceed farther because of the Indians. Notwithstanding, these difficulties, Ezpeleta embarked the artillery and stores, ready to set out by land or by sea, at the first notice.[16]

While Ezpeleta was getting ready in Mobile, the expedition from Havana under Gálvez put to sea on October 16. Unfortunately—fortunately, indeed, for the British!—an autumn hurricane dispersed and damaged the Spanish fleet with nearly four thousand men on board.

By the end of October, ships from the hurricane-shattered expedition began to arrive in Mobile, and two weeks later, deserters from the post at *Barrancas* confirmed the arrival at Pensacola of transports from the Spanish expedition that had been taken as prizes. Notwithstanding the hurricane damage, it appeared certain to Ezpeleta that the expedition would soon be underway. Not having received any news from Gálvez, he discarded all plans of marching overland to Pensacola. He believed that it had been decided to reunite all forces at sea. The artillery and stores having been loaded, Ezpeleta gave orders to embark the men.

On November 14, the forces at Mobile were ready to sail. Ezpeleta turned the government papers over to Captain Enrique Grimarest of his own Regiment of Navarre. Before boarding ship, Ezpeleta intended that Grimarest should be acknowledged governor of Fort *Carlota*. However, Ezpeleta did not embark, and he remained in office for four more months. Successive gales and stormy winds, as well as further arrivals of damaged vessels from the scattered convoy, convinced him that the expedition was over. He prepared for the worse.

The following weeks were characterized by uncertainty and confusion. Day after day Ezpeleta expected the arrival of the expedition from Havana, which he hoped could be reorganized in a short time. This anticipation, and not knowing Gálvez's whereabouts, prevented him from expediting decisions. While Ezpeleta waited, he tried to update his plans for the campaign. It was clear that delays in Havana and the disaster of the autumn expedition had given the British a breathing-spell to improve their defenses. By the end of the year they had completed work on the post at *Barrancas* which they named the Royal Navy Redoubt.[17] As in his previous plans, Ezpeleta would assume responsibility for land operations to seize *Barrancas*. He now had at his disposal, in New Orleans and Mobile, more than eight hundred additional men from the hurricane-shattered ships.

Ezpeleta contemplated two alternatives: a march by land from Mobile, crossing the *Perdido*, and on to *Barrancas*, or a landing of men and artillery at some point not too far from *Barrancas*, and thence by land. Ezpeleta was fully aware of the difficulties involved in the long march, the impracticability of moving the cannon over the roads, and the scarcity of horses. However, he preferred the first alternative over exposing his men and artillery to the perils of a treacherous sea. If a landing by sea were proposed, it would be up to the navy to choose the right place. Ezpeleta preferred the left bank of the *Perdido*, although it was some distance from *Barrancas*. Wherever the site selected, a diversion should be carried out by the navy in order to keep the artillery fire from *Barrancas* pointed towards the sea. In the meantime, the forces from Mobile would approach the rear of the redoubt by land.[18]

Finally, by early January, 1781, Ezpeleta had received news from Gálvez. The general intended to leave Havana for New Orleans with one thousand men. Another five hundred were ready to sail for Mobile. The expeditionary force would be made up of these fifteen hundred men plus the troops already in Mobile and New Orleans from the ships of the ill-fated October expedition and some men to be recruited in Louisiana. Once more Gálvez asked Ezpeleta to plan the initial operations and to draft an itinerary for the march to Pensacola. Difficulties with the navy left no hope for substantial support by men-of-war, so the expedition would have to be carried out by land.[19]

Ezpeleta reassessed and confirmed his plans and wrote Gálvez: the fifteen hundred men from Havana, plus those who had arrived after the hurricane, and the troops from Mobile would form an expeditionary army of three thousand men — the number desired by Gálvez — hence, there was no need to recruit a single man from Louisiana. As the only purpose of Gálvez's presence in New Orleans would be to recruit more men, it would be more expedient for him to come straight to Mobile with the troops from Havana.

Ezpeleta's project contained five main stages: (1) a march by land of a detachment of fifteen hundred men; (2) the transportation by sea of the remaining effectives, artillery, ordnance, and stores; (3) the landing of the artillery on the left bank of the *Perdido*, or on the coast between there and *Barrancas;* (4) the formal attack on the Royal Navy Redoubt; and (5) the entrance of the convoy into the bay, once the battery was captured. Ezpeleta held it indispensable to be able to count upon naval forces superior to those in Pensacola harbor. It would also be expedient to have a ship of the line batter the Royal Navy Redoubt while the land forces were getting ready for their assault, but this could be dispensed with, provided the landing of the artillery was carried out. Ezpeleta's plan coincided in essence with that secretly proposed by Gálvez in Havana, in mid-December, to Captain General Domingo José Navarro and to the commander in chief of the operating army, Victorio de Navia.[20]

Gálvez's plan to sail for New Orleans was never put into action. Five hundred troops destined for Mobile left Havana on December 8. But instead of reaching Mobile, they arrived at New Orleans at the end of the year. Shortly afterwards, on January 7, 1781, the British regulars and Indians attacked the Mobile District (The Village), while frigates from Pensacola sailed into Mobile Bay thus cutting communications between Mobile and New Orleans for several days. Although communications were soon reestablished, fears of a British blockade prevented the authorities at New Orleans from sending to Mobile the recently arrived troops and ships demanded by Ezpeleta. He considered the decision taken in News Orleans unwise, but he protested in vain. Ezpeleta wanted to reunite all these forces in Mobile as soon as possible, in order to be ready to join Gálvez. Judging by Gálvez's last letter, Ezpeleta presumed that he had already put to sea.[21]

During the last week of February, after a silence of nearly two months, Ezpeleta heard again from Gálvez. This time the news was rather comforting: before long the forces gathered at Havana would sail for Mobile. The period of confusion and uncertainty finally seemed over. As time was pressing, Ezpeleta decided not to count upon the troops in New Orleans for the seizure of the post at *Barrancas;* the men from Mobile, supported by naval forces from Havana, would be sufficient.

This decision forced Ezpeleta to make some changes in his plans. Pensacola Bay would become the assembly point for all forces, instead of Mobile Bay. He would march overland with his own men to the *Perdido*. Gálvez's forces from Havana would anchor off the coast between Pensacola Bay and the mouth of the *Perdido*, in the vicinity of Grand Lagoon. The artillery would be unloaded at this point when Ezpeleta appeared on the beach after crossing the *Perdido*. Ezpeleta was overconfident: he thought that once the battery at *Barrancas* was taken, Pensacola could not offer much resistance. With this in mind, Ezpeleta drafted his itinerary as far as the *Perdido* and waited for Gálvez.

When Ezpeleta realized that the coming of the expedition was imminent, he was overjoyed. In a dispatch, he wished Gálvez a safe arrival: nothing had he longed for more eagerly, Ezpeleta wrote, not because of any personal advantage, nor to get out of his post in Mobile, but just to put an end to that enterprise against Pensacola which they had had in hand for so long.[22]

It was not the first time Ezpeleta expressed his feelings regarding the expedition. As early as May, 1780, only a few days after he had been sworn in as governor of Mobile, he had assured Gálvez that he was "dying to set out [for Pensacola], the sooner the better."[23] Some months later, at the end of October, 1780, Ezpeleta had begun to worry about the fate of the expedition. News reported in the *Gazette* arriving in Mobile from South Carolina added apprehensions to those caused by Gálvez's silence. It seemed, according to the *Gazette*, that the combined forces of France and Spain gathered at *Puerto Principe* were intended for an invasion of Jamaica. Ezpeleta suspected that "so large a net would not be meant for such a little bird as this [Pensacola]." He was quite apprehensive of a new delay being imposed on the expedition against Pensacola by the preparation of the one against Jamaica. Ezpeleta commented to Pedro Piernas, the ad interim governor of Louisiana: "If it happens, it would be my last and utmost misfortune." If, furthermore, he could not participate in the expedition against Jamaica, he would "go mad."[24]

In March, 1781, after so many delays and misfortunes, the expedition was at hand. It was not extraordinary that "its proximity and the good weather" would make Ezpeleta "go mad with joy." So he wrote to Gálvez on March 5, and added, "The Carnival begins for us right now."[25] (Technically, the carnival was over; he was writing on Monday of the first week of Lent!).

On the previous day, Sunday, March 4, Ezpeleta had given orders to the troops in Mobile to be ready to depart. Throughout the following days, Mobile began to hear unusual and prolonged drum-beats and came alive with parades, reviews of troops, and inspection of arms. Colorful soldiers buzzed about, going to and fro between their barracks and the boats lined up along the pier. It was rather like a carnival, this getting ready for an expedition for which they had waited for ten long months.[26]

The expedition from Havana had put to sea on the last day of February. On the high seas, Gálvez gave the order to sail, not for Mobile Bay as previously planned, but for Santa Rosa Island instead. On March 9, when Ezpeleta received instructions to join the expedition by sea in order to combine all the forces before *Barrancas*, he was bewildered and feared for the worst. He communicated his fears to Gálvez: Santa Rosa, it was lately reported, was defended by a battery of ten twelve-pounders mounted on *Sigüenza* Point. Gálvez would have to get rid of them before proceeding farther. In any case, the redoubt at *Barrancas* had to be captured to permit the convoy to enter Pensacola Bay safely. In his communication to Gálvez, Ezpeleta insisted on keeping to the original plan and urged him to take the battery at *Barrancas* first. Nonetheless, he assured Gálvez that he was ready to set out by land or sea at the first notice.[27]

The intelligence regarding *Sigüenza* Point proved to be inaccurate. The British had had plans to erect a battery there, but when the troops from Havana arrived there on March 10, they found only some dismounted cannon. On March 13, Gálvez sent his aide, Esteban Miró, to Mobile to discuss with Ezpeleta the junction of their forces. As a result, Ezpeleta changed his itinerary. For fear of British opposition to a crossing of the *Perdido* at the point selected which was some twelve miles up the bay, he decided instead to march along the beach and to cross at the mouth of the *Perdido*. Here he would need boats to ferry the troops across.

On March 14, Ezpeleta gave orders to sail, but three times, on this day and on the following, contrary winds forced the troops to disembark. On the 16th., notwithstanding the continuation of bad weather, the boats set out, rowing for Bon Secour Bay. They landed that night and the following day. After crossing Olivier Bay, they made their way to the seashore and marched along the beach towards the mouth of the *Perdido*. The ferrying was planned for midnight of the 21st., with strict orders to march silently in close formation. Boats sent by the commander of the flagship *San Ramón*, José Calvo de Irazábal, had been waiting at the *Perdido* Bay since March 16. They consisted of twelve armed launches from the warships and transports, protected by the brig *San Pío*. The ferrying of the Mobile troops began at dawn on the 21st. By ten o'clock that morning the operation had been successfully completed.

The forces under Ezpeleta were composed of some nine hundred men from the regiments of the Príncipe, España, Navarra, Havana, and Volunteers of Catalonia. There were also some artillerymen and sappers and, in addition, about twenty-five mounted dragoons lately arrived from Havana via New Orleans, two artillery officers, and one engineer. Two field cannon that had proved difficult to haul were turned over to the navy to be put on board the launches.[28]

The march from Mobile had been a great success. On the 22d., at 9:30 in the morning, Ezpeleta arrived with his forces on Pensacola Bay. They encamped on Tartar Point, facing *Sigüenza* Point. The beach-head had been established by Ezpeleta without opposition from the British, much to General Campbell's regret. The troops from Havana, under Gálvez, could now safely cross the channel from Santa Rosa Island to the mainland. Next day, the 23d., the forces from New Orleans entered the bay in fourteen ships. Three days later, the whole expeditionary army was encamped on the mainland, ready to approach Pensacola and lay siege to the British fortifications.

Ezpeleta had accomplished the mission entrusted to him ten months earlier, but he did not carry out his long-cherished project of seizing the *Barrancas* battery, which remained in the rear, unattacked. Its location had been poorly planned by the British engineers, and its cannon could not hurt the ships entering the bay. Gálvez had recognized that situation and, four days before the arrival of Ezpeleta, had proved to the Navy it was possible to cross the bar safely. He did so in his brig *Galveztown*, accompanied by a galley and two gunboats. This action brought Gálvez world-wide fame and the inclusion of the *Galveztown* on his coat of arms, with the motto: "*Yo Solo.*" Its immediate effect was to encourage the naval officers to cross the bar: the next day, March 19, the frigates led the transports into the bay. Only the flagship *San Ramón* could not enter, in spite of two risky attempts made by her commander, Calvo. Once he had accomplished his mission of seeing the convoy into Pensacola Bay safely, he returned to Havana.[29]

With all three detachments safely on the mainland, the siege of

Pensacola could commence. On March 24, Ezpeleta was named major general.[30] As established in the *Reales Ordenanzas* (Royal Ordinances) by Charles III, the major general was the "voice" of the general commanding an army on campaign and must be obeyed by all.[31] As major general, Ezpeleta was, therefore, second in command only to Gálvez and was his closest collaborator. The death of the other two colonels in the expeditionary army, Luis Rebolo and Francisco Longoria, made Ezpeleta the only senior officer of his class and rank. After Gálvez was wounded, he entrusted Ezpeleta with command of the entire operation.

On March 23, Ezpeleta reconnoitred the terrain in order to encamp in an advantageous place closer to Pensacola. For that site he proposed the field between Sutton's Lagoon and the co-called arroyo *San Miguel*. He recommended that troops be transported there by ship, as soon as possible.[32] Had Gálvez followed his advice, they would very likely have been spared four days of painful marching through marsh and woodland and might have avoided the loss of twenty dead and as many wounded, caused by Indian attacks and errors in the Spanish ranks.

On March 30, early in the morning, Gálvez led the light infantry, etc. around the head of Sutton's Lagoon to occupy the field facing the British fortifications. Ezpeleta led the main body of the army on launches across the lagoon and joined the light troops on the opposite bank. Indians, supported by British regulars and field cannon, attacked to impede the progress of the Spaniards, but Ezpeleta, showing resolute determination, encouraged Gálvez to advance on the attackers and repel them. The British retreated to their forts and the Indians to the woods. One-and-a-half hours later, the Spanish troops were entrenching themselves and mounting cannon in an encampment facing the British defenses.

The siege of Pensacola would not be as easy as Gálvez and Ezpeleta had imagined. On April 4, Ezpeleta reconnoitred the British fortifications and realized how advantageous their position was. With the available resources of men and armament in the Spanish army, it was unlikely that any effective action could be taken against them. The troops were daily engaged in frequent skirmishes with Indian warriors who were often supported by British detachments. The artillery lacked mortars and heavy pieces, as well as sufficient ammunition for a harder and longer siege than had been envisaged. Ezpeleta recommended that eight

DON JOSÉ DE EZPELETA Y GALDEANO (1742-1823), FIRST COUNT OF EZPELETA DE BEIRE. Courtesy of the Academy of Artillery, Segovia, Spain.

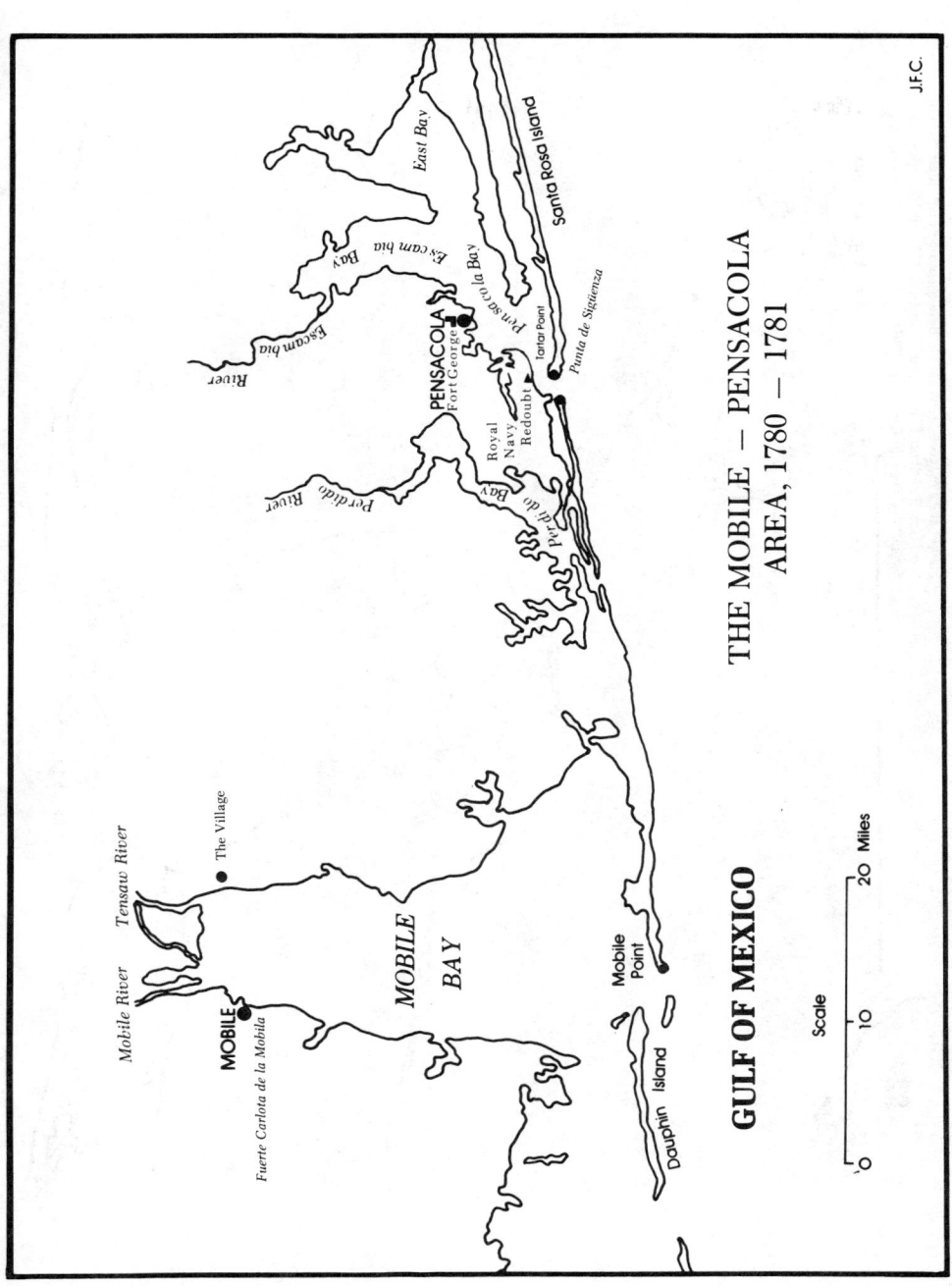

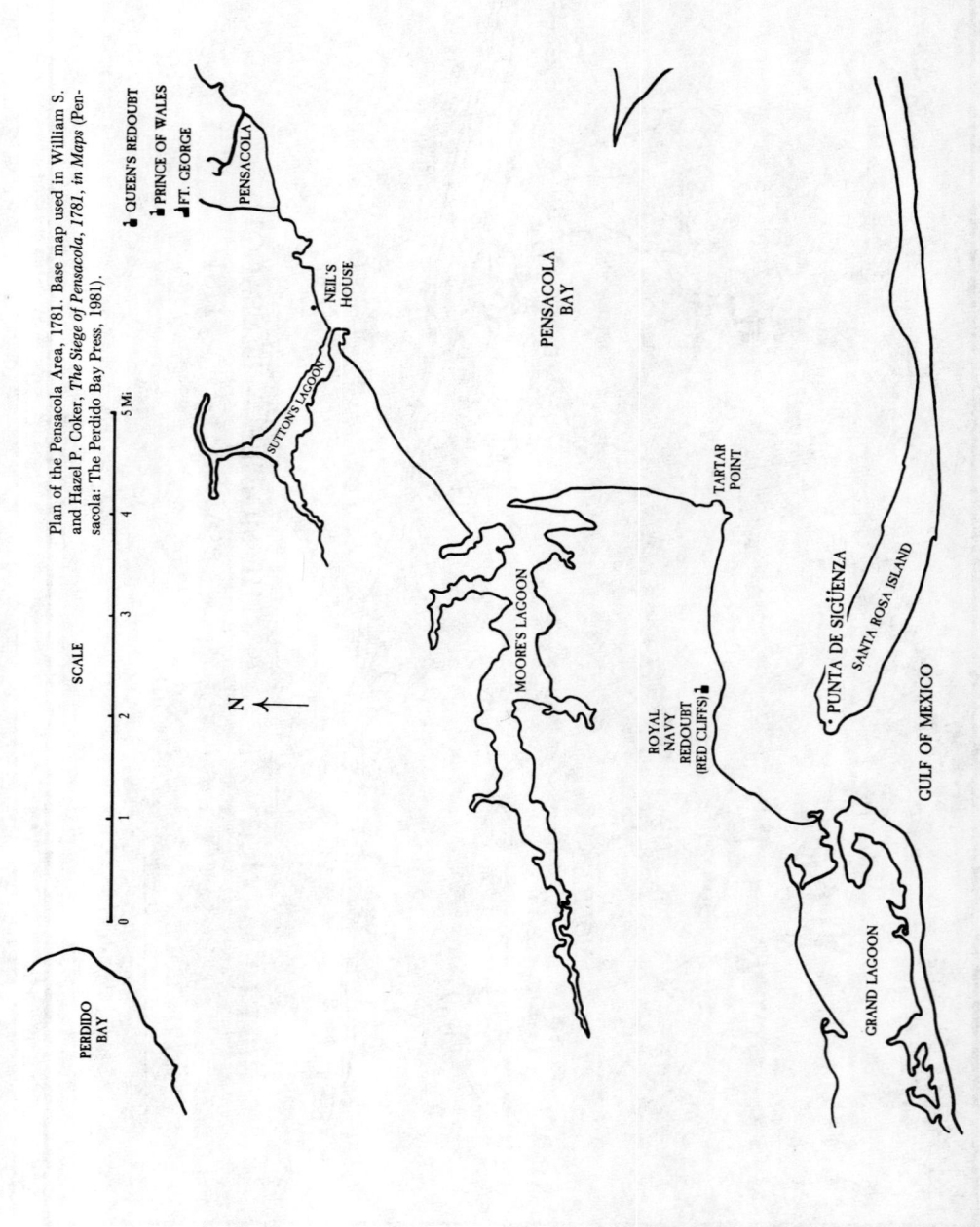

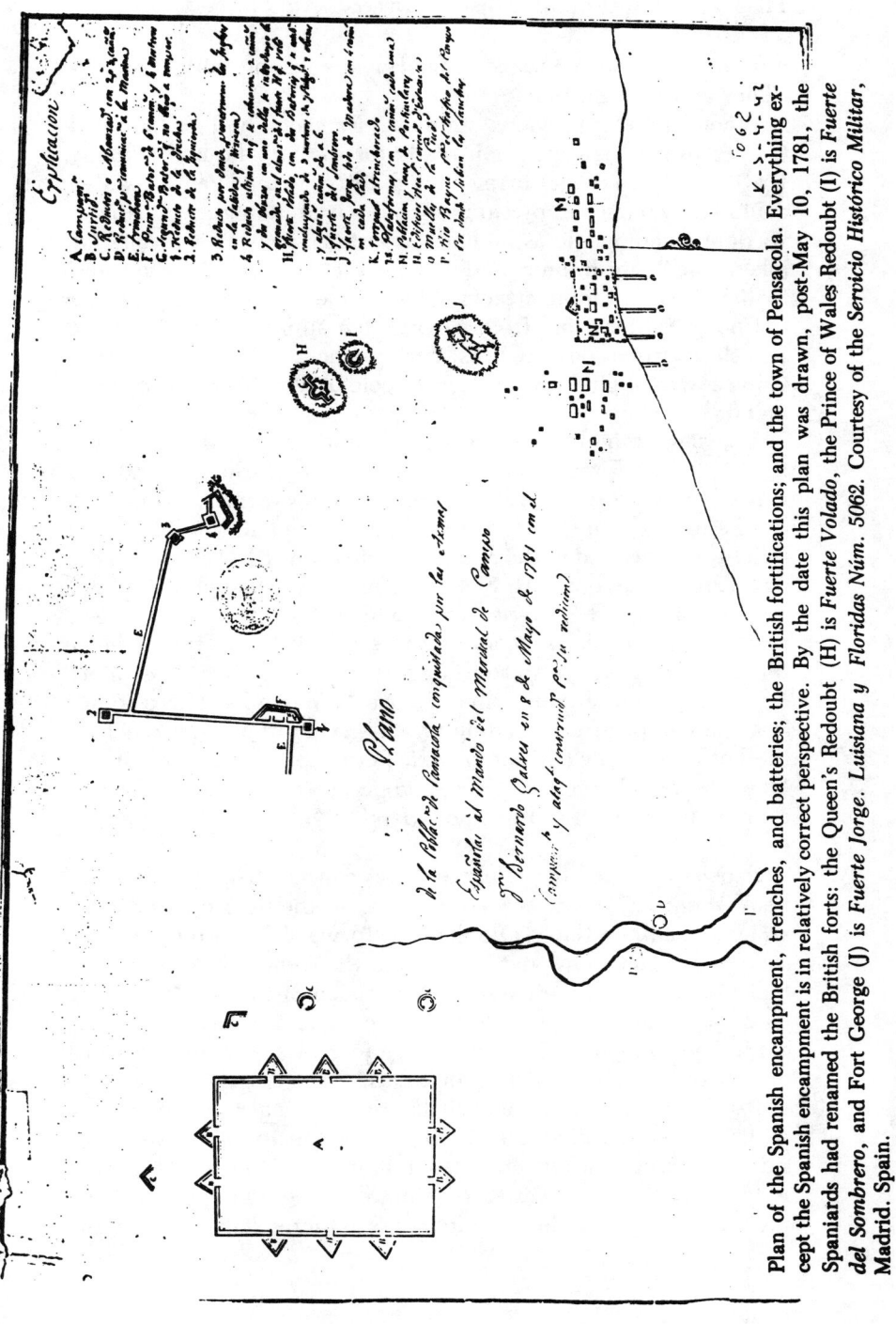

Plan of the Spanish encampment, trenches, and batteries; the British fortifications; and the town of Pensacola. Everything except the Spanish encampment is in relatively correct perspective. By the date this plan was drawn, post-May 10, 1781, the Spaniards had renamed the British forts: the Queen's Redoubt (H) is *Fuerte Volado*, the Prince of Wales Redoubt (I) is *Fuerte del Sombrero*, and Fort George (J) is *Fuerte Jorge*. *Luisiana y Floridas Núm.* 5062. Courtesy of the *Servicio Histórico Militar*, Madrid. Spain.

hundred men be requested from Havana, along with more artillery and ammunition.[33]

When, in the previous summer, Ezpeleta had encouraged Gálvez to get the expedition ready for the fall, he had jokingly written, "If you do not bring enough forces to take Pensacola, we could enjoy ourselves by camping out within its sights."[34] Now it was not as enjoyable as he had suggested, nor was it a time for jokes. The Spanish forces had to move their encampment to avoid British fire and Indian attacks. At the same time, they kept trying to find better locations from whence to mount their attack on the British fortifications. It was during one of these moves that Gálvez was slightly wounded. Ezpeleta was then given command.

The siege might have dragged on and on but the fear of a British relief force from Jamaica pressured the generals in Havana to send strong reinforcements: ships, arms, and men to the besieging army even before they knew of its troubles. The relief forces arrived in the Spanish camp on April 21-22. The next day Ezpeleta set out with Field Marshal Juan Manuel de Cagigal to reconnoitre the point from which the British advanced redoubt—the Queen's—could best be attacked. On the night of the 28th., the troops started digging trenches. Two days later, Ezpeleta personally supervised the work. When he retired to the Spanish camp, after spending twenty-six hours in the trenches, the battery was nearly completed. Four mortars directed at the Queen's Redoubt were in place, and preparations were underway to mount six twenty-four pounders to be used against Fort George.

Ezpeleta worked feverishly and was constantly on the move to help wherever he was needed. On May 4, the British launched a violent assault on the left flank of the forward Spanish trench. As soon as Ezpeleta saw that the men in the trench were under attack, he rushed to their rescue at the head of four companies of chasseurs. Such zeal was criticized by others as excessive self-confidence (*nimia confianza*),[35] but a few days later another incident proved such criticism groundless.

In view of the shortage of shells for the twenty-four pounders which were indispensable for battering the forts, Gálvez considered taking the Queen's Redoubt by escalade. Once it surrendered, it would be easier to reduce the other two forts. At midnight on May 7, the field commanders gathered in Ezpeleta's tent to plan the assault. The forces destined for the operation — some eight hundred men divided in three detachments — set out at one o'clock in the morning. Ezpeleta waited in the trench, ready to help whenever required. The troops had to march around a hillock covered with pines, to avoid being heard, and spent too much time in the diversion. Because of a very bright moon and the approaching dawn, Ezpeleta judged it prudent to call off the attack. He notified Gálvez, and the men returned to the camp without being observed by the British.[36] Ezpeleta showed wisdom in balancing the risks against the possibilities of success. He would not lead his men to slaughter, nor would he compromise an action. If a bold operation had to be carried out, he would not hesitate to assume the responsibility. He would put himself at the head of his men, as he did on several different occasions, notably in the assault and occupation of the Queen's Redoubt.

Ezpeleta also played a significant role in the final capitulation of Pensacola. He forced General John Campbell to put an end to hostilities by refusing to grant him more than three hours to prepare the articles of capitulation instead of the twenty-four hours Campbell had requested. The confrontation is confirmed by official British documents,[37] and was colorfully described by one of Ezpeleta's soldiers, Sergeant 2d Class Manuel Ozcoydi of the Regiment of Navarre. The officer sent by Campbell met Ezpeleta and presented a request for three days in which to come to terms. (No doubt Sgt. Ozcoydi was exaggerating the time requested.) Ezpeleta answered — three hours! On hearing this, the British envoy asked to see the Spanish general, hoping that he would be more generously disposed. Ezpeleta firmly responded that he was the general, and he told the officer that he was wasting too much time. On seeing Ezpeleta's resolution, the British officer did a rightabout-face, probably stamping his foot in the customary British army manner. Sgt. Ozcoydi imputed this violent movement to the officer's regret at having been sent on such a mission. Ezpeleta urged him to obey his orders without delay, otherwise he would rush the British forts with fire and sword and eradicate the entire breed. Those who were listening to Ezpeleta stepped away from him, as it looked as if he were ready to swallow up the whole earth. Gálvez was delighted with Ezpeleta's report of the meeting.[38]

Gálvez upheld the three-hour limit established by Ezpeleta. By seven o'clock that evening, Campbell sent Gálvez the articles of capitulation prepared with Governor Peter Chester's assistance. Gálvez accepted some of them, but rejected others. The next day Brigade Major James Campbell, the general's nephew, arrived at the Spanish camp fully empowered to discuss the articles. Gálvez, being indisposed, entrusted Ezpeleta and his own secretary with the task of replying to Campbell.[39]

Ezpeleta took a hard line. He had suffered much during the last ten months in Mobile, precisely because of Gálvez's leniency in former capitulations, so he pressed for more firmness at Pensacola. In their correspondence, Ezpeleta had more than once expressed his disapproval of Gálvez's milder policies. He had asked the general to "arm himself with a stone heart" — on another occasion the simile had been "an iron heart" — and "to put on the screws in future capitulations." Gálvez had promised to arm himself "with an adamantine heart not to yield to the demands of the British inhabitants in future capitulations."[40] As Ezpeleta had initially taken the position that all inhabitants who took up arms should be treated as prisoners of war, it is interesting to see Ezpeleta's influence in one of the responses to the preliminary articles proposed by Campbell: that all inhabitants who had taken up arms should be treated as prisoners of war — a provision later withdrawn by Gálvez.[41]

It was not a feeling of aversion toward the British that directed Ezpeleta's policy. He esteemed the "English Nation"; it was, in his sight "so noble and so humane."[42] He opposed the methods of making war used by Campbell and others in Pensacola, chiefly with regard to the use of Indians, but also regarding the behavior of some English inhabitants in Mobile. Ezpeleta had written to Campbell that he did not believe he or any commander of a civilized nation would approve of or would consent to deeds such as those committed by the Indians. But, he added, "Whoever authorized the savages to make war, gives cause for their cruelties and is liable for them."[43] As to his attitude toward the inhabitants in general, he would say of one of them, "He is too English to be trusted."[44]

The objections raised by Ezpeleta to some of the articles of capitulation were overcome. The leniency of Gálvez won out again, and the articles were all ratified on the morning of May 10. On the 11th., Spanish troops occupied the Royal Navy Redoubt at *Barrancas Coloradas*. Paradoxically, the first objective in the Spanish plans, the capture of the Royal Navy Redoubt,

Ezpeleta's main objective from the beginning, was the last to fall — without a single shot fired or a single casualty. The battle of Pensacola was over, and with the ceremony of the surrender of this fort, the entire province of West Florida passed effectively to Spain.[45]

In this victory of great consequence for the future of the United States of America, José de Ezpeleta played a very important role. It was reported that when the battle was over, troops and officers in the Spanish regiments took little interest in their own colonels, they talked only of Ezpeleta. Even the French judged him "the best soldier the armies had, unequaled in his courage and dispositions." Our informant, Sergeant Ozcoydi, made an even more emphatic statement: "the only general on the scene during the siege was Ezpeleta." He made it more specific by affirming that after March 30, when the Spaniards repelled the first British attack thanks to Ezpeleta's courage, Gálvez was less a general than a subordinate to Ezpeleta's decisions. Even the British general wanted very much to meet Ezpeleta and looked for him after the capitulation took place. When they finally met, Campbell complimented Ezpeleta for his bravery. Ezpeleta simply replied, "I serve my King."[46]

Perhaps we can never verify the accuracy of these reports. Undoubtedly they contain some exaggerations, the fruits of an understandable admiration for the courage and merit of a chief. But these adulatory comments do point to the fact that Ezpeleta's soldiers were heartily enthusiastic about a commander who made himself appreciated by his men. There was Enrique Grimarest, for example, who in May of 1780 had turned over the command of Mobile to Ezpeleta, "a colonel whom I have always liked."[47] A year later, following the victory at Pensacola, Grimarest wrote Gálvez and congratulated Ezpeleta warmly. All knew at Mobile "how greatly the Cavalier Ezpeleta had behaved at Pensacola." Grimarest added, "I was always very glad that you had such a good companion in arms. We all know what that means from our own experience here at Mobile."[48]

To provide a more impartial and better qualified judgment of Ezpeleta's conduct in Pensacola, we have the official report of Bernardo de Gálvez. In his view, among all the senior officers, Ezpeleta deserved particular commendation. There had been no attack, reconnaissance, or occasion during the expedition in which Ezpeleta had not taken part and in which he had not successfully proven his talents. He had distinguished himself in all of these actions as well as in the discharge of his responsibilities as major general and in the other commissions entrusted to his care, especially the command of the entire army and its operations when the general in chief was wounded.[49]

King Charles III officially acknowledged the meritorious conduct of José de Ezpeleta in the conquest of Pensacola by promoting him to the grade of Brigadier of the Royal Armies with date of rank from February 5, 1781. In the same royal dispatch, the king generously pledged that, once the war was over, he would reward Ezpeleta's outstanding services by appointing him to a post corresponding to his merits.[50]

This royal acknowledgement was the beginning for Ezpeleta of promotions to posts of the highest dignity and responsibility in America as well as in Spain: Deputy Captain General of Louisiana and West Florida during Gálvez's absence (1783-1785); General Inspector of the troops in New Spain (1783-1785); Captain General of Cuba (1785-1789), and of Louisiana and the Two Floridas (1787-1789); Viceroy of New Granada (1789-1797); Governor of the Council of Castile and Captain General of New Castile (1797-1798); Captain General of Catalonia (1807-1808); Viceroy of Navarra (1814-1820); Captain General of the Royal Armies (from 1816); first Count of Ezpeleta de Beire (from 1797).[51] Pensacola was indeed an accolade for José de Ezpeleta. For the newborn United States of America, it was a major step in the drive toward independence. When we think of Pensacola we must remember the names of two men who were closely united and who played major roles in its destiny: Bernardo de Gálvez and José de Ezpeleta.

---

[*]Member of the Jesuit Historical Institute and coordinating editor of Encyclopedia of Jesuit History, Rome, Italy.

[1]Campbell to Clinton, May 12, 1781, Carleton Papers, 30/55, fol. 89, Public Record Office, Kew. This paper is based on my *José de Ezpeleta, Gobernador de la Mobile, 1780-81* (Sevilla, 1980). I am very much indebted to Fr. Charles E. O'Neill for his help with the English composition of this paper and to Mrs. Julita Blasi for corrections of style and typing.

[2]A. Risco, "Don Francisco de Saavedra y la guerra de la Independencia de los Estados Unidos," *Razón y Fe* 88 (1928):216-35, 227.

[3]Manuel Ozcoydi to Joaquín de Ezpeleta Galdeano, Havana, May 19, 1781, *Archivo Ezpeleta, Papeles de Panzacola*, Seville; Borja Medina, *Ezpeleta*, 785-86.

[4]Borja Medina, *Ezpeleta*, 778ff.

[5]J. Dabán, *Revista del Regimiento de Infantería de Navarra*, Havana, Dec. 31, 1780, *AGI Santo Domingo*, 2097; extract of a letter from Capt. Stoney, *Fox*, Havannah, July 21, 1783, C.O. 5/598, PRO; Borja Medina, *Ezpeleta*, pp. lxxvii-lxxviii.
[6]Borja Medina,*Ezpeleta*, 6.
[7]Ibid., 29-30.
[8]Ibid., 4, 50, 395-96.
[9]Ibid., 414-18.
[10]Piernas to Ezpeleta, New Orleans, Jan. 16 and 17, 1781, *AGI Cuba, 114*; Borja Medina, *Ezpeleta*,552-53.
[11]Borja Medina, *Ezpeleta*, 396-413.
[12]Ezpeleta to Gálvez, Mobile, July 4, 1780, *AGI Cuba*, 2; Borja Medina, *Ezpeleta*, 419.
[13]Ezpeleta to Gálvez, Mobile, Aug. 14, 1780, *AGI Cuba*, 2; Borja Medina, *Ezpeleta*, 420.
[14]Ezpeleta to Gálvez, Mobile, Sept. 7, 1780, *AGI Cuba*, 4A; Borja Medina, *Ezpeleta*, 421.
[15]Ezpeleta to Gálvez, Mobile, Oct. 12, 1780, *AGI Cuba*, 4A; Borja Medina, *Ezpeleta*, 452ff.
[16]Ezpeleta to Gálvez, Mobile, Nov. 8, 1780, *AGI Cuba*, 2; Borja Medina, *Ezpeleta*, 453ff.
[17]Borja Medina, *Ezpeleta*, 450-61, 518-19.
[18]Ezpeleta to Gálvez, Mobile, Dec. 30, 1780, *AGI Cuba*, 2; Borja Medina, *Ezpeleta*, 619-23.
[19]Gálvez to Ezpeleta, Havana, Dec. 5, 1780, *AGI Cuba, 1377*; Borja Medina, *Ezpeleta*, 623-24.
[20]Ezpeleta to Gálvez, Mobile, Jan. 6, 1781, *AGI Cuba, 1233*; Borja Medina, *Ezpeleta*, 624, 651-56.
[21]Borja Medina, *Ezpeleta*, 486-91, 533-39, 575-98.
[22]Gálvez to Ezpeleta, Havana, Jan. 30, 1781, *AGI Cuba, 1377*; Ezpeleta to Gálvez, Mobile, Feb. 22, 1781,*AGI Cuba, 107*; Borja Medina, *Ezpeleta*, 669-72, 683-90.
[23]Ezpeleta to Gálvez, Mobile, May 22, 1780, *AGI Cuba*, 2; Borja Medina, *Ezpeleta*, 199.
[24]Ezpeleta to Piernas, Mobile, Oct. 29, 1780, *AGI Cuba*, 4A; Borja Medina, *Ezpeleta*, 451.
[25]Ezpeleta to Gálvez, Mobile, March 5, 1781, *AGI Cuba*, 3A; Borja Medina, *Ezpeleta*, 683.
[26]Borja Medina, *Ezpeleta*, 690-91.
[27]Gálvez to Ezpeleta, *San Ramón* at sea, March 1, 1781, *AGI Cuba, 1377*; Ezpeleta to Gálvez, Mobile, March 10, 1781, *AGI Cuba*, 4A; Borja Medina, *Ezpeleta*, 692, 697-703.
[28]Borja Medina, *Ezpeleta*, 519, 704-705, 716-34.
[29]Ibid., 716, 734-43. In the controversy between Calvo and Gálvez on the issue of the entrance into the bay, Francisco Saavedra, a close friend and confidant of the latter, preferred truth to friendship and honestly admitted that reason was on the part of the naval commander: it was not possible for the *San Ramón* to cross the bar. Risco, "Francisco de Saavedra," 223.
[30]Borja Medina, *Ezpeleta*, 750ff.

[31] *Reales Ordenanzas, Tratado VII, titulo VI, articulo 10.*

[32] Ezpeleta to Gálvez, March 23, 1781, *AGI Cuba, 81;* Gálvez, *Diario de las Operaciones contra la Plaza de Panzacola, 1781,* 2nd ed. (Madrid, 1959), 33; Borja Medina, *Ezpeleta,* 744ff. See ibid., 788 for the two colonels who died.

[33] Borja Medina, *Ezpeleta,* 752-62; Ezpeleta to Gálvez, Pensacola, April 5, 1781, *AGI Cuba 1233.* For the location of the various Spanish campsites, etc. see William S. and Hazel P. Coker, *The Siege of Pensacola, 1781, in Maps* (Pensacola, 1981).

[34] Ezpeleta to Gálvez, Mobile, Sept. 26, 1780, *AGI Cuba, 2;* Borja Medina, *Ezpeleta,* 433.

[35] Borja Medina, *Ezpeleta,* 759-72; "*Diario de lo occurrido en la escuadra, y tropas, que al mando del Gefe de Escuadra Dn. Josef Solano; y del Mariscal de Campo Dn. Juan Manuel de Cagigal, salieron de la Havana el 9 de Abril de 1781, para socorrer al exército español, que atacaba la Plaza de Panzacola,*" Archivo del General Miranda (Caracas, 1929), 1:170.

[36] Borja Medina, *Ezpeleta,* 772ff; Risco, "Francisco de Saavedra," 226.

[37] Campbell to Clinton, May 12, 1781, Carleton Papers, 30/55, fol. 89; Borja Medina, *Ezpeleta,* 780.

[38] Manuel Ozcoydi to Joaquín de Ezpeleta Galdeano, Havana, May 19, 1781, *Archivo Ezpeleta, Papeles de Panzacola;* Borja Medina, *Ezpeleta,* 784.

[39] Campbell to Germain, May 12, 1781, C.O. 5/597, PRO: Borja Medina, *Ezpeleta,* 780.

[40] Ezpeleta to Gálvez, Mobile, June 12, 1780, *AGI Cuba 193B;* Ezpeleta to Piernas, Mobile, Sept. 18, 1780, *AGI Cuba 1377;* Gálvez to Ezpeleta, New Orleans, June 27, 1780, *AGI Cuba 4A;* Borja Medina, *Ezpeleta,* 186, 322.

[41] Ezpeleta to Gálvez, Mobile, March 3, 1781, *AGI Cuba 3A;* Answers to the Articles of Capitulation proposed by His Excellency General Campbell, Carleton Papers, 30/55, fol. 89, PRO: Borja Medina, *Ezpeleta,* 689, 781.

[42] Ezpeleta to Durnford, Mobile, Aug. 25, 1780, *AGI Cuba 2;* Borja Medina, *Ezpeleta,* 335.

[43] Ezpeleta to Campbell, Mobile, Aug. 26, 1780, *AGI Cuba 2;* Borja Medina, *Ezpeleta,* 324-38.

[44] Ezpeleta to Martín Navarro, Mobile, Oct. 26, 1780, *AGI Cuba 2;* Borja Medina, *Ezpeleta,* 191.

[45] Borja Medina, *Ezpeleta,* 781ff.

[46] Ibid., 784ff.; Manuel Ozcoydi to Joaquín de Ezpeleta Galdeano, Havana, May 19, 1781, *Archivo Ezpeleta, Papeles de Panzacola.*

[47] Grimarest to Gálvez, Mobile, May 10, 1780, *AGI Cuba 81;* Borja Medina, *Ezpeleta,* 30.

[48] Grimarest to Gálvez, Mobile, May 12, 1781, *AGI Cuba 114;* Borja Medina, *Ezpeleta,* 784.

[49] Bernardo de Gálvez to José de Gálvez, Pensacola, May 26, 1781, *AGS Guerra Moderna, 6913;* Borja Medina, *Ezpeleta,* 788.

[50] *Real Despacho, San Ildefonso,* Aug. 23, 1781, *Archivo Ezpeleta, Casa Ezpeleta,* 18; Borja Medina, *Ezpeleta,* 789.

[51] Borja Medina, *Ezpeleta,* xlix-lxxv.

DON JOSÉ DE SOLANO Y BOTE (1726-1806), FIRST *MARQUÉS DEL SOCORRO*. Furnished by Eric Beerman through the courtesy of José Luis Santaló and María Isabel Solano.

JOSÉ SOLANO AND THE SPANISH NAVY AT THE SIEGE OF PENSACOLA

Eric Beerman*

Vice Admiral José Solano sailed out of Cádiz Bay on the afternoon of April 28, 1780, commanding a great fleet of seventeen warships which escorted 140 transport vessels carrying nearly twelve thousand crack infantrymen—probably the great concentration of Spanish military power ever sent to the Americas. His expedition was aimed at clearing the British from the Gulf of Mexico and the Caribbean, making that vital region a Spanish lake; his first objective was Fort George at Pensacola. As a result of Admiral Solano's aid or help (*el socorro*) to the embattled Spanish forces at the siege of Pensacola the following year, he would receive the title of Marquis del Socorro.

José Solano y Bote was born in 1726, at the village of Zorita in Estremadura, land of the conquistadors.[1] When it came time to decide on a career, Solano chose the navy and became a *guardia marina* at Cádiz in 1742. He received his baptism of fire off Cape Sicié near Toulon in 1744, and won promotion to ensign. After the war, Solano studied naval science in England, France, Holland, and Russia. In 1754, he began seven long years with the demarcation team in the Amazon region of Venezuela, marking the boundary between the Spanish and Portuguese colonies. He returned home as a thirty-five year old navy captain.

The following year, 1762, Spain entered the Seven Years War. Solano received his first sea command, the seventy-gun ship of the line *Rayo*, which captured two English frigates off Sagres, Portugal.[2] On returning with his prizes to Cádiz, Solano signed a power-of-attorney authorizing his marriage to Rafaela Ignacia Ortíz de Rojas; the ceremony took place—the groom in absentia—in Madrid on June 21.[3] With peace in 1763, Solano became a knight in the prestigious Military Order of Santiago and was named captain general of Venezuela where he expelled the English from footholds along the Caribbean coastline and oversaw the demarcation team in the Amazon region. The Spanish court recognized Solano as an authority on border questions in the Americas. Demarcation lines between the French and Spanish on the island of Hispaniola were in dispute, and in 1770, Solano became captain general of Santo Domingo where he made a classic map of the border between the two colonies. Three years after his arrival, he was promoted to rear admiral.[4]

As war with England approached again, and as his service in Santo Domingo came to a close, Solano requested sea duty. He returned to Spain and was promoted to vice admiral at the outbreak of hostilities in 1779. Spanish strategy made the Gulf of Mexico and the Caribbean principal theaters of operations, and Solano sailed for Havana on April 28, 1780, with 11,752 Spanish infantrymen under General Victorio de Navia. Solano knew that English Admiral George Rodney waited in ambush near the French island of Martinique, but he avoided the trap, thereby winning the title of Viscount of *Feliz Ardid* (Fortunate Maneuver).[5]

The Spanish fleet entered Havana Bay on August 4, and news of Bernardo de Gálvez's capture of Fort Charlotte, Mobile, five months earlier, greeted the admiral. Gálvez had planned a prompt assault on Pensacola, but Admiral Juan Bautista Bonet, Spanish naval commander for Cuba, had insisted upon the Royal Order specifying a minimum of four thousand troops for the Pensacola invasion, and as the army lacked nearly fifteen hundred men, the Mobile veterans were embarked for Havana; they would attack Pensacola another day.[6]

The August briefing brought Solano abreast of the situation. Bonet had failed the powerful Gálvez clan, and Solano received command of the fleet for the second attempt on Pensacola.[7] He and Gálvez planned to launch the invasion in September, but poor weather, and crews and troops not yet recovered from the Atlantic crossing, delayed their departure.

As Solano boarded the seventy-gun flagship *San Juan Nepomuceno* in the early morning hours of October 16, he glanced up at the sky, knowing the danger of hurricanes at that time of the year. Havana's four chief pilots and twelve captains of the ships had met with Solano aboard the *San Juan* and had agreed to sail unless there was a southeastern wind. There was not, so the fleet could sail, but Solano gave sealed orders to each skipper to be opened in case of separation from the rest of the expedition.[8]

The naval force included seven ships of the line, six frigates, a small lugger *Duque de Cornwallis,* escorting fifty-one transports with Gálvez's 3,809 soldiers aboard, many of them veterans of the siege of Gibraltar.[9] Captain José Calvo de Irazábal on his ship of the line *San Ramón,* a key figure in the next invasion of Pensacola, sailed alongside Solano's *San Juan*. The fleet commander's worst fears were realized as the sky turned a frightful color and the wind came up from the southeast. Only a few hours out of Havana, skippers struggled to read their sealed orders: in event of separation, the first assembly point was at *Sonda de Tortuga*, two hundred miles west of the Everglades. If this assembly point was passed, ships should sail northwest to the second point, ten leagues south of the entrance of Mobile Bay.

Disaster struck Solano's sixty-five vessels. The hurricane, at the highest intensity for five days and nights, scattered ships from one end of the Gulf to the other. Transports headed west for protection on the Campeche Bank off Yucatan. The storm finally subsided on October 22. Solano's flagship took a battering and was in a dreadful state, its tiller severely damaged. When the weather improved, Solano found himself three hundred miles south of Pensacola. He sighted Commander Andrés Tacón's frigate *Santa Rosalía*, which had weathered the storm better than the *San Juan*, so Solano changed ships. The flagship was in no shape to go to Pensacola, so he ordered her skipper, José Pereda, to return to Havana and tell Bonet of the disaster, although the Pensacola expedition would continue.[10]

Solano arrived at the second assembly point south of Mobile on October 28, but seeing no warships, he continued west for eight leagues looking for transports. The *Santa Rosalía* returned to the assembly point, and three days later Solano sighted transports and signaled them to assemble. The vessels, including Luis Vidal's schooner *Concepción* carrying artillery, paid not the least attention to the fleet commander but continued southeast to Havana. Lacking sufficient forces below Mobile, where the *Santa Rosalía* searched for fifteen days and gathered only a handful of ships, Solano charted a course to the other assembly point west of the Everglades. No vessels were sighted, and the *Santa Rosalía* sailed for Havana where she arrived on November 19.[11]

Solano's temper flared, no doubt, on seeing many of his ships anchored in the bay. The normally mild-mannered commander instructed all warship skippers to prepare reports and explain why orders had not been followed.[12]

Captain José Pereda, of the *San Juan*, who had arrived in Havana on the last day of October, was cleared of any dereliction of duty, as Solano had ordered him to return.[13] Other warships had returned the same day, while Solano searched for them six hundred miles northwest. Calvo de Irazábal's *San Ramón* had been separated from the expedition the first day of the storm. Her mainmast a shambles, salt in the drinking water, food spoiled, she was in danger of sinking, and Calvo had ordered her return to Havana. The *San Ramón* had little other ballast than her twenty-four-pounders, and eleven of these had been thrown overboard when it was feared the ship might go under.[14]

Captain Pedro Autrán de la Torre's *Dragón* was the last ship-of-the-line to return, her rigging and top-mast battered, water and food spoiled, many of her crew dead or ill when she arrived the last day of November. Solano congratulated the skipper, for *Dragón* had been one of the few vessels to reach the assembly point south of Mobile.[15]

Gabriel de Aristizábal's flagship *Nuestra Señora de la O*, with Gálvez aboard, had her own tale of woe. The frigate had been separated from the fleet the first day and reached Campeche Bank on October 20. *La O* returned east toward the first assembly point at *Sonda de Tortuga* and was joined en route by Commander Miguel Goicoechea's 36-gun frigate *Santa Cecilia*, Commander Pedro Obregón's 22-gun packet boat *San Pío*, and two small transports. The five vessels followed Solano's instructions and, as no other ships were at *Sonda de Tortuga*, set course for Mobile on October 28. Three 70-gun ships of the line came over the horizon—*Guerrero*, *Velasco*, and *Astuto*, commanded respectively by Fidel Eslava, Santiago Muñoz de Velasco, and Estanislao Velasco; they were joined later that afternoon by Commander José Fermín de Rada's 22-gun frigate *Caimán*. Two hundred miles from the assembly point south of Mobile, the naval commanders met aboard *La O* and reached a unanimous decision to return to Havana. Gálvez attended the meeting and took sharp exception, stating that Solano had specifically ordered the expedition to assemble south of Mobile for the invasion of Pensacola. Aristizábal put his objections in writing: *La O* had only twelve days' water and provisions left; it was necessary to return with all possible speed to Havana. Gálvez replied immediately that he had come to fight a war and would follow orders and join Solano. Aristizábal requested the recommendations of the other warship skippers on November 3, and all supported their fellow naval officer. When *La O's* commander advised Gálvez, three days later, of the naval officers' decision, Gálvez retorted that, being so close to Solano, it was a pity the navy did not follow the fleet commander's orders. Gálvez contemplated taking a small boat with his army comrades and continuing northwest as directed by Solano. This threat did not deter Aristizábal who continued on course to Havana with Gálvez still aboard—but no doubt fuming. *La O* sighted two English frigates on November 14, while thirty-five miles northwest of Havana. Joined by the *Santa Cecilia* and *San Pío*, the three Spanish ships closed on the frigates which surrendered after a sharp engagement. The largest prize carried sixty men and twenty-four guns, and the other had thirty-two men and fourteen guns. Their cargo was Jamaica rum, and Gálvez's spirits improved on arriving in Havana with two enemy frigates.[16]

The transports returned later. On December 23, of the fifty-one that left, only eight had arrived, twenty-three were in Campeche, six in Mobile, three in New Orleans, and eleven in ports to the east of Havana.[17]

Bonet, Navia, and captain general of Cuba Diego José Navarro at the *Junta de Generales*, January 28, 1781, approved another invasion attempt against Pensacola. French Caribbean fleet commander, Chevalier de Monteill, arrived in Havana with a squadron of four ships of the line and an equal number of heavy frigates and placed them at the disposal of the Spanish navy. Gálvez replaced Navia as commanding general of operations in the Caribbean and Gulf Coast on February 12, and in the event of his absence from Havana, Field Marshal Juan Manuel de Cagigal would replace him.[18]

On January 22, the *Junta de Generales* assigned Gálvez 1,315 men from various regiments for an assault on Pensacola.[19] Solano offered his naval expertise and estimated that Rodney and Parker had suffered worse than the Spaniards from the October hurricane and that Parker could not offer much naval assistance to Pensacola.

Solano initially assigned only the *Caimán* and *San Pío* to escort thirty-one transports to Pensacola, but when he heard that three large 40-gun English frigates—*Ulysses, Resource, Dutton*—had sailed for Pensacola, he ordered the *San Ramón, Santa Cecilia*, and the 36-gun *Santa Clara*, commanded by Miguel Alderete, to join the expedition, with Calvo de Irazábal as flotilla commander.[20] Bonet instructed Calvo, while Gálvez had overall command of the invasion. As senior naval officer, Calvo had responsibility for the ships.[21] The flagship *San Ramón* had sixty-two guns; it could guard not only against English frigates but, as the lightest ship of the line, it had the best chance of forcing Pensacola Bay and bombarding Fort George with heavy naval firepower. Alderete commanded the *Santa Clara*, Goicoechea the *Santa Cecilia*; *Caimán* and *San Pío* were now under Commander José Serrato and Commander José María Chacón.[22]

The five warships sailed out of Havana escorting thirty-one transports with Gálvez's 1,315 troops on February 28, for the third try at Pensacola.

At two o'clock in the afternoon, March 9, Santa Rosa was in sight. Light infantry and grenadier units stormed ashore at nine o'clock that evening, some three leagues east of Sigüenza Point, but encountered no opposition.[23] Colonel Francisco Longoria led troops west along the beach toward Sigüenza Point, but instead of a battery, he found there just three dismantled cannons. Longoria did capture several sailors from the frigate *Port Royal*, who came to the island to feed the cattle, and Calvo interrogated the prisoners regarding English naval strength at Pensacola. At that moment the *Port Royal* and *Mentor* moved in close to shore and commenced heavy but ineffective fire against Gálvez's camp on the island. Some Spaniards had thought Pensacola would be an easy conquest; the naval attack demonstrated that the English were there to fight.[24]

On the 11th, two 24-pounders from the *San Ramón*, were emplaced at Sigüenza Point and drove off the enemy frigates, leaving the battery at Red Cliffs the major obstacle to forcing the bay. Calvo ordered the *San Ramón* to throw overboard all ballast in preparation for entry. He led the flotilla toward the bar, but the flagship ran aground in shallow water, blocking the channel. The remaining vessels had no alternative but to desist in the attempt. The *San Ramón* later got free, although some damage was done to her hull, and returned to the anchorage off Santa Rosa.[25]

Gálvez, disappointed at the failure to force the bay, went to see Calvo regarding another attempt. The army commander suggested the frigates go first, followed by transports, with the *San Ramón* bringing up the rear. One observer on the *San Ramón* noted that all commanders had wanted to be in the lead the previous day; now they supported Calvo in emphasizing the hazards. Gálvez wanted his troops and vessels inside the bay, however, as he feared the flotilla's departure in the event of a storm.[26]

Calvo wrote to Gálvez on March 14, offering six hundred sailors to implement the initial plan to attack Red Cliffs before forcing the bay. Red Cliffs was a powerful fort surrounded by parapets and moats, with a 140-man garrison with eleven cannons, including five 32-pounders, which fortification required a siege. These cannons covered not only the channel below, but the western end of Santa Rosa, including the encampment on the island. Gálvez replied that he lacked the minimum four thousand troops required by Royal Order to lay siege to Red Cliffs. Calvo retorted that Gálvez might disembark his troops as he had done after the fall of Mobile. He agreed to continue the attack on Pensacola in spite of not having the minimum four thousand troops, but he first wanted to capture Red Cliffs. As Gálvez's channel charts had proved inaccurate and contributed to the *San Ramón* running aground, Calvo feared that even if the flotilla forced the bay, the channel might be a bottleneck, and exit might prove even more dangerous than entry.[27]

The black southeastern horizon on the morning of March 18—which Gálvez feared would force the flotilla to sail and leave his troops stranded on the island—decided him to force the bay on his brig *Galveztown*, accompanied by Riaño's sloop *Valenzuela* and two armed launches.[28] Gálvez still hoped to spur Calvo into forcing the bay. A 32-pound ball was carried by Lieutenant Francisco Gelabert and publicly presented to Calvo on the *San Ramón*, along with the following message:

> that a thirty-two pound ball received in the camp, which he brought and presented, was one of those fired by the fort at the entrance, but that whoever had honor and valor would follow him [Gálvez], for he was going in advance with the *Galveztown* to remove fear.

Calvo was understandably stung by Gálvez's bravado, and Gelabert did not have to wait long for a reply. The skipper of *San Ramón* summoned all hands to the quarter-deck and declared Gálvez a brazen upstart, traitor to king and country; messages such as this ought to be carried by a *ruin* (ignominious) person, not by an officer, in order that the admiral might have the satisfaction of hanging him from a yardarm.[29]

Calvo's reply did not deter "*Yo solo*" that afternoon when the *Galveztown's* twenty 4-pounders were pitted against the mighty battery above on Red Cliffs. The four vessels, unscathed, anchored under the protection of Sigüenza's 24-pounders. The British battery's lack of accuracy was noticed, and naval commanders wanted to follow Gálvez, but Calvo commanded all ships not to move without his explicit order.

Gálvez realized his afternoon message to Calvo was less than diplomatic, and he knew the necessity of the navy's fullest cooperation; he sent his top aide, Colonel Longoria, to soothe Calvo's wounded pride. The colonel did his job well, and Calvo accepted Gálvez's apologies, both commanders forgetting the incident and getting on with the job at hand. Calvo ordered his flotilla into the bay the following afternoon, although the *San Ramón*, without sufficient clearance, remained at the entrance on guard against English ships.[30]

Relations improved until Calvo heard the captain of the *Galveztown* boast that he could take the *San Ramón* into the bay with no problems. On hearing this, Calvo threw overboard all remaining ballast and requested Gálvez to send Rousseau aboard to take full responsibility for the safety of the ship of the line during its entry. Nothing more was heard from Gálvez's French-born skipper; the *San Ramón* remained off the bar, riding dangerously high in the water.[31]

On March 20, and the following day, Gálvez and Campbell negotiated the neutrality of Pensacola; English troops evacuated the village and moved to Fort George and the two outlying redoubts. Gálvez looked on with joy as Mobile soldiers waded into the bay after a long ten-day march, and he ordered his own men, with the exception of a five hundred-man Santa Rosa garrison, to board navy launches and cross the bay.[32]

In high spirits, Gálvez invited the navy boat officers to dine with him. After initial pleasantries, the conversation turned to the work at hand, and words grew heated. Gálvez, in an outburst, charged Minister of the Navy, Marquis de González de Castejón, with responsibility for the navy's slow pursuit of the Pensacola campaign, describing him as a traitor to king and country and under the influence of his wife, a niece of General John Campbell. Gálvez's sharp personal attack on the head of the navy shocked those present; they tried to get the general to change the subject, but to no avail. Infuriated, Gálvez asked if the naval officers were trying to insult him and took his sword and hat in hand. When harbor commander Alderete arrived at the luncheon, the scene calmed for the moment, but the tranquility was brief as Gálvez returned to the subject, complaining that the flotilla had not saluted the *Galveztown* when she forced the bay three days before. Gálvez raved that he did not need the navy; whenever it liked, the flotilla might return to Havana. Alderete, taken aback by these hotheaded remarks, took testimony to send to the Navy Ministry in Madrid.[33]

The arrival of New Orleans' 1,400 reinforcements improved the delicate situation. Alderete told Calvo that Gálvez had offered to dine on the *Santa Clara* in order to reestablish the relationship between the sister services, but the following morning, March 24, Calvo sailed for Havana on the *San Ramón*.[34]

Calvo, while crediting Gálvez with great courage, did not think his military tactics measured up to the same high standard. Gálvez had not followed the original plan to join Ezpeleta at Mobile and to attack the Red Cliffs before forcing the bay. Gálvez had expected a heavy artillery battery at Sigüenza and a weak one at Red Cliffs — and was wrong in both cases. And Gálvez's inaccurate nighttime charting of the channel contributed to the grounding of the *San Ramón*. On the other hand, Calvo felt his flotilla had served Gálvez well. Two previous Pensacola invasions had failed, whereas Calvo had carried Gálvez to Pensacola and established a beachhead without loss of either man or ship. The navy had escorted Ezpeleta across the Perdido, forced the bay, and carried Gálvez's units from Santa Rosa to the mainland without loss. *San Ramón's* cannon, mounted on Sigüenza Point, drove off the British frigates bombarding the island encampment. Warships escorted reinforcements from New Orleans and continued to transport vital supplies and munitions from Havana. The *San Ramón* returned to Havana because she had thrown overboard all ballast, including provisions and drinking water, and her damaged hull made it necessary to seek repairs and supplies in Cuba; she would return to Pensacola if so ordered by the naval high command.[35]

Meanwhile in Havana, Solano met with navy officers and the French fleet commander Monteill, who offered ships for a joint operation against Pensacola. On March 21, a large Spanish and

French fleet—fifteen ships of the line and two frigates—sailed from Havana to reconnoiter the Florida Straits for a rumored English fleet sailing to Campbell's relief. Solano commanded one line from aboard his powerful 80-gun *San Luis;* Monteill was on the 74-gun *Palmier,* and Bonet was aboard his flagship *Guerrero.* The English fleet did not materialize, however, so the allied fleet took the opportunity to practice maneuvers for an eventual attack on Pensacola. The fleet returned to Havana Bay on March 26.

Monteill complained that the Spanish fleet lacked aggressiveness. If Pensacola was not an immediate objective, Monteill would return to Guarico and protect French shipping in Haitian waters. Bonet, not wanting to lose the valuable French squadron, replied that the *Junta de Generales* would make a decision in four days.[36]

On that date, an English naval force of eight ships of the line, several frigates, and various transports with troops and artillery was reported to have rounded Cape San Antonio, on the western tip of Cuba, heading with Jamaican reinforcements for Pensacola.[37] On receiving this report, the *Junta* met in emergency session on April 7, and ordered Solano's fleet to sail immediately with Cagigal's army reinforcements and deliver succor to Gálvez's embattled forces.[38] Monteill joined with four ships of the line and an equal number of frigates. Cagigal's 1,600 infantrymen boarded the vessels rapidly, and Solano sailed in a record two-day time after the report of the English fleet.[39]

A week at sea and a hundred miles south of Pensacola, Aristizábal's *Nuestra Señora de la O* sighted the 40-gun *Ulysses* and a transport with four hundred men, artillery, and munitions, returning to Jamaica on finding that Gálvez had won the race to Pensacola. Without being ordered, the captain of the frigate *Unicornio* took up the chase—only to be captured after a three-hour nighttime battle.[40]

Solano sighted Santa Rosa on April 19. The *Andromaque,* patrolling close to the southern shore and more concerned with English ships than shallow water, ran aground a mile off shore. Drinking water and twelve cannons were thrown overboard, and the evening tide allowed its captain, the Chevalier de Ravenel, to get his frigate out to deep water.

Solano's powerful fleet anchored off Santa Rosa two days later. Alderete went out to Solano's *San Luis* that afternoon for a strategy meeting joined by Cagigal and Francisco Saavedra.

Leaving Solano, the group boarded the French cutter *Serpent* and entered the bay, in spite of the Red Cliffs' barrage, as the Spaniards wanted a firsthand account of the battle from Gálvez himself.[41]

The cutter anchored at Sutton's Bayou, where two naval batteries protected the vital waterway leading to Gálvez's camp. The group boarded a small launch, entered the upper arm of the bayou, and proceeded to a landing, from whence they walked a half league to the camp. Gálvez, overjoyed to see them, greeted Cagigal especially warmly. Gálvez remarked that he had not asked Havana for help, nor did he expect it; when he saw the great fleet arrive off Santa Rosa, he had had no reason to think them over than English ships—which meant disaster. The general confirmed that Campbell had mounted a tougher defense than anticipated and that the Indians were especially fine warriors, accounting for most of the Spanish casualties. Gálvez admitted that his troops were nearly exhausted after moving their camp for the seventh time.[42]

At Solano's request, Cagigal inquired about the English navy at Pensacola. Gálvez stated that the frigates *Port Royal* and *Mentor* had gallantly awaited the entire flotilla on March 11, and bombarded the Spanish encampment on Santa Rosa. When Gálvez forced the bay seven days later, the two frigates pulled back abreast of the village of Pensacola. *Mentor* skipper Robert Deans had removed all cannons and men for the defense of Fort George, leaving aboard a skeleton crew to hide the frigate in the Middle River (Blackwater Bay). Gálvez had ordered Alderete, on April 3, to capture the abandoned *Port Royal* near Pensacola, and he had received a pleasant surprise on finding on board nearly a hundred Spanish prisoners. Rousseau took the *Galveztown* and went up the Middle River in an unsuccessful attempt to find *Mentor*, which was later burned and scuttled. Gálvez reiterated his desire to cooperate fully with Solano, for the fleet had saved him from probable disaster.[43]

On April 22, Solano's fifteen ships of the line and seven frigates, arrayed off the southern shore of Santa Rosa, presented an intimidating sight for the English defenders of Pensacola. Forty launches forced the bay with 1,600 of Cagigal's troops, 1,500 of Solano's men volunteering to serve on land, and 700 of Monteill's Frenchmen joining the siege of Fort George. Solano ordered two frigates east toward Cape San Blas to guard against English ships.

The remaining frigates took up station in the entrance of the bay, while the majestic ships of the line spread out along the coast in an impressive show of force. Gálvez's siege units totaled 8,000 men; Spanish and French forces inside and outside the bay numbered 14,000 — a powerful force assembled against Campbell's garrison of 1,300 men without naval protection. Solano's timely arrival with help for Gálvez sealed the fate of Fort George; nevertheless, the garrison steadfastly resisted until the end, in true English military tradition, making the Spaniards fight for everything they obtained.

Solano planned initially to transport Cagigal's men to Pensacola and then depart for Guarico. However, two intercepted letters from Campbell to the Red Cliffs mentioned the imminent arrival of Admiral Rodney with eight ships of the line and fourteen frigates, and Solano told Gálvez that the navy would guard Pensacola Bay until the final surrender — a gracious act which gratified Gálvez.[44]

Cagigal reconnoitered the terrain around Fort George and the two redoubts. His findings, supported by English deserters and later verified by Campbell himself, led to a strategy for forcing the surrender of Pensacola with minimum casualties, cost, and time — in contrast with Gálvez's siege strategy.

Cagigal shrewdly observed that Fort George and the two redoubts were in range of naval artillery in the bay. He believed that the most elementary student of military science would understand that a mortar mounted on a vessel, or a bomb launch protected by a frigate, could move close off shore, and at the first incendiary ball, Campbell would have no other alternative than immediate capitulation. The English general knew that incendiary balls would ignite the inflammable walls, set off the powder magazine, and cause the destruction of fort and garrison. Cagigal was quick to observe another flaw in the English fortifications: Fort George, the Prince of Wales, and Queen's redoubts were in the line of fire from ships positioned off the village. It was obvious that Campbell had expected an attack such as Gálvez's, not the one that Cagigal planned. Gálvez was sceptical of any strategy other than his own; therefore, the Gibraltar veteran decided on a practical demonstration to convince him.[45]

On Tuesday noon, April 24, Cagigal, Alderete, Goicoechea, Serrato, and other naval personnel boarded a bombardment brig and sailed off the village; Fort George was less than a mile away.

Opening fire with two 24-pounders, the Spanish shot hit not only Fort George but further inland by the Prince of Wales redoubt. The fort returned the fire, as did two howitzers mounted on the waterfront. With his point proven, Cagigal ordered the brig out of range. He was convinced that Gálvez would send in two frigates to finish the job and force the surrender of Fort George. Cagigal took soundings and found fourteen feet of water, more than adequate for frigates. Landlubber Gálvez, however, was not impressed and ordered the land siege to continue. English testimony later corroborated Cagigal's observations: if the naval attack had been followed up, Campbell would have had no other alternative than to surrender, as an incendiary ball would have ignited his powder magazine.[46]

The following morning, Gálvez received the English commissioner, John Stephenson, with a letter from Governor Peter Chester expressing concern over the bombardment of the previous day and noting that the neutrality of the village had been guaranteed by both Gálvez and Campbell. Gálvez defended Cagigal on the ground that the village had suffered no damage, the balls passing harmlessly overhead. Stephenson countered that if a round fell short, death and destruction would result to innocent civilians. Chester was obviously concerned about the welfare of the villagers, but his true reason may have been that he recognized the fort's tenuous position if the navy pressed its attack. Gálvez's soldiers had required herculean efforts to get one 24-pound cannon into position, whereas Cagigal had sailed in, almost effortlessly, with two 24-pounders and bombarded Fort George.[47]

As a result of a fierce English counterattack on April 26, causing heavy casualties, Gálvez decided to implement part of Cagigal's plan. Solano concurred, and the *Santa Clara*, *Santa Cecilia*, Cagigal's bomb brig, and two armed launches with one 24-pounder each moved into position off the village. Gálvez did not give the order to open fire, for initially he wanted the ships as a diversion to draw attention away from his suffering siege units. Solano instructed Alderete to await the arrival of the repaired *Andromaque* before firing on Fort George. On the morning of April 30, the 36-gun French frigate sped toward the bar, and as she passed below Red Cliffs, the *Andromaque* fired on the English battery and did more damage than any other ship, thus reinforcing Cagigal's concept of the effectiveness of naval artillery against land targets.[48]

On May 1, Gálvez opened fire with artillery below and west of the Queen's Redoubt which returned a heavy barrage, wounding Captain López Carrizosa, commander of the naval brigade. The following morning, Cagigal and Alderete met aboard the *Santa Clara* and planned a naval bombardment of Fort George. They took the plan to Gálvez, who approved it. Solano not only concurred, he also offered two ships of the line — Captain Pedro Autrán de la Torre's 62-gun *Dragón* and Captain Deidier de Pierrefeu's 64-gun *Tritón,* the lightest in their respective classes and therefore those with the best chance to cross the shallow bar.[49]

On the morning of May 5, their ballast thrown overboard, the two ships prepared to cross the bar and participate in the naval bombardment of Fort George. At that moment a violent storm arose, and the mission was aborted, as Solano ordered all ships to cut their moorings and set sail for fear of being blown onto the coast. Just before setting a course southwestward, Solano informed Gálvez that the fleet would return as soon as the weather permitted.[50]

At nine o'clock on Tuesday morning, May 8, a Spanish howitzer round struck the Queen's Redoubt, setting fire to inflammable walls, causing the powder magazine to explode, and killing 105 defenders. Cagigal received Gálvez's approval, and the *Santa Clara, Santa Cecilia,* and *Andromaque* prepared to open fire on Fort George. At that moment, Campbell ran up a white flag, and the epic siege ended.[51] Formal surrender ceremonies took place at Fort George on May 10. At that moment, Solano was riding out the storm on the *San Luis*, some miles south of Mobile Bay. Commander of the naval brigade, López Carrizosa, recovered from his wounds, represented Solano at the ceremony.[52]

One week after the surrender, and twelve days at sea, Solano returned and was overjoyed to see that the Spanish flag flew over Fort George. The fleet gathered the anchors and launches cut loose on its hasty departure. The victorious troops embarked on Solano's ships and sailed for Havana on May 20, arriving nine days later to a hero's welcome, a three-day victory celebration and a *Te Deum* Mass at Havana Cathedral.[53]

Gálvez proved magnanimous in the hour of his greatest triumph. He laid to rest any differences with the navy, writing to his uncle of Solano's opportune and vital help.[54] Gálvez also wrote to Navy Minister González de Castejón, telling him of Solano's invaluable aid, the courageous participation of the naval brigade, and the outstanding leadership of Alderete who led the naval units into the bay and was responsible for the naval artillery used against Fort George. Gálvez ended, "The navy had on every occasion demonstrated valor and outstanding conduct, officers and sailors alike, and merit the highest tribute in an operation far removed from their own usual professional competence."[55]

Pensacola battle diaries arrived in Cádiz aboard Serrato's *Caimán* on July 27, providing details of one of Spain's finest hours. Solano wrote to the Navy Minister and recommended López Carrizosa, Alderete, and Serrato for promotion. The *Gaceta de Madrid* published these promotions and added a fourth—Solano's own promotion to full admiral.[56]

Solano continued his brilliant naval career after Pensacola and obtained the highest rank in the navy, *capitán general*. In addition to his martial talents, his ability in affairs of state resulted in his appointment as a member of the King's Council of State, and he was named to the prestigious Order of Carlos III. He died in Madrid in 1806.[57]

Bernardo de Gálvez and the Spanish Army received due recognition for the battle of Pensacola which contributed in no small measure to the success of the American Revolution. José Solano and the Spanish Navy's equally crucial roles are far less known. There is no substitute for victory in war, and Gálvez won the land battle of Pensacola with a long siege—although, had naval artillery been used against Fort George at the earliest possible moment, it is interesting to conjecture if the course of the battle might have been different. José Solano fully merits the title of Marquis del Socorro for the Spanish Navy's opportune help to Gálvez at the battle of Pensacola in 1781.

*Spanish archival consultant, Madrid, Spain.

[1] José Solano was born March 6, 1726, and baptized March 11, at San Pablo Church Zorita; he was the son of Agustín Solano and María Bote; his godfather was his maternal grandfather Juan Bote de Escobar. Baptismal document, *expediente* 7802, *Orden Militar de Santiago, Archivo Histórico Nacional, Madrid* (hereafter cited as *AHN*); original certificate, Book of Baptisms (1726), San Pablo Church, Zorita.

² "Memorias de don José Solano y Bote, dictadas a uno de sus hijos," copy in possession of María Isabel Solano, to whom the author expresses his gratitude. See also José Luis Santaló Rodríguez de Viguri, *Don José Solano y Bote: Primer Marqués del Socorro, Capitán General de la Armada* (Madrid, 1973).

³Copy of marriage document, *AHN, Orden Militar de Santiago, expediente 74-moderno;* original certificate, San Justo Church, Madrid, Book of Matrimonies (1762). The bride's father, Domingo Ortiz de Rozas, was captain general of Chile, knight in the Military Order of Santiago, and Count de Poblaciones. Solano and his wife had thirteen children.

⁴"*Memorias de Solano.*" For his *residencia* as captain general of Caracas (1771-1784), see *AHN, Consejo de Indias, legs. 20551-20561;* for his *residencia* as captain general of Santo Domingo (1778-1781), see *AHN, Consejo de Indias, leg. 20766.* Solano's map of Santo Domingo, *AHN, Estado (Mapas, Planos y Dibujos).*

⁵"*Expediente personal de don José Solano y Bote,*" Archivo-Museo Bazán, El Viso del Marqués, Sección de Marina de Guerra. "*Plan de operaciones,*" Marquis de González de Castejón to Solano, *El Pardo,* April 8, 1780, *AGI Santo Domingo,* 2086. "*Estado general de la expedición de mar y tierra que salió de Cádiz, con destino a América en 28 de Abril de 1780,*" Biblioteca Nacional, Madrid (hereafter cited as *BN), MS 19445;* Robert Beatson, *Naval and Military Memoirs of Great Britain from 1727 to 1783* (London, 1804), 6:226-27. Victorio de Navia y Ballet was born in Turin, where his father José de Navia (Marquis of Santa Cruz de Marcenado and Viscount del Puerto) was ambassador. *AHN, Orden Military de Alcántara, expediente 1059.*

"*La esquadra de dn. José Solano, salió de Cádiz el 28 de Abril de 1780,*" Colección de Clonard, leg. 31, Servicio Histórico Militar, Madrid (hereafter cited as *SHM*). For title papers of I Viscount de Feliz Ardid, *AHN, Consejos Suprimidos, libro 629, año 1784.*

⁶"*Estado mayor del Ejército destinado para la conquista de Panzacola,*" Gerónimo Girón, Mobile, April 1, 1780, *Colección de Clonard, leg. 31, SHM.* Bonet to Gálvez, Mobile Bay, April 6, 1780, *AGI Santo Domingo, leg. 2543.* Bonet was born in 1709, at Valletta, son of Spanish naval captain Miguel Bonet; commissioned ensign in Spanish navy, 1728; admiral, 1779; died, 1786. Copy of Bonet's will, *Archivo Histórico de Protocolos, Madrid* (hereafter cited as *AHP); expediente 1146, Orden Military de Santiago, AHN;* naval service record, *Archivo-Museo Bazán.*

⁷Royal Order, May 11, 1780, attached to José de Gálvez to Bonet, Aranjuez, May 14, 1780, *AHN, Estado, leg. 4202.* José de Gálvez was the omnipotent Minister of the Indies; Matías was captain general of Guatemala; Miguel was member of the King's Council of War; Antonio commanded the army garrison in Cádiz; Bernardo's brother-in-law Luis de Unzaga was captain general of Venezuela.

⁸Bonet to Solano, Havana, Sept. 9, 1780, *Archivo General de Simancas* (hereafter cited as *AGS), Marina, leg. 420, doc. 220.* Aristizábal, born in Madrid, was a knight in the Order of Alcántara, and as a result of outstanding service at Pensacola, he became full admiral; he died in 1805, while commanding the naval base at Cádiz. See his *expediente* for entry in the Order of Alcántara and his naval service record at *Archivo-Museo Bazán, Marina de Guerra, leg. 10, no. 139.* Solano, "*Expedición contra Panzacola, 1780,*" Havana, Dec. 1, 1780, *AGS, Marina, leg. 420, doc. 221.*

[9] Gerónimo Girón, "*Estado que manifiesta el numero de oficiales y tropa de que se compone la expedición encargada al mando del Mariscal de Campo Dn. Bernardo de Gálvez,*" Oct. 8, 1780, SHM, *Colección de Clonard, leg. 31.*

[10] Solano to Bonet, aboard *San Juan*, Gulf of Mexico, Oct. 23, 1780, "*Expedición contra Panzacola, 1780."*

[11] Solano to Bonet, aboard *Santa Rosalia*, Havana Bay, November 19, 1780, ibid.

[12] Solano to all naval commanders, ibid.

[13] Pereda to Solano, aboard *San Juan*, Havana Bay, Nov. 19, 1780, ibid.

[14] Calvo de Irazábal to Solano, aboard *San Ramón*, Havana Bay, Nov. 19, 1780, ibid.

[15] Autrán de la Torre to Solano, aboard *Dragón*, Havana Bay, Nov. 19, 1780, ibid.

[16] Aristizábal to Gálvez, aboard *Nuestra Señora de la O*, Nov. 3, 6, 1780; Gálvez to Aristizábal, Nov. 3, 6, 1780; Miguel Goicoechea, Pedro de Obregón, José Orozco et al. to Aristizábal, aboard *La O* at $27°$ $10'$ N, SSE of Mobile Bay, Nov. 3, 1780; Aristizábal to Bonet, aboard *La O*, Havana Bay, Nov. 16, 1780, ibid; *Gaceta de Madrid*, no. 14 (February 16, 1781), 124-26.

[17] Solano to Bonet, Havana, Dec. 23, 1780, AGS, *Marina, leg. 420, doc. 22022.* In addition to Solano's "*Expedición contra Panzacola, 1780,"* see Gálvez, "*Diario de lo acaecido desde el 16 de Octubre de 1780 en que salió del Puerto de la Havana la Esquadra que conducian la expedición al mando del Mariscal de Campo Dn. Bernardo de Gálvez hasta el 18 de Noviembre en que se regresó al expresado Puerto la Fragata de S.M. la que conducía a dicho jefe,*" SHM, *Colección de Clonard, leg. 31.*

[18] *Junta de Generales*, Havana, Jan. 22, 1781, AGI *Santo Domingo, leg. 1233.* Royal Order, El Pardo, Feb. 12, 1781, AGI *Santo Domingo, leg. 2083-B.* José de Gálvez to Bernardo de Gálvez, El Pardo, Feb. 12, 1781, AGI *Santo Domingo, leg. 2083-A.* Cagigal was born in Santiago de Cuba, 1739, while his father, General Francisco Antonio Cagigal de la Vega, served as governor. Cagigal entered the army in Cuba, was captain of the Havana infantry regiment, and went to Spain and served in the 1762 invasion of Portugal. Four years later he was colonel of the *Príncipe* regiment in Oran, and in 1775, he accompanied O'Reilly at the invasion of Algiers. The following year Cagigal went to Brazil as brigadier in the attack on Santa Catalina and was promoted to field marshal the following year. He sailed with Solano in 1780, and was second in command to General Navia. Promoted to lieutenant general and captain general of Cuba, he led the invasion of the Bahamas in 1782. He differed with Bernardo de Gálvez, was accused of indirect involvement in contraband, and was imprisoned four years in Cádiz. Released, he fought in the Pyrenees against the French, 1793-1795, and died in Valencia in 1811.

[19] "*Diario de Gálvez.*" The troops included: 126 from *Rey* regiment, 63 from *Navarra*, 63 from *Príncipe*, 63 from *España*, 231 from *Soria*, 77 from *Guadalajara*, 308 from *Hibernia*, 77 from *Aragón*, and 307 from *Flandes*, according to Pedro Rodríguez de la Buria to Floridablanca, Havana, Feb. 24, 1781, AHN, *Estado, leg. 4201.* This total number supports the "*Diario de Gálvez,*" but José Calvo de Irazábal lists only 1,153 in "*Estado que manifiesta los Buques de Guerra y Convoy, del mando del Capitán de Navío Dn. José Calvo de Irazábal, en el que se conduce el Ejercito que a las ordenes del Sor. Dn. Bernardo de Gálvez, Mariscal de Campo de ellos, se dirije al socorro de la Movila y conquista de Panzacola*" (hereafter cited as "*Estado de Calvo*"), AGS, *Marina, leg. 421.*

[20] "*Extracto del Diario de la Navegación del Capitán de Navio de la Real Armada Don José Calvo de Irazábal, comandante de todos los buques dirigidos a la conquista de Panzacola en el que se contienen las hechas cartas de correspondencia con el Sr. Don Bernardo de Gálvez, y demás documentos que justifican en todas sus partes su conducta*" (hereafter cited as "*Diario de Calvo*"), Havana, May 30, 1781, AGS, Marina, leg. 421, doc. 378. See also AGI Indiferente General, leg. 1578.

[21] Bonet to Calvo, Havana, Feb. 6, 1781, "*Diario de Gálvez*."

[22] "*Diario de Gálvez*" numbers the transports at twenty-five and "*Estado de Calvo*" has twenty-seven, while thirty-one (plus the five warships) figure in the map, "*Convoy de 36 Buques de Guerra y transportes que bajo las órdenes del Capitán de Navío de la Real Armada Dn. José Calvo de Irazábal, el dirigió a auxiliar las Tropas del Rey destinadas a la conquista de Panzacola,*" Museo Naval, Madrid (hereafter cited as MN), Mapas, sig. Bandeja VI, Carpeta B, Num. 16. Miguel Alderete assumed control of the flotilla after Calvo de Irazábal left for Havana on March 24, and after Solano arrived on April 19, Alderete commanded the naval forces within the bay. He was born in Cádiz, 1738, entered the navy as a *guardia marina* in 1751, and served for many years in Caribbean waters; commanded the 32-gun frigate *Matilde* in the October 1780 attempt on Pensacola; promoted to captain and died in Havanna in 1796.

[23] "*Diario de Calvo*"; map, "*Toma de la Plaza de Panzacola con ella la Rendición de la Florida Occidental a las Armas del Rey Carlos Tercero, Año de 1781,*" MN (hereafter cited as "*Toma de Panzacóla*").

[24] "*Diario de Gálvez.*"

[25] "*Diario de Panzacola*"; "*Diario de Calvo*"; "*Toma de Panzacola.*"

[26] "*Diario de Panzacola*"; Donald E. Worcester, trans., "Miranda's Diary of the Siege of Pensacola, 1781," *Florida Historical Quarterly* 29 (1951):163-96.

[27] Calvo to Gálvez, *San Ramón*, Pensacola coast, March 14, 1781, "*Diario de Calvo.*"

[28] Maury Baker and Margaret Bissler Haas, eds., "Bernardo de Gálvez's Combat Diary for the Battle of Pensacola, 1781," *Florida Historical Quarterly* 56 (1977):180.

[29] John Walton Caughey, *Bernardo de Gálvez in Louisiana, 1776-1783* (Berkeley, 1934), 203. Caughey erred in translation regarding Calvo's threat of hanging Gálvez (although Calvo might have wanted to do so). Francisco Gelabert, an engineering officer, continued in Florida after the war, made many maps of the region, and became colonel of engineers; he was involved in 1805 with border questions between Spanish West Florida and the United States. Gelabert's military *expediente*, AGMS.

[30] "*Diario de Panzacola,*" 144.

[31] Calvo to Gálvez, Pensacola Bay, March 19, 1781, "*Diario de Calvo.*"

[32] "*Diario de Gálvez.*"

[33] "*Diario de Panzacola,*" 145-46. Pedro Castejón, marquis de González de Castejón (1719-1783) served like Solano and Calvo de Irazábal at the battle of Cape Sicié and at Havana in 1762; he commanded the fleet during O'Reilly's invasion of Algiers in 1775, and was made Minister of the Navy, which position he held at the time of his death.

[34] "*Diario de Panzacola,*" 146-47.

[35] "*Diario de Calvo.*" On arrival at Matanzas, Cuba, April 2, Calvo wrote to Bonet explaining his differences with Gálvez, AGI Santo Domingo, leg. 2083.

[36] Copy of *"Diario de Francisco de Saavedra,"* original at *Colegio de Jesuitas* in Malaga. The French ships of the line at Havana were *Palmier, Destin, Triton, Intrepide;* frigates were *Licorne, Andromaque;* brigs were *Gustave, Levrette, Bienfaisant,* schooners were *Petite Minerve, Souris;* and cutter *Serpent.* Rènè Quatrefages, *"La participación militar de Francia en la toma de Pensacola," Revisita de Historia Militar,* 21, no. 42 (1977):12-13. See also William S. Coker and Hazel P. Coker, *The Siege of Pensacola, 1781, in Maps* (Pensacola, 1981), App. M, p. 113.

[37] *"Diario de la ocurrido en la esquadra y tropas, que al mando del Gefe de Esquadra Dn Josef Solano; y del Mariscal de Campo Dn. Juan Manuel de Cagigal, salieron de la Havana el 9 de Abril de 1781 para socorrer al exército español, que atacaba la plaza de Panzacola"* (hereafter cited as *"Diario de Solano"), Archivo del General Miranda,* 1:150. Cagigal later stated that Gálvez floated this rumor in Havana so that Solano would go to the help of Pensacola. Cagigal testimony, Mardird, 1790, *"El Señor Fiscal con El Teniente General Dn. Juan Manuel de Cagigal sobre la Conquista de la Isla de la Providencia"* (hereafter cited as *"Fiscal con Cagigal"). AHN, Consejo de Indias,* leg. 20170, no. 4.

[38] Diego Josef Navarro to José de Gálvez, Havana, April 8, 1781, *AGI Santo Domingo,* leg. 2083-B.

[39] *"Fiscal con Cagigal"; "Diario de Solano."* Monteill commanded the 74-gun *Palmier,* Du Maitz de Goimpy the 74-gun *Destin,* Duplessis Parscau the 74-gun *Intrepide,* Deidier de Pierrefeu the 64-gun *Triton,* and Chevalier de Ravenel the 36-gun frigate *Andromaque.* Odet-Julien Le Boucher, *Histoire de la Derniere Guerre entre la Grande Bretagne, et Les Estats-Unis de L'Amérique, La France, L'Espagne et al Hollande* (Paris, 1787), 216. Landing units under the command of navy captain Boiderut included troops from the French regiments of Orleans, Poitou, Agenois, Gatinois, and Cambresis. Bernardo to José de Gálvez, Pensacola, May 26, 1781, *AHN, Estado,* leg. 4211.

[40] *"Diario de Solano,"* 155-56.

[41] Ibid., 158. Cagigal's units were from the following regiments: *Rey, Soria, Guadalajara, España, Navarra, Hibernia, Aragón, 2º Cataluña, Flandes, Fixo de Havana,* and sixty-two artillerymen. *Relación* from Cagigal, Havana, April 9, 1781, *AHN, Consejo de Indias,* leg. 20909, no. 6.

[42] *"Diario de Gálvez"; "Diario de Solano,"* 160.

[43] Alderete to Gálvez, Pensacola Bay, April 4, 1781, *AGI PC,* leg. 2; Alderete to González de Castejón, Pensacola, April 4, 1781, *Gaceta de Madrid,* no. 48 (June 15, 1781):502; *Logbook of the H.M.S. Mentor,* eds. Robert R. Rea and James A. Servies (Gainesville, 1982); *"Diario de Solano,"* 160.

[44] *"Diario de Solano,"* 160; Cagigal to Gálvez, Santa Rosa, April 22, 1781, *AGI PC,* leg. 2; Solano to González de Castejón, *San Luis,* Santa Rosa, May 18, 1781, *Gaceta de Madrid,* no. 63 (August 7, 1781):633-34. Coker and Coker, *Siege of Pensacola, 1781, in Maps,* 116-17.

[45] *"Fiscal con Cagigal."*

[46] Ibid.; *"Diario de Solano,"* 162, 177; Baker and Haas, "Gálvez's Combat Diary," 189; "A Journal of the siege of Pensacola, West Florida, 1781," *Archivo del General Miranda,* 1:186. Most of the Pensacola diaries mention Cagigal's naval bombardment on April 24, although, perhaps significantly, the *"Diario de Gálvez"* does not.

[47] *"Diario de Solano,"* 163; *"Diario de Gálvez."*

[48] *"Fiscal con Cagigal"; "Diario de Solano,"* 167; Solano to González de Castejón, Santa Rosa, May 18, 1781, *Gaceta de Madrid,* no. 63 (Aug. 7, 1781):633-34.

⁴⁹"A Journal of the siege of Pensacola West Florida 1781," 187-88; *"Diario de Solano,"* 168.

⁵⁰*"Diario de Solano,"* 171; Solano to González de Castejón, Santa Rosa, May 18, 1781, *Gaceta de Madrid*, no. 63 (Aug. 7, 1781):633-34; *"Toma de Panzacola* (map)."

⁵¹*"Toma de Panzacola* (map)"; *"Vista de Panzacola y Su Baia, Tomada por los Españoles año de 1781* (map)," BN, Geografia y Mapas; *"Diario de Solano,"* 174-75; *"Fiscal con Cagigal"*; Cagigal to Alderete, Panzacola, May 8, 1781, *Archivo del General de Miranda*, 1:148. Both maps show three frigates—*Santa Clara, Santa Cecilia,* and *Andromaque*—off the village, May 8, preparing to fire.

⁵²*"Artículos de las capitulaciones convenidas entre D. Bernardo de Gálvez . . . y los Excmos. Señores D. Pedro de Chester, Juan Campbell . . . 12 Mayo 1781,"* AGS, Guerra Moderna, leg. 6912; Gálvez to González de Castejón, Pensacola, May 26, 1781, *Gaceta de Madrid*, no. 63 (Aug. 7, 1781): 635-36.

⁵³*"Toma de Panzacola* (map)"; Solano to González de Castejón, Santa Rosa, May 18, 1781, *Gaceta de Madrid*, No. 63 (Aug. 7, 1781), 633-34; Solano to González de Castejón, Havana Bay, April 29, 1781, *Gaceta de Madrid*, no. 56 (July 13, 1781):574.

⁵⁴Bernardo to José de Gálvez, Pensacola, May 26, 1781, *Gaceta de Madrid*, no. 63 (Aug. 7, 1781):631-32.

⁵⁵Gálvez to González de Castejón, Pensacola, May 26, 1781, *Gaceta de Madrid*, no. 63 (Aug. 7, 1781):635-36.

⁵⁶Serrato to González de Castejón, Cádiz, July 27, 1781, ibid., 630; Solano to González de Castejón, Pensacola Bay, May 18, 1781, AGS, Marina, leg. 421, doc. 378; *Gaceta de Madrid*, no. 67 (Aug. 21, 1781):675.

⁵⁷Alfonso de Figueroa y Melgar, "Solano," *ABC* (Madrid), September 11, 1973; *"Expediente personal de Solano"*; Solano was buried with decorations of the Orders of Santiago and Carlos III at Carmen Descalzo Convent in Madrid. *"Testamento del Exmo. Sr. Marqués del Socorro,"* AHP, Protocolo 21260.

FRENCH AND SPANISH MILITARY UNITS IN THE 1781 PENSACOLA CAMPAIGN

Jack D. L. Holmes*

The 1781 campaign against Pensacola was an important part of the Spanish strategy which developed against England following the 1779 Spanish declaration of war. As with other decisive military encounters throughout history, that campaign formed a microcosm of a more important, world-wide conflict of far-reaching importance, and, as with the participants in such battles, the bloody field at Pensacola honed the skills of future military leaders whom Spain named to command her far-flung frontier outposts in America. If American historians have played down the West Florida campaigns of Bernardo de Gálvez, the same is not true of Spanish and Mexican historians who realize its true importance in the military history of the several nations involved.

It is not an easy matter to define such weighty matters as the date of the Spanish declaration of war, inasmuch as seven different dates are given, depending on a variety of circumstances; but the declaration of war which seems to have had the greatest impact on Bernardo de Gálvez, Louisiana's ad interim governor, was that of May 18, 1779.[1] Still more confusing is the question of whether Spain actually recognized the independence of the United States during the conflict, or whether, as one historian stated, it did not take place until October 27, 1795.[2] Both the American government and English officers believed that Spain recognized American independence at New Orleans in August, 1779.[3]

Armed with royal orders to defend Louisiana as best he could, reinforced with general approbation from the Louisiana creoles, and with a heterogeneous force of regulars, militia, whites, blacks, and Indians, Governor Gálvez launched the first of his campaigns against the English forts Bute at Manchac and New Richmond at Baton Rouge, both of them falling in the early fall of 1779.[4] The youthful commander's uncle, Joseph de Gálvez, the chief minister of Carlos III in Spain, had outlined Spain's aims during the war with England at the same time Bernardo was leading his men against the English forts on the Mississippi.

"Mobile and Pensacola are the keys to the Gulf of Mexico," Joseph wrote, and the English should be driven from those posts as well as the banks of the Mississippi River. Louisiana, he noted, in what was to become the key-stone of Spanish policy toward that frontier province for a decade, "should be considered the bulwark or barrier protecting the vast empire of New Spain."[5]

Joseph de Gálvez expected some three thousand troops from the United States to attack St. Augustine and possibly make a diversion on the Mississippi, since Congress had suggested that if Spain would finance such an expedition it would be undertaken.[6]

In his instructions to Viceroy Martín de Mayorga, Joseph de Gálvez urged that troops and money be sent to Havana for the combined expeditions being launched against both Mobile and Pensacola. Should additional troops be needed, he added, the French on the Island of Santo Domingo could supply the necessary forces. To throw off suspicion by the English as to the ultimate destination of the Mexican expeditionary forces, they were to pretend they were assembling troops at Veracruz for a campaign against British Jamaica.[7]

Carlos III of Spain and his nephew, Louis XVI of France, had renewed the 1761 Family Compact on April 12, 1779, thus binding the Bourbon monarchies to the alliance against their common foe, England.[8] France hoped to persuade Spain to recognize the independence of the United States — as France had done in 1778, on signing an alliance with the young American republic.[9] The common cause, often referred to by Americans, Spaniards and Frenchmen, was their mutual war against England, although Spain and the United States were never allies.

France and Spain were allies, however, and the French sent some 725 troops to cooperate with the Spanish forces sent from Havana on February 28, 1781.[10] The Regiment du Cap troops served in the fighting at Pensacola, and on May 11, 1781, following the surrender, a company of French troops, composed of their officers and 139 men, occupied the British battery at Red Cliffs.[11] Following the surrender of the English at Pensacola, Bernardo de Gálvez reported to his uncle on the outstanding French officers deserving of reward for their service during the campaign. There were naval and artillery units, as well as troops from the Poitou, Angenois, Gatinois, and Cambresis infantry regiments, and a picket of *cazadores* or foresters from Angenois.[12]

In addition to these French soldiers who remained under the

jurisdiction of their French officers and units, a number of French officers chose to transfer to Spanish units prior to the Pensacola campaign, and these "reformed" officers continued to render yeoman service to the Spanish crown throughout the colonial dominion of Louisiana.[13] Pedro de Marigny is, perhaps, the quintessential representative. At Pensacola he served as aide-de-camp to Bernardo de Gálvez and was characterized as "very intelligent and capable of military or political command," both of which he fulfilled after the American Revolution in Louisiana.[14]

The Mexican contribution to American independence has not received its due, but from the very beginning, Mexican monetary support was of paramount importance to the success of the combined Franco-Spanish fleet and for the land forces from Havana and New Orleans. Mexican sources have noted this aid,[15] but the United States has forgotten it, in much the same way it has neglected Spanish aid.[16] The point to recall is that the history of the Gulf of Mexico and the Caribbean holds a unity which transcends national boundries. Just as Prof. Alfred Barnaby Thomas urged historians to adopt a larger view of the area's background some twenty-five years ago, so we must adjust our own analysis of the American Revolution in the southern theater of operations to extend as far as Campeche, Veracruz, and Havana.[17]

In order to trace the role of the various Spanish units in the Pensacola campaign, it is essential to divide the campaign into its various expeditions, each of which took place at different times and under different commands. It was the wish of Carlos III that Bernardo de Gálvez, the governor of Louisiana, take complete command of all expeditions, but the jealousy of officers of superior rank and seniority often frustrated the united effort of the Spaniards, not to mention the frustration of the French commander.[18] The struggle between land and naval forces, between French and Spaniard, and between Cuban, Mexican and Louisianian would characterize the Pensacola campaign and render the Spanish efforts as inefficient at times as those of the out-manned British defenders.

The question of numbers always causes problems when wartime losses are discussed. Pensacola, two hundred years ago, was no exception to this axiom. How many troops did the Spaniards have? How strong was the British garrison? The answers to these questions are many and charged with prejudice and jingoism.

An interesting total is given by Conrotte as 112,748 men in the Spanish service, of whom 10,887 joined the Army of Operations under Gen. Victorio de Navia in 1780.[19] Several thousand troops were already in Mexico, Cuba and Louisiana, and these must be added to the total. The destruction caused by the 1780 hurricanes, however, must be deducted from the total, and here we have a problem: how many people were on both sides of the Pensacola line?

"The army, including militia and blacks, amounted to 3,701 men, of whom, 500 were *hors de combat*," wrote a diarist in one expedition's log. "The defending garrison consisted of 800 regulars, 200 sailors, and 1,000 savages roaming through the woods," concluded the Spanish estimate. "Our forces included 1,504 sailors or marines, 725 Frenchmen, and a total of 7,803 effective men," concluded the Spanish scribe.[20] A typical "black-legend," jingoistic, anti-Spanish version would have it believed that a defending British force of 1,000 regular troops, "some provincials," and servants, faced 15,000 men under Gálvez.[21] The *London Gazette* represented the official English version of the conflict: "the combined Regular Land Troops of the Enemy on Shore did not consist of fewer than 7800 Men, besides Seamen and Marines, to which being added the Consideration of 15 Ships of the Line and 6 Frigates, King's Snows, Sloops, &c. &c. being so long employed on this Service." The "General Return of the Garrison of the Royal Navy Redoubt" and other rosters given in the same issue reveal the final strength of the English defenders as 1,116 regulars; 90 killed; 46 wounded; and 83 deserted.[22]

Whatever statistics we use, the fact remains that a variety of international regiments and detachments, white and black, served in the Spanish campaign against the English at Pensacola. From Louisiana and Mobile came a number of interesting units, black, white, brown, and even red!

As with all Spanish colonies, the motherland dictated certain organizational rules regarding the establishment of line regiments of infantry, artillery and cavalry. The Louisiana Infantry Battalion, organized at Havana in 1768, consisted of less than four hundred men. By the time of the American Revolution, however, the Louisiana battalion was supplemented with at least ten militia companies. Louisiana had universal military training, under which young creole men had the opportunity to serve in the New Orleans or district militia companies. These men were untried until the 1779 campaign against the English along the Mississippi River, but in subsequent campaigns at Mobile and Pensacola, they were prominent.[23]

Typical of their number was Pedro (Pierre) de Marigny, a native of New Orleans. He first organized the Canary Islands immigrants at a settlement known as *San Bernardo* (in honor of the Louisiana governor) and fought in the campaigns of Fort Bute, Baton Rouge, and Mobile. At Pensacola, Marigny served Gálvez as aide-de-camp and showed the same leadership skills he had employed in directing the free Negro and mulatto militia units at Mobile the previous year.[24]

Following the Seven Years War, Spain's Irish military genius, Alexander O'Reilly, organized militia units for the Caribbean and in Louisiana where free blacks came under the same universal military training rules as whites. A number of the blacks who served in the Baton Rouge campaign of 1779 received special medals for valor, and at Mobile, in 1780, the first Spanish casualty was a free Negro. The force of 4,400 troops mustered by Lt. Col. Gerónimo Girón included 278 free black and mulatto militiamen from Havana. On February 28, 1781, Martín Navarro mustered almost 300 free blacks and mulattoes from Havana and an additional 200 from the Louisiana Negro and mulatto militia units. Another force of 90 free blacks and mulattoes joined 75 Negro slaves in marching overland to Pensacola. In all, Gálvez had more than 500 colored troops during the siege, and General Joseph de Ezpeleta directed four companies of them in building the Half-Moon battery to attack the Queen's Redoubt defenses.[25] These blacks and mulattoes joined white militiamen and the grenadiers, dragoons, and foresters of the Louisiana Infantry Regiment in an expedition which left New Orleans on March 3, and arrived off Pensacola on March 23, 1781. Lt. Col. Cayetano de Salla of the Soria Infantry Regiment called the roll and noted there were 1,348 men ready for action.[26]

When Gálvez was in Havana, during the fall of 1780, he tried to organize various military units for his Pensacola expedition. The uncooperative Cuban high command delayed the departure of the assembled troops, now reinforced by thousands of men, fresh from the unsuccessful siege of Gibraltar, who had joined the expedition under Lt. Gen. Victorio de Navia.[27] The worst series of hurricanes to strike the Caribbean during the eighteenth century struck the fleet on the night of October 16/17, and for five days the tempest tossed ships from the mainland of North America as far south as the peninsula of Yucatan.[28] Gálvez was forced to return to Havana and regroup his forces.

Chief of Squadron Josef Solano, Marqués del Socorro, arrived on November 19, 1780, aboard the frigate *Santa Rosalía*, and Gálvez found this naval commander's ideas more in keeping with his own than those of the Cuban naval officers.[29] Capt. Joseph de Rada's convoy of troops, dispatched to reinforce Mobile, found the sandbars at Mobile Bay too dangerous to risk, so he returned to Havana, after making an astonishing voyage as far as the Mississippi.[30]

Solano sent José de San Martín to make a reconnaissance of the northern Gulf Coast from Cape San Blas to the Mississippi River in order to determine where the invasion force would sail in the spring of 1781.[31] Finally, on February 28, 1781, the expedition was ready. Martín Navarro compiled a list of twenty ships and a total of 1,637 men under the command of Lt. Col. Cayetano de Salla.[32] On March 5, the famous brig *El Galveztown*, which became Gálvez's flagship when he ran past the guns into Pensacola Bay,[33] joined the expedition which began to unload troops on Santa Rosa Island, March 9.[34]

A major portion of the troops belonged to the Havana Infantry Regiment, the unit which had restored Spanish rule to Louisiana under Alexander O'Reilly in 1769. "The Noble" regiment was among the oldest in America, having been organized by Governor Diego de Velázquez in 1515. In 1753, Viceroy conde de Revillagigedo had sent troops from it to garrison forts at St. Augustine and St. Marks, Florida, and O'Reilly increased its size and efficiency in 1763. In 1778, some fifty men arrived in New Orleans under the command of Lt. Col. Manuel González, and the following year the Havana regiment earned a sash for its bravery in the conquest of the British posts along the Mississippi. It suffered the hurricane of 1780, but the following year units joined Gálvez both from New Orleans and from Havana.[35]

The Navarra Infantry Regiment was founded on July 21, 1705, with the motto, "The Triumphant." Stationed in Havana when Gálvez organized the Pensacola expedition, members of the fifth, seventh, and eighth companies of the first battalion fought bravely at Pensacola. Col. Joseph de Ezpeleta, wartime commander of Mobile and right-hand-man to Gálvez at Pensacola, directed some of these men from Mobile overland on March 18, while 12 officers and 280 men joined Salla's naval expedition.[36]

The Príncipe Regiment, "The Bold," was organized in 1537, and, from 1704 to 1776, it was known as the Lombardy Regiment. Inspector O'Reilly praised these troops at Havana in 1771, and Gálvez found them capable and heroic soldiers during the 1779 and 1780 campaigns. At Pensacola this regiment played an even greater role when the grenadiers under Colonel Francisco de Longoria occupied the British battery on *Punta de Sigüenza*, Santa Rosa Island. They continued the attack at Fort George, acting with a brigade from the Regiment of the King.[37]

The *Regimiento Inmemorial del Rey*, or King's Regiment, dated from 1632, and had battle honors from Spain's greatest eighteenth-century campaigns. They joined General Navia's expedition and left Cádiz for Havana on April 13, 1780. They furnished two companies of grenadiers, three riflemen, and three detachments of troops in the 1781 expedition of Gálvez. They saw fierce fighting at the Half-Moon battery and joyously "replaced the vanquished English leopard with the Castillian lion on the battlement of Fort George."[38]

"The Bloody" Soria Infantry Regiment was also represented at Pensacola, two officers and fifty-five men having come with Salla's expedition. Salla himself was a lieutenant colonel in this unit. Created in 1591, as the *"Tercio Departmental del Bravante,"* it boasted as one of its commanders, Luis de Velasco, sixteenth-century viceroy of New Spain. The Soria Regiment served during the siege of Gibraltar before coming to America to take part in the Pensacola campaign.[39]

For three-quarters of a century no Spanish regiment wrote the annals of glorious combat more than the Irish brigades, and some 580 officers and men of the Hibernian Infantry Regiment fought at Pensacola in 1781. Approximately 14 percent of the casualties sustained by the French and Spanish troops were suffered by the Irish, whose motto, taken from the 18th Psalm, seemed prophetic: "Their fame throughout the land."[40] Organized by Irish soldiers who had fled their homeland to France and Spain, it was in 1709 that the first battalions were created in Aragón. They fought and died on the beach at Algiers in 1775, and restored Spanish power two years later in Buenos Aires. Some 1,232 troops arrived at Havana in the early part of August, 1780, and, among the 580 joining Gálvez at Pensacola, Lt. Col. Arturo O'Neill remained as the Spanish commandant of Pensacola after the war.[41]

Reconstructed Uniform of the Navarra Regiment used at Pensacola in 1781. The regimental banner is used in the 1980 Gálvez stamp instead of the proper castle-and-lion standard. Copyright 1982 by Jack D. L. Holmes. Published with his permission.

Spanish Troops in the Siege of Pensacola; Navarra Regt.

Reconstructed Uniforms of Four Units Represented at Pensacola in 1781. Original water colors by Francisco Ferrer Llull of Montevideo, Uruguay. Copyright 1982 by Jack. D. L. Holmes. Published with his permission.

Another commandant and governor of Pensacola was Vicente Folch y Juan, who joined the Second Regiment of Catalonian Volunteers as part of General Navia's expedition in 1780.[42] "The Sublime and Heroic" *Regimiento de Cataluña* mustered a detachment of dragoons under Girón at Havana on October 8, and Lt. Col. Antonio de Llano of the light infantry fought so well at Pensacola that he received a pension of 4,000 *reales*.[43]

The *Regimiento de España*, "The Martyr," furnished 700 men from the second battalion for the first Gálvez campaigns of 1779. They were shipwrecked at Mobile Bay the following year, but survived to form the backbone defense of The Village in the bloody battle there on January 7, 1781. Because they were battle-hardened veterans, they were useful for garrison duty, although many complained there was not enough action to suit them. That was prior to Pensacola, however, and during four separate attacks by the English and their Indians, they performed heroically.[44]

"The Tiger," as the Guadalajara Regiment was called, came in the expedition of José Solano, which left Cádiz on April 28, 1780, and joined the French troops on Martinique until July 5, when they joined the troops organized at Havana for the Pensacola campaign.[45]

Although the Mallorca Infantry Regiment was known as "The Invincible," the furious fighting at Pensacola on May 4, 1781, resulted in the death of Capt. Salvador Requerols and Ensign Francisco Aragón, and the wounding of Lt. Juan Xaramillo. The Mallorca Regiment had seen action at Baton Rouge, and members accompanied Capt. Juan de la Villebeuvre to raise the Spanish colors over Fort Panmure de Natchez in October, 1779. Four companies from the first battalion and two of grenadiers fought at Pensacola in 1781.[46]

"The Formidable" Aragón Infantry Regiment earned the praise of friend and foe alike for its stout defense of Havana's Morro Castle against the British attacking force from June 8 to July 30, 1762. On April 28, 1780, a detachment left Cádiz with General Navia's expedition. One of its colonels, Francisco Longoria Flores, commanded 1,000 men who passed muster in Havana on February 16, 1781.[47] Perhaps its most famous member, however, was a captain of fusiliers who kept a diary of the Pensacola campaign, Francisco Miranda, later known for his role as precursor of the Venezuelan independence movement.[48]

A small detachment of the Toledo Infantry Regiment, "The Prophetic," joined Gálvez in the Pensacola campaign, and Capt. Francisco de Eguía was breveted lieutenant colonel for his role.[49]

Created in 1572, the Naples Regiment, "The Distinguished," sent a small detachment with the Army of Operations leaving Cádiz on April 28, 1780.[50]

The British were impressed by the Spanish artillery at Pensacola, and Gálvez depended upon such officers as Lt. Julián Álvarez, who had directed the effective batteries at Baton Rouge and was promoted to brevet captain in command of the Royal Artillery Corps at Pensacola. In addition to the veteran gunners who sailed with Álvarez to Pensacola, four marched overland to the fray.[51]

Both Spanish and French marines landed with the army units and served with distinction. Other units had token representation, such as Sgt. Manuel Rodríguez who had defended the royal cattle herd on Dauphin Island, and then joined Gálvez at Pensacola.[52]

The character of Gálvez's forces was obviously varied and included men of many nationalities and colors. To career officers, the Pensacola campaign was an important entry on their service records, and the list of military commandants, municipal officials, and governors includes some of the most important in North America: Hugo O'Conor, who succeeded Bernardo de Gálvez in command of the Mexican *Provincias Internas;* Louisiana governors or lieutenant governors Esteban Miró, baron de Carondelet, marqués de Casa-Calvo, and Francisco Bouligny; Cuban captains-general Joseph de Ezpeleta and Juan Manuel de Cagigal; Pensacola commandants Arturo O'Neill, Mauricio de Zúñiga, José de Soto, and Francisco Maximiliano de St. Maxent; Mobile district commandants Enrique Grimarest, Juan Antonio Bassot, and Antonio Palao; Natchez commandants Phelipe Treviño and Francisco Bouligny; Juan Antonio de Riaño and Manuel de Flor, both brothers-in-law of Bernardo de Gálvez and subsequently governors of Guanajuato and Puebla in Mexico.

By way of conclusion, one of Pensacola's outstanding early citizens, Joseph Noreiga, whose brickyard furnished the building stones of many an early structure, and who served in various government positions, was a native of Asturias who came with Gálvez to Pensacola in 1781, served as long-time adjutant during the Spanish domination, and as schoolmaster for the cadets.

Noreiga was an ensign in the Louisiana Infantry Regiment during the campaigns of Gálvez against Baton Rouge, Mobile, and Pensacola. He was one of the 1781 veterans who remained.[53]

---

*Director, Louisiana Collection Series of Books and Documents on Colonial Louisiana, Birmingham, Alabama.

[1] Royal Order, "Declaration of War Against His Britannic Majesty," Aranjuez, May 18, 1779, *AGI Cuba, leg. 569*. For a discussion of the various dates of the declaration see J. Horace Nunemaker, "Louisiana Anticipates Spain's Recognition of the Independence of the United States," *Louisiana Historical Quarterly* 26 (1943):755-69. The major cause of the war, as Spain saw it, was English violation of neutral rights. George Bancroft, *History of the United States*, Centenary ed., rev. (London, 1876), 6:229-49.

[2] Nunemaker, "Louisiana Anticipates," 755-69; Manuel Conrotte, *La intervención de España en la independencia de los Estados Unidos de la América del Norte* (Madrid, 1920), 211, gives the later date. When Bernardo de Gálvez received the royal order naming him "*gobernador en propiedad*" of Louisiana, he took the occasion, August 20, to recognize American independence, to the sound of drum rolls and "various demonstrations of joy and '*Vivas al Rey*.' " Minutes of the New Orleans Cabildo, New Orleans Public Library Archives, fols. 171(b)-172(b).

[3] Oliver Pollock, the American agent in Louisiana, wrote to the inhabitants of Natchez from Fort Bute at Manchac, Sept. 8, 1779, that Spain had declared "the independency" of the United States, as well as war against "our tyranical Enemy Great Britain." *AGI Cuba, leg. 192*; Jack D.L. Holmes, "Juan de la Villebeuvre: Spain's Commandant of Natchez during the American Revolution," *Journal of Mississippi History* 37 (1975):113-14; William B. Willcox, ed., *The American Rebellion: Sir Henry Clinton's Narrative of His Campaigns, 1775-1782* (New Haven, 1954), 421.

[4] John Walton Caughey, *Bernardo de Gálvez in Louisiana, 1776-1783*, reprinted, foreword by Jack D.L. Holmes (Gretna, La., 1972), 149-70; Jack D.L. Holmes, *The 1779 "Marcha de Gálvez": Louisiana's Giant Step Forward in the American Revolution* (Baton Rouge, 1974).

[5] Gálvez to Virrey of New Spain [Martín de Mayorga], No. 122, Aug. 29, 1779, *Archivo General de la Nación (México), Reales Cédulas, vol. 117, fols. 225-27*; Jack D.L. Holmes, "*La última barrera: la Luisiana y la Nueva España*," *Historia Mexicana* 10 (1961):637-49.

[6] Gálvez to Mayorga, Aug. 29, 1779. The idea of an American expedition against Pensacola dates from 1776, when Capt. George Gibson discussed it in New Orleans with Governor Luis de Unzaga. Benedict Arnold and George Morgan considered it in 1777, when they reasoned that fifteen hundred men, armed and provisioned from New Orleans, could accomplish the task and leave the United States with long-term advantages through access to Mobile and Pensacola and the Gulf of Mexico. Max Savelle, *George Morgan, Colony Builder* (New York, 1932), 176-77; Edmund C. Burnett, ed., *Letters of Members of the Continental Congress* (Washington, 1923), 2:421-23, 443-49.

[7] Gálvez to Mayorga, Aug. 29, 1779. Joseph also wrote to his nephew, Bernardo, concerning the relative superiority of the combined Bourbon forces against

England—double the treasury and triple the population—and the fact that the American Revolution forced England to divide forces it might otherwise use against France and Spain. It is obvious that Spain held no great fear or "blind respect toward the British colossus." Gálvez to Bernardo de Gálvez, No. 314, Aug. 30, 1779, AGI Cuba, leg. 174-A.

[8]Conrotte, *Intervención de España*, 231-35.

[9]Herbert Ingram Priestley, *France Overseas Through the Old Regime: A Study of European Expansion* (New York, 1939), 284-87.

[10]French zeal in "the common cause" is described in Bernardo de Gálvez to Joseph de Gálvez, Pensacola, May 26, 1781, *Gazeta de Madrid*, Aug. 7, 1781. Eric Beerman, "'*Yo Sólo*' not '*Sólo*': Juan Antonio de Riaño," *Florida Historical Quarterly* 58 (1979): 181, states that 750 French troops arrived at Pensacola on April 19, 1781. On the differing number of French troops see also William S. Coker and Hazel P. Coker, *The Siege of Pensacola, 1781, in Maps* (Pensacola, 1981), App. M.

[11]Diary of Francisco de Saavedra, Jesuit College, Malaga, Spain.

[12]Bernardo de Gálvez to Josef de Gálvez, No. 25, Pensacola, May 26, 1781, *Archivo Histórico Nacional (Madrid), Sección de Estado, leg. 4211*, transcript supplied through the courtesy of Dr. Eric Beerman of Madrid. See also Réne Quatrefages, "La participación militar de Francia en la toma de Pensacola," *Revista de Historia Militar* 21 (no. 42, 1977):7-30. I am grateful to Prof. Lee Kennett, University of Georgia, author of *The French Forces in America, 1780-1783* (Westport, Conn., 1977), and Jonathan R. Dull, Yale University, author of *The French Navy and American Independence: A Study of Arms and Diplomacy, 1774-1787* (Princeton, 1975), for tips to the following archival sources on the Chevalier de Monteuill's forces at Pensacola: "*Expedition dans le Golf a Mexique*," an excerpt from a diary of the expedition, *Archives Nationales, Paris, Marine*, B^4, Vol. 184, fols. 304, 285-87, copies in the Manuscripts Division, Library of Congress.

[13]See the list of "*oficiales reformados*" serving in the Mobile siege of 1780, *AGI Cuba, leg. 113*.

[14]Jack D.L. Holmes, *Honor and Fidelity, The Louisiana Infantry Regiment and the Louisiana Militia Companies, 1766-1821*, vol. 1, Louisiana Collection Series (Birmingham, 1965), 205.

[15]Andrés Cavo, *Los tres siglos de México durante el gobierno español . . . con notas y suplemento, por el Lic. Carlos María de Bustamente* (México, 1836-1838), 3:38; Jorge Ignacio Rubio Mañé, "*Las tropas de Campeche en la toma de Pensacola*," *Revista de Historia Yucateca* 13 (1973):156-59. Mexico also supplied a company of mounted dragoons for Pensacola and increased the financial subsidy by 315,000 pesos. After learning of Bernardo's success at Pensacola, a *Te Deum* mass was sung in Mexico City. Joseph de Gálvez to Virrey, Nos. 127-28, Aug. 30, 1779, vol. 117, fols. 237-38; No. 13, June 11, 1781, vol. 121, fols. 36-37; No. 177, Nov. 18, 1781, fols. 357-59, *Archivo General de la Nación (México), Reales Cédulas*.

[16]Buchanan Parker Thomson, *Spain, Forgotten Ally of the American Revolution* (North Quincy, Mass., 1976); *Ayuda española en la guerra de la independencia norteamericana* (Madrid, 1967); José Montero de Pedro, marqués de Casa Mena, *Españoles en Nueva Orleans y Luisiana* (Madrid, 1979), 34-44.

[17]Professor Thomas's ideas are cited in Jack D.L. Holmes, ed., *Documentos inéditos para la historia de la Luisiana, 1792-1810*, Vol. XV, *Colección Chimalistac de Libros y Documentos Acerca de la Nueva España* (Madrid, 1963),

pp. xvii-xviii. Spanish recognition of the strategic connection of the Gulf of Mexico and Caribbean is indicated in the Conde de Ricla's *"Dictamen,"* Feb. 20, 1780, *Archivo General de Simancas, Guerra Moderna*, leg. 7303-1. Similar ideas are expressed in the diary of Francisco de Saavedra.

[18] Joseph de Gálvez to Virrey of New Spain, No. 122, Aug. 29, 1779, *Archivo General (México)*; Quatrefages, "La participación militar," 13-14.

[19] Conrotte, *Intervención de España*, 235-36.

[20] "Diario de lo ocurrido en la escuadra de . . . Josef Solano," *Archivo del General Miranda, 1750-1785* (Caracas, 1929-1950). 1:160.

[21] Richard L. Campbell, *Historical Sketches of Colonial Florida* (facsimile reprint, intro. by Pat Dodson (Gainesville, 1975), 152.

[22] *London Gazette*, October 9-13, 1781.

[23] Holmes, *Honor and Fidelity*, 20-26.

[24] Ibid., 205.

[25] Holmes, "Black Participation in the Battle of Pensacola," paper presented at the University of Florida Center for Latin American Studies, March 1, 1976; Roland C. McConnell, *Negro Troops of Antebellum Louisiana* (Baton Rouge, 1968), 20-22.

[26] Rosters signed by Cayetano de Salla, *San Francisco de Paula Escardó*, off Pensacola, March 23, 1781, *AGI Cuba*, leg. 81.

[27] Ricla's *"Dictamen,"* Feb. 20, 1780; summary of the diary for the convoy which left Cádiz for Havana April 28, 1780, under command of Squadron Chief Josef Solano; Navia to Ricla, Havana, Oct. 23, 1780, *Archivo General de Simancas, Guerra Moderna*, leg. 7303.

[28] "Tornadoes," *DeBow's Review*, After-the-War series, 5, no. 2 (Sept., 1868):815; Ivan Ray Tannehill, *Hurricanes, their Nature and History, Particularly Those of the West Indies and the Southern Coasts of the United States* (Princeton, 1938), 145-46; David M. Ludlum, *Early American Hurricanes, 1492-1870* (Boston, 1963), 71-72; Jack D.L. Holmes, "Who's The Greatest Hurricane of All?" *Pensacola Journal*, Aug. 12, 1980.

[29] Navia to Ricla, Oct. 23, 1780; Jacobo de la Pezuela, *Crónica de las Antillas* (Madrid, 1871), 102.

[30] *Diario de las operaciones contra la Plaza de Panzacola, 1781*, 2d ed. (Madrid, 1959), 10. The original manuscript, together with Bernardo de Gálvez's official reports, list of casualties, and inventory of captured property left Pensacola on June 3 and reached Cádiz on July 27, 1781. One copy was set in print at the official newspaper, *Gazeta de Madrid* and offered for public sale on Aug. 13, 1781. There were several contemporary editions, at least one of which was published in Mexico City. Jack D.L. Holmes, "Bernardo de Gálvez: Spain's 'Man of the Hour' During the American Revolution," *Cardinales de dos independencias (Noreste de México-Sureste de los Estados Unidos)* (Mexico, 1978), 169.

[31] San Martín's report, Jan. 1, 1781, *Museo Naval (Madrid)*, MS vol. 291, fols. 172-74.

[32] "Report of Troops Used in the Pensacola Expedition" and "Statistics on the Pensacola Expedition," Lawrence Kinnaird, ed., *Spain in the Mississippi Valley, 1765-1794* (Washington, 1945), 1:421-24.

[33] Raymond J. Martinez, *Rousseau—the Last Days of Spanish New Orleans*, 2d ed. rev., foreword by Jack D.L. Holmes (New Orleans, 1975), iii-iv, 5-9; Beerman, *"Yo Solo,"* 174-84.

³⁴*Diario de las operaciones*, 13-14.

³⁵María de Sotto Serafín, conde de Clonard, *Historia orgánica de las armas de infantería y caballería españolas* (Madrid, 1851-1862), 11:420-49; Hylario Ramíres Estenos, Roster of Havana Infantry Regiment, New Orleans, Nov. 8, 1779, *AGI Cuba, leg. 159-A*.

³⁶Clonard, *Historia orgánica*, 11:237-82; Beerman, "José de Ezpeleta," *Revista de Historia Militar* 21 No. 42 (1977):97-118; F. de Borja Medina Rojas, *José de Ezpeleta, Gobernador de la Mobila, 1780-1781* (Seville, 1980).

³⁷Clonard, *Historia orgánica*, 7:423-523; Pezuela, *Crónica de Antillas*, 101.

³⁸Clonard, *Historia orgánica*, 9:58-59.

³⁹Ibid., 8:455-516; Salla's roster, March 23, 1781, *AGI Cuba, leg. 81*.

⁴⁰Clonard, *Historia orgánica*, 11:315-50; W.S. Murphy, "The Irish Brigade of Spain at the Capture of Pensacola, 1781," *Florida Historical Quarterly* 38 (1960):216-25.

⁴¹Holmes, "Some Irish Officers in Spanish Louisiana," *Irish Sword* 6 (1964):243-44.

⁴²Holmes, "Three Early Memphis Commandants, Beauregard, DeVille DeGoutin, and Folch," *West Tennessee Historical Society Papers* 18 (1964):14-26.

⁴³Clonard, *Historia orgánica*, 10:447-85; Gerónimo Girón's roster, Havana, Oct. 8, 1780, *AGI Cuba, leg. 113*; Pablo Figuerola's roster, Cádiz, April 2, 1780, *Archivo General de Simancas, Guerra Moderna, leg. 7303*; *Gazeta de Madrid*, Aug. 21, 1781.

⁴⁴Clonard, *Historia orgánica*, 10:33-81; Manuel Serrano y Sanz, *Documentos históricos de la Florida y la Luisiana, siglos xvi al xviii* (Madrid, 1912), 352; Holmes, "Alabama's Bloodiest Day of the American Revolution: Counterattack at The Village, January 7, 1781," *Alabama Review* 29 (1976):208-19; Gálvez to Navarro, No. 208, Baton Rouge, Oct. 15, 1779, *AGI Cuba, leg. 1232*.

⁴⁵Clonard, *Historia orgánica*, 9:264, 287.

⁴⁶Ibid., 10:82-136; *Gazeta de Madrid*, Aug. 21, 1781; *Diario de las operaciones*, 83; Holmes, "Juan de la Villebeuvre," 103.

⁴⁷Clonard, *Historia orgánica*, 11:374, 386-87; Navia to Josef de Gálvez, No. 53, confidential, Havana, March 1, 1781, copy supplied by W.S. Murphy.

⁴⁸William Spence Robertson, ed., *The Diary of Francisco de Miranda: Tour of the United States (1783-1784)* (New York, 1928), xiii-xvii; Miranda's diaries are in the *Archivo del General Miranda*, 1:150-79; Donald E. Worcester, "Miranda's Diary of the Siege of Pensacola, 1781," *Florida Historical Quarterly*, 29 (1951):163;96.

⁴⁹Clonard, *Historia orgánica*, 9:490-91; *Gazeta de Madrid*, Aug. 21, 1781.

⁵⁰Clonard, *Historia orgánica*, 8:151, 169.

⁵¹*Gazeta de Madrid, Suplemento*, Jan. 14, 1780; Bernardo de Gálvez to Josef de Gálvez, No. 325, confidential, New Orleans, Oct. 16, 1779, *AGI Cuba, leg. 223-B*; Martín Navarro's roster, New Orleans, Feb. 28, 1781.

⁵²Holmes, "Alabama's Bloodiest Day," 213. More than 13,000 head of Texas cattle from ranches near *San Antonio* and *La Bahía* were driven overland to Louisiana for the Gálvez campaigns in West Florida, and the beeves on Dauphin Island were undoubtedly from this "Longhorn" variety. Robert S. Weddle and Robert H. Thonhoff, *Drama & Conflict: The Texas Saga of 1776* (Austin, 1976), 171; Holmes, *Honor and Fidelity*, 213.

⁵³Holmes, *Honor and Fidelity*, 138.

LOYALIST RESISTANCE AFTER PENSACOLA: THE CASE OF JAMES COLBERT

Gilbert C. Din[*]

Following the surrender of Fort George at Pensacola on May 10, 1781, and the subsequent yielding of the Natchez insurrectionists in June, military action for the Spaniards in the Mississippi Valley did not end. In 1782 and 1783, the Spaniards experienced further hostility from persons they called Natchez rebels and pirates. The most important of these was James Logan Colbert. Of the few studies which have examined Colbert's activities in this period, D. C. Corbitt provides the longest account and states that Colbert seriously hindered Spanish use of the Mississippi. In Corbitt's words, Colbert "travers[ed] at will the area in question, and [made] it unsafe for the Spaniards to use the Mississippi except with heavily armed convoys." Corbitt also asserts that Colbert threatened the Arkansas Post for months, towards the end of the war, and made good the English claim to the Mississippi's east bank from the Yazoo River to the Ohio (which was subsequently ceded by Britain to the United States).[1] These statements, however, demand a closer examination of Colbert's true strength on the Mississippi and the extent of the damages he actually inflicted on the Spaniards.

James Logan Colbert, a Scotsman and trader, began his residence among the Chickasaws before 1740, when he was about the age of twenty. Over a period exceeding forty years, he married three Chickasaw women who bore him eleven children. His sons — William, George, Levi, Samuel, Joseph, and James — in time became the principal spokesmen among the Chickasaws. The elder Colbert, during these years, acquired considerable wealth, lived in an imposing house, and reputedly owned 150 Negro slaves.[2]

Upon the outbreak of the American colonial rebellion, General Thomas Gage ordered John Stuart, Superintendent of Indian Affairs of the Southern District, in October, 1775, to rally the Chickasaws and other tribes against the enemies of His Britannic Majesty. Overall, Colbert seems to have done little until 1780. He, his sons, and a number of Chickasaws were said to have been at the defense of Mobile, retiring shortly before its surrender.

Later in 1780, Colbert led the Chickasaws against the newly established American post of Fort Jefferson, five miles below the mouth of the Ohio, destroying farms around the fort but failing to seize it. Colbert claimed to have received three wounds there. The Chickasaw attacks, however, forced the Americans to abandon the fort. Almost immediately after besieging Fort Jefferson, if all of Colbert's activities may be believed, he descended to Pensacola to bolster its defenses with his sons and Chickasaw warriors. He left before Pensacola surrendered in May, 1781.[3] Thereafter, Colbert was not heard from for nearly a year.

Shortly before the Pensacola commander, General John Campbell, yielded to the Spaniards, he ordered the Tory settlers of Natchez on the Mississippi to mount a diversionary action against Spain. Obedient to his instructions, on April 22, they rose up and forced the Spanish garrison of Fort Panmure to surrender on May 4. But their victory was made futile by Campbell's defeat and the suspension of all military action in West Florida. In June, Spanish forces reoccupied Natchez and arrested John Blommart and several other leaders of the insurrection. Their imprisonment became an important factor in Colbert's subsequent actions.[4]

The Spaniards regarded the insurrectionists as guilty of civil rebellion and did not consider them prisoners of war. In 1779, after Spain had occupied the Natchez district as part of the terms of surrender of Baton Rouge, the British residents who remained in possession of their homes and property took oaths of fidelity to Spain. In rising to assist Campbell, the Natchez loyalists committed civil rebellion in the eyes of Governor Bernardo de Gálvez of Louisiana. Blommart and a half dozen other leaders were taken to New Orleans, tried for rebellion, found guilty, and sentenced to death. Gálvez, however, appeared more angry at General Campbell who authorized the uprising and then denied complicity in it. Inasmuch as the shedding of blood at Natchez had been minimal, Gálvez declined to exact the supreme penalty from the leaders but merely detained them in New Orleans.[5] Colbert, not knowing Gálvez's true intentions, began committing depredations on the Mississippi, which at least in part were motivated by his efforts to compel the Spaniards to release the condemned men.

The whereabouts of Colbert in the second half of 1781 are not definitely known. He appears to have been in the Chickasaw country when British sympathizers from Natchez, Georgia, the Carolinas, and probably Pensacola arrived there seeking refuge.

A number of them, angry at the Spaniards, wanted to continue fighting. A month after Natchez fell to the Spaniards they sent a threatening message to the Arkansas Post, claiming their readiness to seize it.[6]

The Arkansas Post, a midway station between Natchez and Spanish Illinois, possessed only a modest garrison, a tiny civilian population, and few Quapaw allies. It was the most vulnerable of the Spanish posts on the Mississippi.[7] Initially, the Arkansas inhabitants feared the Chickasaws more than the rebels, as the Indians had vexed the west-bank natives and white hunters for years. At that time, Fort Charles III at Arkansas was still not completed, despite eighteen months of construction. In July, 1781, the civilians and soldiers quickly resumed work but again did not finish it. The Arkansas commandant, Captain Balthazar de Villiers, alerted Acting Governor Pedro Piernas of the possibility of further loyalist action. In response, in August, 1781, Piernas prepared three heavily loaded boats to take supplies to Arkansas and St. Louis,[8] but the Natchez rebels seemed to have vanished in the second half of 1781.

Of equal concern to the Spaniards was the role of the Chickasaws among whom Colbert and the Natchez rebels lived. At this time, full-blooded chiefs such as Payamataha were trying to break the hold on the tribe by the half-bloods, among whom Colbert's sons stood out. The collapse of British resistance in West Florida had a telling effect on Payamataha and the other chiefs who were determined not to fight the Spaniards. By September, 1781, Captain Villiers at the Arkansas Post reported the peaceful intentions of the Chickasaws.[9]

But the Chickasaws could not give up their time-honored practice of hunting on the Mississippi's west bank and taking occasional prisoners and scalps. When Villiers heard of one such Chickasaw party in November, 1781, he sent out four soldiers to recall the hunters to the Post, but his men never returned. In February, Villiers received the distressing news that three bodies had been found on the St. Francis River, above the Arkansas Post, and the commandant concluded that they were his soldiers. Four months later it was learned that the Chickasaws had captured three of his men, while the fourth had probably been killed. For the moment, however, Villiers feared that the rebels were responsible, as they were reported to be nearby.[10]

The first definite news of Colbert, after Pensacola, placed him at the Chickasaw Bluffs, the site of modern Memphis, about February, 1782, where he started hindering river traffic, although not stopping every boat. When Villiers learned of the presence of brigands there, he quickly sent messages to the governor telling him of the Post's weakness. Before a terminal illness overtook Villiers that spring, he kept up a stream of letters recounting the dangers he faced.[11]

Colonel Esteban Miró, who assumed the office of acting governor of Louisiana on March 1, 1782, replied to Villiers' warning by stating that he would take measures to see that boats going to Illinois that spring would journey together. However, the most important vessel bound for St. Louis, that of Sylvestre L'Abbadie, had already departed alone. In all, about a half dozen boats left New Orleans in February and March, most of them traveling alone or becoming separated while ascending the river.[12] Although the upper Mississippi was considered the most dangerous part of the voyage, the first assault on Spanish navigation came not far above Natchez.

On April 19, twenty-five leagues above Natchez and eight above the Yazoo River, John Turner, a Natchez fugitive, with ten Englishmen and three Negroes, seized the flatboat of Eugene Pouré. Four hours later, the captives, who had been made to row their own vessel, turned on the rebels, killing six whites and two Negroes with oars. Turner and one slave alone managed to evade the oar blows and escape. Pouré then took his boat downstream where he encountered those of François Vallé and Eugenio Álvarez; together they descended to Natchez to inform Commandant Carlos de Grand-Pré of Turner's attack.[13]

On April 22, the three boats of Pouré, Vallé, and Álvarez resumed their journey, traveling together. To assist them, Grand-Pré sent one party of Indians to escort them part way and another overland to the Yazoo River to search out and destroy the remaining fugitives. Grand-Pré also informed Governor Miró that Turner boasted of plans to seize L'Abbadie's vessel which had preceded Pouré's and carried six thousand pesos in coin, military supplies, trade goods, and Indian presents. Also traveling on board were Anicanova Ramos de Cruzat, wife of the lieutenant governor of Spanish Illinois, Francisco Cruzat, and her four young sons.[14] Grand-Pré's warning, however, came too late.

In March and April, 1782, L'Abbadie's barge slowly made its way up the Mississippi. At the Arkansas Post, Joseph Hortiz left the craft to go overland to inform Cruzat of the vessel's approach. On May 2, without incident or warning of pirates, L'Abbadie reached the Chickasaw Bluffs. Two boats going downriver, one belonging to Joseph Motard of Illinois, the other American, reported that all was quiet. Joseph Meson, a former New Orleans resident returning there from Virginia aboard the American boat, said nothing about having been detained by Colbert and then released under an oath of silence. Both L'Abbadie and Señora Cruzat later censured Meson severely for keeping his word of honor to pirates instead of alerting the Spaniards.[15]

At 11:00 A.M. on May 2, a man named Thomas hailed L'Abbadie's boat from the west bank, alleging to have letters from Lieutenant Governor Cruzat for his wife. When the boat approached land, forty Englishmen and one mestizo, armed with carbines, knives, and clubs, leaped out of the vegetation and quickly seized the craft. Colbert, who claimed to have a British captain's commission, told Señora Cruzat that her person would be respected and she would soon be allowed to proceed to St. Louis. His forces were estimated at one hundred to three hundred whites, with no Indian allies. When two hundred and fifty Chickasaws arrived a week later and received a share of the booty, they avoided direct involvement with Colbert. For most of their nineteen days in captivity, Señora Cruzat and the other prisoners were kept about five leagues up the Chickasaw (Margot) River and thirty leagues from the Chickasaw village, an estimated two days' journey away. She observed little discipline among the whites, periodic drunkenness, and confusion and indecision on Colbert's part. At times the captain, disgusted by the conduct of his own men, threatened to leave them. The captives learned that a spy in Natchez, François La Grange, sent frequent messages to Colbert about Spanish river traffic. By May 15, Colbert determined to release Señora Cruzat, her children, and several other persons and to inform the governor that the remaining captives would be released when the insurrection leaders arrived at the Chickasaw village. Señora Cruzat insisted in traveling on L'Abbadie's larger and more comfortable boat, which the rebel captain reluctantly supplied. He first obtained an I.O.U. from L'Abbadie for 400 pesos for the boat which the former owner had to pay to Blommart upon the latter's release. On May 21, Señora Cruzat, her children, a Negro servant, L'Abbadie (who had been stripped of all his clothing save his leather breeches), and eight other persons left the Chickasaw Bluffs going downstream.[16]

The released prisoners carried several messages from Colbert. He demanded the release of Blommart, John Alston, Joseph Holmes, Jacob Winfree, John Green, and William Eason. He also included Parker Carradine, John Smith, and John Turner, but the first two had already been released, and the third was never a prisoner. Colbert also asked Governor Gálvez to release Judith Holston, an elderly woman Grand-Pré had arrested for aiding the fugitives. In return, Colbert promised to free five captives. Alexander McGillivray, who momentarily visited Colbert on the Mississippi, appears to have written these letters for the loyalist captain.[17]

The day after leaving Colbert, the former captives encountered the three boats of Vallé, Pouré, and Álvarez thirty leagues above the Arkansas River. They all quickly retired downstream where, at the mouth of the Arkansas, they parted company. Señora Cruzat, in L'Abbadie's boat, continued to New Orleans to sound the alert to Governor Miró, while the approximately ninety men in the other three boats traveled up to the Arkansas Post to reinforce it. In a parting boast, Colbert had declared his intention of seizing it, and Natchez afterwards.[18] With a presumed force of three hundred men, the Spaniards believed him capable of doing so; but they overestimated Colbert's real strength, and he abandoned the Mississippi for the rest of the year. Meanwhile, Señora Cruzat reached New Orleans on May 30, and immediately made a lengthy deposition of what had occurred.

Six days after learning of Colbert's audacious attack, Governor Miró reported to Gálvez that rebels had disrupted the navigation of the Mississippi between Arkansas and Spanish Illinois. Miró dismissed any possibility of attacking them, as they were 300 leagues away and would melt into the forest if pursued. In any case, he calculated that he would require 1,000 soldiers, 400 hunters, numerous Indian auxiliaries, and large sums of money to do so. He did plan to lead a column of soldiers to reinforce Natchez, and he proposed to Gálvez the establishment of several new forts on the Mississippi in order to minimize future attacks. From Natchez he intended to send additional soldiers to the Arkansas Post, issue a pardon to the fugitives who appeared before him, and try to win over the Chickasaw Indians to the Spanish camp. Although they were not directly supporting Colbert, the

Chickasaws harbored the rebels. The governor believed that Colbert should not be regarded as a duly commissioned officer authorized to wage war, as he had placed himself at the head of rebels whose oaths of fidelity to Spain had invalidated their right to engage in further hostilities. While Miró originally planned to take 200 soldiers to Natchez, he left on June 17, with only half that number.[19]

The first Spanish action against Colbert was launched from St. Louis. On May 30, Joseph Hortiz arrived there overland from Arkansas with the news that L'Abbadie's boat was coming loaded with money, goods, and passengers and that rebels were at the Chickasaw Bluffs. Cruzat quickly sent Sub-lieutenant Diego Blanco, nine soldiers, fourteen militiamen, and two merchants downstream to escort L'Abbadie safely to St. Louis. After they left, Cruzat learned from Loup Indians on June 5, that rebels had seized L'Abbadie's craft as well as that of Monsieur Lafon who had left Illinois going downriver. He then sent Captain Jacobo Dubreuil and a party of soldiers to Ste. Geneviève to reinforce that garrison and community. In Ste. Geneviève, Dubreuil dispatched a delegation of twenty-two Loup, Kaskaskia, and Peoria Indians to the Chickasaws to recover the prisoners, to ask the Chickasaws not to protect the brigands, and to get the natives' assistance in clearing the river of rebels. To escort the friendly Indians, Dubreuil sent militia Lieutenant Carlos Vallé, with eight militiamen and an interpreter, down to the Chickasaw Bluffs.

On June 12, eighteen leagues below Ste. Geneviève, Vallé's party encountered Blanco's detachment as he was returning to St. Louis after failing to find L'Abbadie. When Vallé informed Blanco of the fate of L'Abbadie's vessel and the objective of his mission, Blanco immediately joined with his soldiers and three militiamen. The others chose to return to St. Louis. On June 17, Blanco, Vallé, and their men arrived at the Chickasaw Bluffs, which they found deserted. After reconnoitering, they discovered a prison and huts built by the rebels a quarter of a league from the river. The next day, the friendly Indians left on their mission to the Chickasaws, asking that the soldiers wait for them below the Ohio River, as remaining at the bluffs was dangerous. After burning the rebel encampment, Blanco retired upstream. About July 4, the Indians not having returned, he took his men up to Ste. Geneviève.

The Indian party returned on July 25, with six prisoners and a group of Chickasaws, but without Colbert's captives. The Chickasaws, who had held the six prisoners, assured Cruzat that they wanted peace and friendship, which he said would be theirs if they expelled the rebels and cooperated with the Spaniards. The Chickasaws also asked Cruzat to call off the raids of his Indian allies whom the lieutenant governor had recently incited against them. In return, the Chickasaws, led by their great chief Payamataha, pledged to restore all their Spanish prisoners and those who had escaped from Colbert.[20]

Before leaving New Orleans, Governor Miró launched a vigorous effort to separate the Chickasaws from Colbert's influence. He ordered messengers sent to Chief Payamataha. From Arkansas, the acting commandant dispatched the Quapaws, and from Mobile, Commandant Henrique Grimarest sent the Choctaw large medal chief Paulous to the Chickasaws, where he was well received. Seven other nations were then attempting to persuade the Chickasaws to join the Spaniards in an alliance. Payamataha, reportedly sick, said he would visit Miró in Natchez when he recovered his health. The chief regretted Colbert's action and said that the whites were many leagues away, but this probably was not accurate. Another report from the Chickasaws stated that Payamataha had gone to make peace with the Choctaws, and Colbert, instead of being far away, was at home.[21]

On July 1, Governor Miró arrived at Natchez, where he planned to talk with the Chickasaws and shore up Spanish defenses on the Mississippi. He remained there for three and a half months. Although he released Judith Holston and pardoned the fugitives who appeared before him, he refused to negotiate with Colbert whom he regarded as a criminal unlawfully leading a gang of pirates. In a letter to Colbert, July 29, in which Miró claimed that he was not using the Indians, the governor explained that the Natchez leaders were political, not military, prisoners. As for the hostages Colbert retained, Miró hoped to use the Chickasaws to secure their release. In order to help Cruzat in Illinois, the governor also re-opened the Mississippi which, it seemed, was not closed, as Colbert's band had retired from the river.[22]

Easier to assist than St. Louis, which needed Indian presents and trade goods, was the Arkansas Post. There, temporary commandant Lieutenant Louis de Villars erroneously feared a rebel attack, as he believed that they were still at the Chickasaw Bluffs interfering with river traffic.[23] When Miró discovered that Villars had permitted Quapaw bands to war on Colbert (although they did not do so), the governor sent an express with orders to take the rebels prisoner and not to kill them.[24] Miró also sent Sublieutenant Antonio Soler of the Royal Artillery Corps and thirty-three soldiers to the Arkansas Post to reinforce and rebuild the fort.[25] In July, Villars learned that the Chickasaws desired peace; several of their chiefs returned with a Quapaw party and declared their intentions of visiting Miró at Natchez. On their way down-stream, however, the Chickasaws spotted Soler and his soldiers journeying upriver and fled back to their village with this information. From St. Louis, Villars learned that rebel strength consisted of 130 men who were living five leagues away from the Chickasaw village because the tribe refused to have them in the village. But he distrusted the Chickasaws because reports stated that they were with a party of rebels on the Chickasaw River, consuming forty casks of brandy, and constantly drunk.[26] In August, the likelihood of an attack on the Arkansas Post diminished. By then Miró had appointed Captain Jacobo Dubreuil to replace Villars as commandant at the Arkansas Post.[27]

In October, Miró felt confident that Colbert was no longer a menace to the Spaniards and prepared to return to New Orleans. Three boats had gone up to Illinois and three more had come down the river without incident. Miró believed that he had carried out his principal objectives of tranquilizing the province, opening the river, and reinforcing the garrisons and forts, but he had failed to talk with the Chickasaws and to obtain the freedom of the captives. Two Englishmen, however, one a long-time resident at the Chickasaw village and the other a fugitive who returned for a pardon, provided him with information. They reported that the Chickasaws refused to help Colbert attack the Arkansas Post or seize boats on the Mississippi. They calculated that only twenty-eight whites supported the captain. With this news, Miró concluded that he could safely return to New Orleans. He told Cruzat in St. Louis to discharge the militia and to cease worrying about Colbert.[28]

Two weeks after Miró left Natchez, five Chickasaws and a teen-age boy, Carlos Lafon, seized on the Mississippi, brought Colbert's reply to the governor.[29] Colbert resented Miró's accusation of harboring rebels and asserted that the fugitives had always been English, never Spanish, subjects. He reminded Miró of

Spanish assistance to James Willing in 1778, after he had plundered British settlements along the Mississippi. Colbert insisted that he had the right to destroy his king's enemies. As for the hostages, he intended to keep them until Miró exchanged them for those held in New Orleans. Colbert, who appreciated the governor's claim of not using Indians to wage war, as the struggle was purely between whites, crowed, "I have prevald with my Indians to make Peace both with you & the Americans & with all The world as it is proper that no Indians ought to interfare with what Concerns None but white [people]." The statement, however, conflicted with reports Miró had received about Chickasaw refusal to help the rebels. As for the Natchez fugitives, Colbert wrote surprisingly, "I must blame them for not Remaining in Peace till war was desided between great Brittain & Spain."[30] He insisted, nevertheless, that Blommart had General Campbell's authority to wage war and therefore should be regarded as a military prisoner.

Colbert's inactivity lasted until December, 1782, when he returned to the Mississippi at the Chickasaw Bluffs to resume his depredations. With twenty-five men, he attempted to seize the boat of Benito Vásquez, a St. Louis trader. Soon the merchant Antonio Pino reported that the rebels were camped on the river.[31] In response to this news, Commandant Jacobo Dubreuil at the Arkansas Post sent Quapaw scouts to learn more about them. One report stated that sixty to eighty Englishmen were then on the St. Francis River, opposite the Chickasaw Bluffs, but that number was an exaggeration. More reliable information came from Baptista Ringuet and Baptista La Framboise, men captured with L'Abbadie the year before. In February they escaped and informed Dubreuil that Colbert had only thirty men but was waiting for one hundred more from the Ohio. They incorrectly placed his Chickasaw allies at two hundred warriors led by his son. Both men said that Colbert planned to attack the Arkansas Post, as well as seize the convoy to Illinois, that spring. Dubreuil, in turn, sent Quapaw Chief Angaska, twenty-three wariors, and eleven white inhabitants to reconnoiter and attack the rebels if the opportunity arose.[32]

In addition to his thirty whites, Colbert had only perhaps a dozen Chickasaws, all of whom were related to him, but he was recruiting men from the American boats he stopped and pillaged. One victim who later testified to the Spaniards, Henoc Wales, left Ohio for Natchez with his wife and children aboard a flatboat loaded with furniture, animals, and flour. On December 26, Colbert's brigands at the Chickasaw Bluffs despoiled him of everything he had.[33] Other Americans encountered similar treatment, although Colbert recruited a number of them to aid in his plundering. The Spaniards, however, did not suffer losses, as they had detained their boats in Illinois.[34] Despite reports that provided Dubreuil with considerable information about Colbert, the captain's attack at the Arkansas Post still caught the Spaniards partially by surprise.

In April, Colbert felt sufficiently strong to carry out his long-promised attack on the Spanish post. His Chickasaws deceived the Quapaws, whose village on the lower reaches of the Arkansas River was supposed to block the entry of unwanted persons. The rebels then rapidly ascended the stream to the vicinity of the Arkansas Post, seizing along the way the pirogue and property of Antonio Pino. At daylight on April 17, they assaulted the Arkansas village, taking a number of prisoners, including Lieutenant Villars and his family, pillaging whatever they could find, and engaging in a fire-fight with a Spanish patrol. The rebels killed two soldiers, wounded a third, and took prisoner six more. Sergeant Alejo Pastor alone of the patrol managed to escape and entered the fort with news of what had happened. When the attackers appeared at the fort's gate, Commandant Dubreuil commenced firing both cannons and fusils, driving the rebels to cover behind a ridge. With only carbines, Colbert's force was unable to inflict any damage on the fort, but the captain tried to use his captives to compel Dubreuil to surrender. At about 9:00 A.M., under a flag of truce, Colbert sent one of his officers and Señora María Luisa Vallé de Villars, wife of Lieutenant Villars, with a message.[35]

Colbert's efforts to parley with Dubreuil, however, came at the same moment that the commandant unleased a sally of eleven soldiers and four Quapaws, all of whom let out Indian war cries as they exited the fort. The remaining soldiers covered them with a barrage of gunfire. Colbert's officer immediately deserted Señora Villars who was quickly brought within the fort and reported to Dubreuil. Colbert claimed to have five hundred Chickasaws, two boatloads of whites, and cannons with which he intended to assault the fort at noon; he also intended to kill his prisoners if Dubreuil used the Quapaws against him. But

Colbert's men, frightened by the Indian war cries, fled to their boats. There, the captain released the women and children prisoners and repeated his boast that he would attack at noon. Instead, he embarked his men and the remaining prisoners and moved downriver.

Although the siege of the fort was over, Colbert did not abandon the vicinity immediately. After his retreat from the Arkansas Post, he camped on the river, not far above its mouth, and retained the hostages, as they protected him against Spanish attack. The Quapaws, who had failed to detect Colbert's penetration of their river and who had not helped in the fort's defense, now belatedly came to Dubreuil's assistance. A party of one hundred Indians and twenty soldiers went in pursuit of Colbert to recover the prisoners. After negotiations on April 24, the captain surrendered Lieutenant Villars and his other prisoners, except for four soldiers, three slaves, and the son of Anselmo Layones. In return he expected Governor Miró to release Blommart and several other prisoners in New Orleans. If Miró failed to do so, then Villars would owe Colbert two thousand pesos for his freedom.[36] Shortly after releasing the prisoners, he hurriedly left the Arkansas, as the convoy from New Orleans was nearing.

On retreating upriver, Colbert continued his depredations. He briefly detained a flatboat belonging to Mr. Goutyrs, on which two of his men deserted. In New Orleans, one of them, Malcom Clark, testified that Colbert had seized boats whenever he was strong enough to do so, but many of his men now wavered in their loyalty and sought asylum, fearful of Spanish reprisals and the approach of the convoy. Through both seizure and purchase, Colbert amassed seven to eight hundred barrels of flour, half of which he conducted to the Chickasaw village.[37] About now, Colbert left the Mississippi for the last time, leaving a twenty-man detachment under his second-in-command, McGillivray, to bring up the rest of the flour.

The convoy to Illinois, which frightened Colbert away from the Arkansas, had left New Orleans in February, rendezvoused with nine other boats at Pointe Coupée, and proceeded slowly up the Mississippi. In late March it left Natchez, and it was still eighteen leagues below the Arkansas River on April 17, when Captain Joseph Valliere, who commanded a guard of thirty soldiers, learned of Colbert's plan to attack the Arkansas Post. Despite Valliere's attempt to bottle up Colbert on the Arkansas, the rebels had escaped when he arrived at the river's mouth. Because of a shortage of food on the Arkansas, the convoy resumed its journey upriver on May 3, with twenty-four Quapaw scouts.[38]

Seven days later, Valliere's scouts reported the presence of Colbert's men on the Chickasaw River. With one hundred whites and twenty-four Indians, Valliere marched up the river to engage the rebels. After nearly a league, Valliere encountered them and, in a skirmish, killed McGillivray and wounded another; a third rebel drowned. The rest fled into the wilderness. Valliere recovered three Spanish soldiers taken at the Arkansas Post, an armed flatboat, three pirogues, and about four hundred barrels of flour. He destroyed most of the flour and all the boats except a pirogue.[39] He believed that the rebels still had two armed flatboats, but he was unable to continue searching for the remaining fugitives. In spite of Valliere's superior strength and the willingness of his soldiers and boat crews, the merchants insisted that his duty was to escort their boats safely to St. Louis. Consequently, Valliere resumed the voyage to Illinois and arrived without further incident.[40] By this time, Colbert was no longer on the Mississippi, and the war was over.

News of the peace reached New Orleans in April. Governor Miró immediately gave the Natchez insurrection leaders the freedom of the city until a ship from Jamaica should arrive to evacuate them. Gálvez had pardoned them on condition that they leave Spanish territory.[41] Miró sent the news to Arkansas with orders to inform Colbert of the end of hostilities and for him to return both the prisoners and booty taken on his raid against the Arkansas Post, as it had been made after the war had ended. The governor also declared Villar's I.O.U. of two thousand pesos to Colbert for his release null and void. In early July, Dubreuil sent two Spanish soldiers with copies of letters to the Chickasaws.[42]

By August the Spanish messengers were in the Chickasaw village where they delivered the letters to Colbert. In a terse reply, Colbert rejected the return of the property and said that he had already written to Miró on this matter. Moreover, he no longer had the prisoners. Upon learning of the war's conclusion from the British governor of St. Augustine, he had disbanded his men and sent the remaining Spanish prisoners to Mobile—they arrived in New Orleans before August 1—but he retained the slaves and other property as legitimate prizes of war.[43] Privately, however, Colbert was not confident of the legitimacy of his military operations with the British governor.

Meanwhile, the Chickasaws continued in their peace efforts with the Spaniards. In August a Chickasaw delegation arrived at the Arkansas Post claiming that everyone in the tribe, excepting Colbert's family, desired harmonious relations. They branded Colbert's promises as deceitful and pointed out "a thousand" of his lies. Chief Payamataha persisted in his friendly overtures to the Spaniards, although Colbert's sons sought to create further mischief. In the spring of 1784, the chief journeyed to the Chickasaw Bluffs where he fell mortally ill with fever. As he lay dying, he told Anselmo Billet, an Arkansas-based trader, that he had counseled the young men to maintain friendly relations with the Spaniards and that he was dying a Spaniard. He requested that upon his death his body be draped with a Spanish flag and thus cremated. It was done.[44]

James Colbert preceded Payamataha in death. About the end of summer, 1783, Colbert laboriously journeyed to St. Augustine as his health deteriorated. He arrived on October 5, and conferred with the governor about Spanish claims to the property he had seized in his last raid. Ill health then prevented him from leaving. Feeling uncertain about his fate, on November 12, he dictated a letter ordering that whatever property he had be given to his son James whom he was concerned about and had placed in the counting office of Panton, Leslie and Company. Anthony Hutchins, a Natchez resident who wrote the letter for Colbert, described him as:

> much dispirited and no less apprehensive of his loss of life; having as he said enemies in every quarter, aggravated by various causes, as well as by his pointed exertions in the cause and Interest of his sovereign against such as he conceived to be his duty to oppose and to annoy; which he said made his situation very unsafe.[45]

Colbert's premonition was correct. Within weeks after dictating his letter to Hutchins and visiting Alexander McGillivray, he died in a horsefall as he was returning home.[46]

In assessing Colbert's wartime activities, his loyalty to his sovereign can be admired: he undoubtedly exceeded the norm for British subjects on the Mississippi. His effort to obtain the release of the Natchez leaders was commendable, as was his freeing of prisoners in the expectation that Governor Miró would reciprocate. But his integrity as a military leader breaks down because he often operated as a brigand, stopping civilian boats, seizing private property, looting at the Arkansas Post, and threatening to kill hostages if he did not achieve his objectives. Colbert's strength, too, has been exaggerated, as he rarely had over thirty men in his command. Nor did he enjoy the allegiance of the Chickasaw tribe in 1782 and 1783, only that of his kin within the nation. Moreover, his stays on the Mississipi were brief, particularly in 1782. Although he remained on the river for a longer period in 1783, his principal victims were weakly-armed American boats. As the war closed, the Spaniards repelled his attack at the Arkansas Post, and Captain Valliere's force routed the last of his men on the Mississippi. In light of this, it is difficult to accept Corbitt's contentions that Colbert cancelled the Spanish claim to territory north of the Yazoo River as he "travers [ed] at will the area in question" and that, because of Colbert, Britain controlled this region when it was ceded to the United States in the peace treaty of 1783.

---

*Professor of History, Fort Lewis College, Durango, Colorado.

[1]D.C. Corbitt, "James Colbert and the Spanish Claims to the East Bank of the Mississippi," *Mississippi Valley Historical Review* 24 (1938):472; John W. Caughey, "The Natchez Rebellion of 1781 and Its Aftermath," *Louisiana Historical Quarterly* 16 (1933):57-83. Corbitt's and Caughey's studies on Colbert are the only ones to use Spanish documentation. I wish to thank Professor Emeritus A.P. Nasatir of San Diego State University for the use of many of the Spanish documents cited herein.

[2]A.M. Gibson, *The Chickasaws* (Norman, 1971), 65; Harry Warren, "Some Chickasaw Chiefs and Prominent Men," *Publications of the Mississippi Historical Society* 8 (1904):555-70; Guy B. Braden, "The Colberts and the Chickasaw Nation," *Tennessee Historical Quarterly* 17 (1958):222-49, 318-35; H.B. Cushman, *History of the Choctaw, Chickasaw, and Natchez Nations* (Stillwater, 1962); James H. Malone, *The Chickasaw Nation, A Short Sketch of a Noble People* (Louisville, 1922); James Adair, *Adair's History of the American Indians*, ed. Samuel Cole Williams (Ann Arbor, 1967), 398.

³Gibson, *The Chickasaws*, 71-73; Caughey, "Natchez Rebellion," 69-70; Lawrence Kinnaird, ed., *Spain in the Mississippi Valley, 1765-1794* (Washington, 1949), 2:21-34. Colbert claimed to have suffered three wounds while attacking Fort Jefferson, which prevented him from seizing newly-appointed Lieutenant Governor Francisco Cruzat's boat as he headed upstream in 1780, but this might have been characteristic boasting. For the Chickasaw attack on Fort Jefferson see Zachariah Frederick Smith, *The History of Kentucky* (Louisville, 1886), 160-61; Lewis and Richard Collins, *History of Kentucky* (Louisville, 1924), 2:39-40. Although R.S. Cotterill, *The Southern Indians: The Story of the Civilized Tribes Before Removal* (Norman, 1954), 43, calls Colbert the British commissary with the Chickasaw tribe, I have found no such evidence. To the contrary, John McIntosh signed himself as commissary in a letter from the Chickasaw country to the Spanish commandant at the Arkansas Post, Sept. 2, 1779, *AGI Cuba, leg. 192*. Caughey, "Natchez Rebellion," 69, calls Farquhar Bethune the British deputy superintendent of Indian affairs for the Mississippi district, and Anicanova Ramos de Cruzat also names Bethune commissary of the Chickasaws, Louis Houck, ed., *The Spanish Regime in Missouri* (Chicago, 1909), 1:230.

⁴Caughey, "Natchez Rebellion," 57-65; Kinnaird, *Spain in the Mississippi Valley*, 1:428. Charles Gayarré paints a pathetic and imaginative picture of the flight of the Natchez fugitives, *History of Louisiana* (New York, 1972), 2:148-51.

⁵Caughey, "Natchez Rebellion," 57-62; Wilbur H. Siebert, "The Loyalists in West Florida and the Natchez District," *Mississippi Valley Historical Review* 2 (1916):465-83.

⁶Kinnaird, *Spain in the Mississippi Valley*, 1:429-31; J. Barton Starr, *Tories, Dons, and Rebels: The American Revolution in British West Florida* (Gainesville, 1976), 217-18; Robert V. Haynes, *The Natchez District and the American Revolution* (Jackson, 1976), 143-52 (the latter must be used carefully as it contains many errors). In 1781, Capt. Jacobo Dubreuil took a detachment of soldiers to reinforce St. Louis. On his way past the Chickasaw Bluffs, the Chickasaws attacked his party. It is not known if Colbert was present. Dubreuil to Miró, Fort Charles III, May 20, 1783, *AGI Cuba, leg. 107*.

⁷Gilbert C. Din, "Arkansas Post in the American Revolution," *Arkansas Historical Quarterly* 40 (1981):3-30.

⁸Kinnaird, *Spain in the Mississippi Valley*, 1:429-31; Piernas to Gálvez, New Orleans, Aug. 22, 1781, *AGI Cuba, leg. 1376*. On the condition of the Natchez rebels in the Chickasaw country, see Villiers to Piernas, Fort Charles III, Sept. 16, 1781, *AGI Cuba, leg. 194*.

⁹See a second letter of Villiers to Piernas, Sept. 16, 1781, *AGI Cuba, leg. 194*; Piernas to Villiers, New Orleans, Oct. 12, 1781, *AGI Cuba, leg. 114*. For the struggle between full-blooded and half-blooded Chickasaws over control of the tribe, see Gibson, *The Chickasaws*, 61-67.

¹⁰Villiers to Piernas, Fort Charles III, Jan. 9, Feb. 4, 13, 27, 1782, *AGI Cuba, leg. 195*; Cruzat to Miró, St. Louis, Aug. 4, 1782, *AGI Cuba, leg. 9*.

¹¹Din, "Arkansas Post," 13-17. By May, 1782, Villiers was seriously ill. Lt. Louis de Villars, who was going to Ste. Geneviève with his father-in-law François Vallé, took command at the Arkansas Post and sent Villiers to New Orleans in early June. Villiers died on June 19, after undergoing an operation the day before. Villars to [Miró], Fort Charles III, May 29, 1782, *AGI Cuba, leg. 195*; Piernas to Gálvez, No. 36, New Orleans, June 22, 1782, *AGI Cuba, leg. 1377*. In the spring of 1782,

Villiers also had to contend with a conspiracy to butcher the Arkansas Post garrison. Four persons were subsequently executed in New Orleans for their roles in it. Stanley Faye, "The Arkansas Post of Louisiana: Spanish Domination," *Louisiana Historical Quarterly* 27 (1944):671.

[12]Gálvez to the New Orleans Cabildo, Havana, Jan. 22, 1782; Piernas to Gálvez, New Orleans, March 1, 1782, *AGI Cuba, leg. 1377*; Faye, "Arkansas Post," 673.

[13]Grand-Pré to Miró, No. 232, Natchez, April 22, 1782, *AGI Cuba, leg. 9*; Eugene [Pouré] to [Miró], Fort Charles III, June 8, 1782, *AGI Cuba, leg. 195*.

[14]Ibid.

[15]Houck, *Spanish Regime*, 1:219-31; Kinnaird, *Spain in the Mississippi Valley*, 2:21-34; Jack D.L. Holmes, "Spanish-American Rivalry Over the Chickasaw Bluffs, 1780-1795," *Publications of the East Tennessee Historical Society* 34 (1962):26-57.

[16]Ibid.

[17]Ibid., John W. Caughey, *McGillivray of the Creeks* (Norman, 1938), 16, believes that Alexander McGillivray wrote the letters for the captain. Copies of the letters are in *AGI Cuba, leg. 2359*. A *"palabra de honor"* or promise to return to Colbert's custody given by the released captives is in *AGI Cuba, leg. 133*, dated May 15, 1782.

[18]Villars to [Miró], below the White River, May 22, 1782, *AGI Cuba, leg. 195*.

[19]Miró to Gálvez, New Orleans, June 5, 1782, *AGI Cuba, leg. 151A*; Piernas to Gálvez, New Orleans, June 22, 1782, *AGI Cuba, leg. 1377*; Miró to Cruzat, Natchez, July 20, 1782, *AGI Cuba, leg. 3*. Gálvez concurred in Miró's decision not to regard Colbert as duly commissioned to wage war; he approved Miró's actions and ordered the Natchez leaders sent to Havana or Veracruz. Gálvez to Miró, Guarico, July 21, 1782, *AGI Cuba, leg. 9*.

[20]Kinnaird, *Spain in the Mississippi Valley*, 2:49-54; Cruzat to Miró, St. Louis, Aug. 8, 1782; Diego Blanco to Miró, St. Louis, Aug. 13, 1782, *AGI Cuba, leg. 9*.

[21]Miró to Villiers, No. 108, New Orleans, May 22, 1782; Miró to Henrique Grimarest, No. 67, New Orleans, June 3, 1782, *AGI Cuba, leg. 3*; Kinnaird, *Spain in the Mississippi Valley*, 2:57-58, 62-63.

[22]Miró to Cruzat, Natchez, July 20, 1782, *AGI Cuba, leg. 3*; Kinnaird, *Spain in the Mississippi Valley*, 2:60; Cruzat to Miró, St. Louis, July 28, 1782, *AGI Cuba, leg. 9*.

[23]Two letters of Villars to Miró, Arkansas, July 5, 1782, *AGI Cuba, leg. 2359*.

[24]Miró to Villars, Natchez, No. 180, July 9, 1782, *AGI Cuba, leg. 3*.

[25]Two letters of Villars to Miró, Arkansas, Aug. 12, 1782, *AGI Cuba, leg. 195*. Villars originally wanted to carry out extensive repairs, even move the fort, as Sub-lieutenant Soler recommended, but Miró said it was too expensive. [Miró] to Villars, No. 111, Fort Panmure, Oct. 3, 1782, *AGI Cuba, leg. 3*.

[26]Villars to Miró, Arkansas, July 6, 1782, *AGI Cuba, leg. 2359*; Villars to Miró, Arkansas, Aug. 4, 6, 1782, *AGI Cuba, leg. 195*.

[27]Miró to Jacobo Dubreuil, No. 140, Natchez, July 20, 1782, *AGI Cuba, leg. 117A*.

[28][Miró] to Cruzat, Fort Panmure, Oct. 18, 1782, *AGI Cuba, leg. 115*; Miró to Gálvez, New Orleans, Nov. 7, 1782, *AGI Cuba, leg. 1*; [Miró] to Bellisle, New Orleans, Nov. 2, 1782, *AGI Cuba, leg. 195*.

[29]Piernas to Miró, Natchez, Nov. 3, 1782, *AGI Cuba, leg. 9*.

[30]Kinnaird, *Spain in the Mississippi Valley*, 2:60.

³¹Dubreuil to [Miró], Fort Charles III, Jan. 8, 1783, *AGI Cuba, leg. 116;* Piernas to Miró, Natchez, Jan. 10, 1783, ibid., *leg. 9;* Miró to Dubreuil, No. 134, New Orleans, Feb. 5, 1783, ibid., *leg. 3.*

³²Dubreuil to Miró, Arkansas, Feb. 18, 21, March 1, 1783, *AGI Cuba, leg. 107.* Dubreuil to Miró, Jan. 9, 1783, ibid., *leg. 116,* reported that he had arrived at the Arkansas Post on Jan. 5, and assumed command on Jan. 8; Lt. Villars remained temporarily as second in command.

³³"Declaration of Henoc Wales," New Orleans, April 9, 1783, *AGI Cuba, leg. 196.* Wales identified Colbert's partisans as Simon Burney, Ziblan Mathews, James Clonketin, Juan Holsten, Ricardo Hall, Betnigo Swallen, Patricio Rogers, Joel Starn, Jame Mchim, William Windright, and Patricio Maar. See also Dubreuil to Miró, Arkansas, March 26, 1783, *AGI Cuba, leg. 107.*

³⁴Cruzat to Miró, St. Louis, March 2, 1783; Piernas to Miró, Natchez, March 21, 1783, *AGI Cuba, leg. 9.*

³⁵For two accounts of Colbert's attack see Dubreuil to Miró, Fort Charles III, May 5, 1783, *AGI Cuba, leg. 107,* and a shorter version, Dubreuil to Martín Navarro, Fort Charles III, May 4, 1783, *AGI Cuba, leg. 602A.* See Din, "Arkansas Post," 23-25, for a longer description. The account in Anna Lewis, *Along the Arkansas* (Dallas, 1932), 174-86, suffers from poor translations of the Spanish documents.

³⁶Dubreuil to Miró, Fort Charles III, May 5, 1783, *AGI Cuba, leg. 107;* Villars's I.O.U., April 24, 1783, *AGI Cuba, leg. 2360.* In addition to the release of Blommart, Colbert wanted Jacob Winfree, Jean Olsen (John Alston), William Utoy (probably William Eason), and William Williams freed.

³⁷Piernas to Miró, Natchez, May 9, 18, 1783, *AGI Cuba, leg. 9.* Based on Malcom Clark's information, Miró stated that Colbert then had seventy whites, twelve Indians, and five Negroes. Miró to Dubreuil, New Orleans, May 17, 1783, *AGI Cuba, leg. 107.*

³⁸Instructions to Captain Joseph Valliere, Feb. 10, 1783, *AGI Cuba, leg. 2;* Valliere to Miró, Natchez, March 28, 1783; Valliere to Piernas, 18 leagues below the Arkansas River, April 18, 1783, *AGI Cuba, leg. 196;* Piernas to Miró, Natchez, April 23, 1783, *AGI Cuba, leg. 9;* Valliere to Miró, Arkansas, April 28, May 2, 1783, *AGI Cuba, leg. 196.*

³⁹Valliere to [Miró], Chickasaw Bayou, May 11, 1783, *AGI Cuba, legs. 196 and 2360;* Dubreuil to Miró, Arkansas, May 22, 1783, *AGI Cuba, leg. 107.* Valliere gave the Quapaw chief, Patrimeny, a small medal for his assistance and asked for Miró's approval. Valliere to [Miró], at the Balur St. Martain, May 12, 1783, *AGI Cuba, leg. 196.*

⁴⁰Valliere to Miró, Ecors à Margot, May 20, 1783, and St. Louis, July 18, 1783, *AGI Cuba, leg. 196.* Miró explained the work of Valliere's expedition to Gálvez in his No. 95, New Orleans, Aug. 1, 1783, *AGI Cuba, leg. 2.*

⁴¹Gálvez to Miró, Guarico, April 7, 1783, *AGI Cuba, leg. 1377;* Miró to Dubreuil, No. 207, New Orleans, April 28, 1783, *AGI Cuba, leg. 3.* The six leaders being held—J. Blommart, John Alston, Jacob Winfree, W. Williams, Will Eason, and Samuel Benjamin— promised to remain in the New Orleans vicinity. New Orleans, April 28, 1783, *AGI Cuba, leg. 196.*

⁴²Miró to Dubreuil, New Orleans, May 16, 1783, *AGI Cuba, leg. 3;* [Miró] to Gálvez, New Orleans, No. 86, May 18, 1783, *AGI Cuba, leg. 224A.* Miró wrote that if Colbert continued his depredations, he intended to treat him as a "ban-

dolero." Dubreuil to Colbert, [Arkansas], July 5, 1783; Dubreuil to Miró, Fort Charles III, July 18, 1783; *Noticia de los efectos y Esclavos que ha tomado Jaime Colbert . . . en este Río y Puesto de Arkansas los Días 16 y 17 de Avril*, Fort Charles III, Aug. 26, 1783. The value of the property Colbert took, without counting Antonio Pino's losses, amounted to 3,703 pesos, 3 *reales*. *AGI Cuba, leg. 107*.

[43]Pedro Classin returned from the Chickasaw country, but Antonio Longinos stayed behind due to an injury to his leg. Dubreuil to Miró, Arkansas, Aug. 26, 1783; Colbert to Dubreuil, Chickasaw Country, [August] 3, 1783, *AGI Cuba, leg. 107*.

[44]Kinnaird, *Spain in the Mississippi Valley*, 2:89-91; Dubreuil to Miró, Arkansas, Aug. 26, 1783, April 20, 1784, *AGI Cuba, leg. 107*.

[45]Anthony Hutchins' deposition, Natchez, Mar. 7, 1791, with enclosed statement of James Colbert, St. Augustine, Nov. 12, 1783, Natchez Court Records, Chancery Court, Spanish Translations, vol. F, fols. 154-56 (provided by Dr. Jack D.L. Holmes). On Colbert's son James, see Braden, "The Colberts and the Chickasaw Nation," 223, 234; Warren, "Some Chickasaw Chiefs," 559.

[46]Caughey, "Natchez Rebellion," 82; Caughey, *McGillivray of the Creeks*, 68. McGillivray wrote, "[Colbert] had been at St. Augustine, concerning demands that was made on him by the Governor of New Orleans for damages he did on the Mississippi: he got full powers to Clear up that Complaint."

THE QUEEN'S REDOUBT EXPLOSION IN THE LIVES OF WILLIAM A. BOWLES, JOHN MILLER AND WILLIAM PANTON

J. Leitch Wright, Jr.*

A red hot Spanish shot rolled into the magazine of the Queen's Redoubt on May 8, 1781, touching off an unprecedented explosion on the Gulf Coast and forcing the British garrison defending Pensacola to surrender. Although not obvious at the time, hostilities of the American Revolution and of the international conflict associated with it were drawing to a close. The general peace settlement in 1783, recognized sweeping changes. Spain received title to both East and West Florida; the United States won its independence; and boundaries throughout the world were redrawn. Looking ahead to the storming of the Bastille in 1789, one realizes that upheaval and change were continuing. For good reason the latter decades of the eighteenth century are known as a revolutionary era.

It is not my purpose to dwell on international diplomacy and great matters of state but instead to focus on three men whose lives were affected by the destruction of the Queen's Redoubt and by the ensuing turbulent years. Only one of them, William Augustus Bowles, was actually in Pensacola when the magazine went off; John Miller had left some months beforehand; and William Panton was alternating between Georgia and East Florida. Yet because of the American Revolution, Panton moved to Pensacola in 1785, and, though still a British subject, became one of the most influential citizens of Spanish West Florida. The destruction of the Queen's Redoubt transformed the careers of these three who at one time or another so influenced the economy and political development of Pensacola and of the expansive hinterland depending on this port.

In most respects John Miller is the least known, though if Bernardo de Gálvez had not captured Pensacola, Miller doubtless would have been remembered as one of the founding fathers of English-speaking West Florida. But he has remained a secondary, often obscure figure, and only the broad outline of his life is clear. He was from Elgin in the northern part of Scotland, apparently of the middle class and reasonably well educated. Like thousands of young eighteenth-century Scotsman, he emigrated to the American colonies, and perhaps he first settled in Virginia, Georgia, or some other colony on the Atlantic Coast.[1]

At some point after 1763, he arrived in West Florida to take advantage of opportunities in this newly-acquired British colony. The first definite mention of Miller in the province is in 1771, when he was elected to the West Florida assembly as a delegate from Mobile.[2] After a few years he moved to Pensacola to represent the West Florida capital in the assembly and to expand his varied business ventures. Identified with the province's commercial and political elite, Miller emerged as one of the most conscientious and industrious members of the lower house, serving on a variety of committees. He had a personal interest in government beyond the public welfare. For example, he concerned himself with the details necessary to establish a ferry over the Perdido River, thereby improving land communication between Pensacola and Mobile. With business interests in both towns, Miller appreciated that his own well-being was identified with the public good. He also was a justice of the peace, settling minor disputes among the growing civilian population.[3]

Above all, Miller was a merchant. For centuries Scotland had been poor, but in the eighteenth century Scots were allowed — encouraged — to go to all parts of the expanding British empire. Like other Scots, Miller picked West Florida, and Scots dominated all aspects of the province's commercial life. Many of them were Miller's partners or in some way closely associated with him. He was a member of several firms: John McGillivray, John Miller, and Company; John Miller, Peter Swanson, and Company; and he had his own firm, John Miller and Company. He was linked with Scottish merchants such as William Struthers, Peter Swanson, James McIntosh, and the McGillivrays — John, James, Daniel, Donald, and Lachlan. Miller provided supplies for the province's civilian and military populace, speculated in lands, traded (legally or not) with Spanish Louisiana, and engaged in the Indian trade.[4] As time passed, the Indian commerce became more important, though in the 1770s the most prominent Scottish name associated with the southern Indian trade was not John Miller but Lachlan McGillivray. Lachlan had come to Georgia in Oglethorpe's day. For long periods he had lived among Indians in the interior, trading with them and begetting a mestizo progeny, eventually emerging as one of the most successful Indian traders in the Georgia and South Carolina back country. When Britain acquired West Florida in 1763, Lachlan sent nephew John McGillivray to Mobile to supervise the westerly branch of the Indian trade. Lachlan employed other McGillivrays as well, but John, based in Mobile, was the most important. When the elderly Lachlan, who was a Tory, retired to Scotland during the Revolution, he made John his heir and turned over everything to him in return for an annuity.[5]

When Miller came to Mobile and became a partner of John McGillivray, Miller immediately became deeply involved in the Indian commerce and had influential contacts in Augusta, Savannah, Charleston, and other southern commercial centers. It is probable — or at least we may speculate — that Miller knew the McGillivrays in Scotland and that they, more than anyone else, brought him to West Florida.[6] The southern Indian trade involved an enormous area, much of the region between the Appalachian Mountains and the Mississippi River and below the Ohio River. Deerskins and furs — perhaps by river transportation, though usually by trains of packhorses — made their way from the interior to some coastal port. Charleston long remained the most important one. After the founding of Georgia, Savannah and Augusta won the growing portion of this commerce, and when Britain acquired West Florida, Mobile, and especially Pensacola, exported a growing share of the skins and peltry. In the long run — though not until the American Revolution and the ensuing years can we see this clearly — Pensacola became the pre-eminent port for the Indian trade, surpassing Charleston, Savannah, and all other competitors. When the young merchant John Miller came to Mobile and Pensacola, he fully appreciated the significance of the Gulf Coast ports. The capture of Fort George and convulsions associated with the French and American Revolutions did not make him forget Pensacola's magnificent harbor and the fortune awaiting traffickers with Indians in the interior.

But we have gotten ahead of our story because Miller, as he was establishing himself in West Florida, no more than anyone else envisioned that in 1776, the thirteen colonies would proclaim their independence. By virtue of his own efforts and his Scottish connections, he assumed that his various undertakings would prosper. As has been mentioned, he was involved in more ventures than the Indian trade, and it was almost inevitable that land speculation was one. After 1763, Britain actively encouraged emigration to the Floridas in the south and to Canada in the north, while the large area in between remained Indian country. Promotional tracts appeared, extolling Florida's attractions. Soldiers and sailors, promised bounties, along with others who had headright grants or used political influence, were urged to take up lands in West Florida. Miller was not a veteran and had no large family to win headright grants, but he purchased the headrights and bounty lands of others and used his influence in government to obtain large tracts: 2,200 acres on the Tensaw River, lands along the strategic Iberville canal waterway connecting Mobile with the Mississippi River, town lots in Manchac, Pensacola, and similar property.[7] During the 1770s, the most dynamic and attractive part of West Florida was the Natchez District on the Mississippi, and the growing Mississippi settlements were one reason Miller was so interested in acquiring property at Manchac and along the Iberville canal route. Anthony Hutchins, who remained in Natchez under British, Spanish, and American domination, was Miller's agent at Natchez during the British era.[8]

Miller himself remained at Pensacola, while his partners, agents, and employees sold his wares on the Mississippi, at Mobile, and in the Indian country. As a member of the assembly and a justice of the peace, Miller understood governmental procedures, and he assisted his partners and associates in a variety of ways: by speeding up the process of buying, granting, and selling lands, securing prompt clearances for ships, registering bills of credit and exchange, settling estates in which he had an interest, obtaining Indian trading licenses, and in a multitude of other ways expediting routine but essential business details.

A rejuvenated Spain entered the war in 1779, and one of her objectives was to seize the British Floridas and make the Gulf of Mexico once again a Spanish lake. The governor of Spanish Louisiana, young Bernardo de Gálvez, got off to an auspicious start in 1779, by capturing Baton Rouge and Britain's other posts on the Mississippi, and the following year by forcing Mobile to capitulate. Gálvez's success and the enterprise of the Spanish and French navies wreaked havoc with Miller's business. His friend, General Montfort Browne, had been lieutenant governor of British West Flordia before he became governor of the Bahamas. In 1780, Browne offered Miller a seat on the Bahamian council, an offer which Miller, seeing most of West Florida under Spanish control, accepted. Presumably he arrived in Nassau in the latter half of 1780. He became one of the earliest British loyalists to move from Florida to the Bahamas.[9] He was not the last. Before long, thousands of Florida exiles joined him, including William Panton and William Augustus Bowles.

Regardless of precisely when Miller left Pensacola, he had gotten out before the Spanish attack. Gálvez's powerful army and navy sailed into Pensacola harbor in March, 1781, to begin a two month's siege. During this campaign, Miller was in Nassau, and as the Spanish lines drew tighter about the West Florida capital, he may have been a bit smug, pleased with himself for having escaped in time. Many of Miller's friends and business associates were at hand when Pensacola fell on May 10.

There was no reason for Miller to feel so complacent, because within almost a year to the day, the Spaniards also captured Nassau, and he was included in the surrender terms. After Nassau's fall, the Spaniards accused him of outfitting privateers to prey on Spanish shipping. As a result, they imprisoned him, first in Nassau and subsequently in Havana. For the time being we must leave this furious British merchant who, in his confinement in 1782-83, painfully realized that the victorious Spanish ensign snapped in the breeze over Nassau, Havana, and Pensacola.[10]

William Augustus Bowles was in Pensacola when it fell. Had he stepped into the Queen's Redoubt five seconds earlier, the young British officer would have been blown into the air, mangled, or killed, as were over a hundred of his comrades. But by this narrow margin his life was spared, and we must examine his career more closely. Born at Frederick, on the Maryland frontier, in 1763, he was a generation younger than Miller. When the American Revolution broke out, Bowles's family remained loyal to the crown, and at the first opportunity William, the eldest child, made his way to the British lines in Philadelphia. Only fourteen years old in 1777, he secured a commission as ensign in the Maryland Loyalist regiment. This unit was ordered to Pensacola to help defend British West Florida, and the destinies of Bowles and the Floridas converged. In late December, 1778, the Maryland Loyalists debarked at Tartar Point commanding the entrance to Pensacola Bay.[11] Like other newly-arrived soldiers he was anxious to see the capital six miles away and joined them on an excursion which sailed over to Pensacola. But William missed the return boat, thereby being absent without leave, and as a result he was dismissed from the service. There was probably more to his dismissal, because disputes among the provincial officers were common, and Bowles was not the only one to resign or be dismissed. Nevertheless, sixteen-year-old William suddenly found himself penniless in Pensacola, bereft of friends and over a thousand miles from home.

At this juncture the paths of Bowles and Miller probably first crossed. To support himself and satisfy his curiosity, Bowles became an Indian trader, joining a party of Lower Creeks who were returning to the Chattahoochee River after visiting the West Florida capital. For some two years Bowles lived among and traded with these Indians, and it is likely, though we really do not know, that he got his trading goods from Miller or his associates.[12] One could engage in the Indian trade at various levels. The lowest was that of a packhorseman who led a string of horses several hundred miles into the interior, turned over his wares to resident factors in native villages, and returned to the coast, laden with skins and furs. At the highest level was someone like Sir William Johnson of New York who, before his death in 1774, lived close to or among the Indians on the frontier, traded with them and bought their lands, became enormously wealthy, and in the process sired an extensive mestizo progeny. He was made a baronet for his many services to the crown and was one of a handful of titled British noblemen to die in the American colonies. Though Bowles began his career as a packhorseman and resident factor in a Lower Creek village, he aspired to be the Sir William Johnson of the southern Indians; like Sir William he acquired Indian wives and proceeded to father mestizo children.

Periodically Bowles returned to Pensacola. Once when he reached the eastern edge of Pensacola Bay he found an abandoned hogshead, made a mast of a tree branch and a sail out of a blanket, and in this unwieldy craft sailed over to Pensacola's wharf. When he visited the West Florida capital in 1780, several hundred warriors accompanied him, and the swarthy Bowles, dressed as a Lower Creek, was indistinguishable from them. British authorities had urged Lower Creeks and other southern Indians to come to Pensacola to help defend the province against Spain. Bowles's war party joined British forces which marched overland from Pensacola to Mobile. Gálvez had captured Mobile in 1780, and the immediate British objective was The Village, an outpost across the bay from Mobile. The attack failed, but Bowles distinguished himself: "Glory was his passion, and war he considered the path which led to it."[13] As a result, he was reinstated in his regiment. It was Ensign Bowles, again dressed in a British officer's uniform and not as a Creek warrior, who in 1781, saw Spanish forces land at the entrance to Pensacola Bay and methodically make their way toward the town; and it was Bowles's regiment which was in the Queen's Redoubt and suffered the highest casualties when the magazine exploded.

The Pensacola garrison was paroled and sent off to British-occupied New York where Ensign Bowles spent the remainder of the war. An out-spoken loyalist, Bowles realized he could not remain in New York or return to Maryland at the conclusion of peace. The Revolution had disrupted his life. Joining thousands of other loyalists, particularly those with Florida ties, he sought refuge in the Bahamas. Bowles did not know what the future might bring, but he had not forgotten his native family or the heights to which Sir William Johnson had soared in the Indian country.[14]

The vagaries of the Revolution brought Bowles and Miller to the Bahamas and, for a brief time, also William Panton. Panton subsequently moved to Pensacola, but before 1784, he had never set foot in Pensacola or anywhere else in West Florida. Even so, he had much in common with his fellow Scot John Miller. Panton had emigrated to Charleston in 1765, and both in South Carolina and in Georgia he engaged in the Indian trade, land speculation, and commerce with the growing white populace. In 1763, Britain won a large area in the south which she organized into the two Floridas. Panton saw an opportunity in British East Florida, Miller in British West Florida. From Charleston, Savannah, and Frederica, Panton sent his ships laden with Indian goods to the St. Marys and St. Johns Rivers in East Florida to trade with those Creeks who had drifted into Florida and had become known as Seminoles. With his far-flung commercial involvement in South Carolina, Georgia, and East Florida, Panton emerged as one of the more successful Georgia and South Carolina merchants — until 1775.[15] Like most Scots who had come to America, Panton was an outspoken loyalist, and the Georgia Patriots or Whigs thought Panton's trading with the southern Indians "dangerous to the liberties of America," as indeed it was.[16] To escape imprisonment or tarring and feathering, Panton sought refuge in loyal East Florida. When he reached St. Augustine in 1776, he found that he was but one of many who had been forced to abandon Georgia, South Carolina, and other rebellious colonies.

He did not expect to remain permanently in East Florida: as soon as Britain sent over troops and assisted Americans loyal to the crown, this mad rebellion must be suppressed. In the meantime, he was in East Florida and had to make a living. Through friendship with East Florida's governor, Patrick Tonyn, and Colonel Thomas Brown, a prominent Georgia-South Carolina loyalist exile commanding the East Florida Rangers, Panton was authorized to manage East Florida's Indian trade. The province's boundaries counted for little as far as Indian commerce was concerned. Panton trafficked with Seminoles, Creeks, Cherokees, and any other Southern Indians in East Florida, Georgia, or South Carolina. Most southern Indians sided with Britain during the Revolution, and, as George III's loyal subject, Panton resolved to use the natives to help crush the rebellion and punish those who had confiscated his property and forced him into exile.[17]

The principal undertaking that Panton, Miller, and Bowles had in common was trading with the southern Indians, and again it is necessary to take a closer look at this commerce. The area involved was enormous, embracing much of the region between the Appalachian Mountains and the Mississippi River and south of the Ohio River — the Old Southwest as it came to be known after 1783. For the most part this was Indian country, and the tens of thousands of Indians involved were commercial hunters, ranging hundreds of miles over the Old Southwest and at times crossing the Mississippi in quest of furs and skins. The white man's powder, guns, and much more were essential to the natives. After they returned to their villages from winter hunts lasting months, the local factor exchanged manufactures for furs and skins, and made the latter up into packs which in time were sent away to the coast by packhorse trains. Though some ports were more convenient than others, it did not make much difference whether it was Charleston, Savannah, St. Augustine, Pensacola, or Mobile. Before the Revolution, Charleston — and to a lesser extent Savannah — dominated southern Indian commerce. Most of the South Carolina and Georgia Indian traders were loyalists who, like Panton, fled either to East or West Florida. They continued trading with the southern Indians, the main difference being that peltry was exported from St. Augustine or Pensacola in the loyal Floridas.[18]

In the long run, Pensacola replaced Charleston as the most important port for the southern Indian trade. One indication of this is the career of John Stuart, Britain's Indian superintendent for the Southern Department, the region south of the Ohio River. Before the Revolution, Stuart lived in one of Charleston's finest houses, but when hostilities broke out Stuart, like many others, sought refuge in East Florida. He subsequently made his way to Pensacola where he remained until his death in 1779.[19] The point to keep in mind is that it was possible for Stuart to supervise and trade with the southern Indians from either Charleston or Pensacola. After Stuart's death, Britain divided the Southern Indian Department. The western division included the Chickasaws and Choctaws, and Pensacola was the key port; the eastern division incorporated the Creeks and Cherokees whose goods came from St. Augustine or some other convenient port on the Atlantic coast.[20]

Panton took advantage of the fact that Britain had decreed that half of the goods for the southern Indians must be funneled through St. Augustine or some other port on the Atlantic coast and that his friend, Thomas Brown, was Indian superintendent for the eastern division. For an interval it appeared that Panton would not have to stay in East Florida, because British forces, including provincial troops and Indians, recaptured most of Georgia and returned the royal governor to Savannah. Panton moved back to Georgia, served as a member of the representative assembly, and continued trafficking with the Indians.[21] But Cornwallis's surrender at Yorktown in 1781, shattered Britain's hopes of retaining the thirteen colonies. Even before signing the definitive peace treaty in 1783, Britain evacuated Charleston and Savannah. As a result, William Panton, his friend Superintendent Thomas Brown, and other loyalists returned to East Florida. Once again Panton found himself in St. Augustine, still trading with as many of the southern Indians as possible, supplying the needs of the white populace through his store in St. Augustine,[22] but realizing that his Georgia exile was permanent.

That Britain had lost the war was reflected in the general peace settlement of 1783, when she not only conceded independence to the American colonies but also relinquished title to East and West Florida. This had little effect on West Florida, because by 1783,

Gálvez had already captured it; but for East Florida, still under British control and swarming with loyalists, it was another matter. Panton, like most loyalists, wanted to remain in America, certainly until he had restored his fortune. The way to achieve this was to do what he knew best: trade with the Indians. As well as anyone, he realized that Indians were addicted to and dependent on the white man's goods. Enormous profits lay waiting, and even though Spanish forces were planning to sail over to St. Augustine from Cuba, Panton realized that with foresight and luck he might turn his misfortunes to advantage.

The immediate issue in 1783 was who was going to furnish goods to the southern Indians. Pensacola's fall had meant that Britain's Indian superintendents no longer could use that port as a center to trade with and manage the natives. As British forces in the South suffered repeated setbacks, a commercial vacuum had developed among the Indians. Relying on Spanish or French merchants, Gálvez, with little success, had tried to ensure that manufactures continued to reach Indian villages. Yet in 1783 a commercial void still existed.[23] Panton's solution was for him and his associates to remain in Florida with Spanish approval and to continue trading with the Indians. All three—Spain, the natives, and Panton and his loyalist associates—held in common a resolve to check the expansion of aggressive American republicans. Panton's dream, which largely came true, was to expand his trade with the Indians from his base in East Florida so that with Spain's blessing it included most of the Old Southwest.

He and his loyalist partners—John Leslie, Thomas Forbes, Charles McLatchy, and William Alexander—saw their chance. Despite the slowness of eighteenth-century communications, they were remarkably effective on both sides of the Atlantic as they negotiated with the Spanish and British governments and pressed their case among the natives in the interior. Leslie remained in St. Augustine where he and, until his departure in 1785, Thomas Brown courted the new Spanish governor with felicitous rhetoric and money, explaining how only their loyalist friends were able to supply the southern Indians and keep them contented and in Spain's interest.[24] Forbes went to London and made the same arguments to the Spanish ambassador.[25] In 1783, McLatchy moved to the vicinity of the abandoned fort at St. Marks Apalachee where he could better trade with the more westerly Indians, and he hoped that Spain would condone his activities or at least close one eye.[26] Panton himself, in 1784, joined the exodus from East Florida to the Bahamas, and Nassau became the center of his firm's operations. From this British port, if Spain agreed, he could trade legally with the southern Indians, or, if Spain proved uncooperative, he could conveniently smuggle wares over to the mainland.[27]

All signs indicated that Spain would cooperate. She allowed Leslie to stay in St. Augustine, McLatchy in St. Marks, and most important of all, she permitted Panton to move to Pensacola and establish a warehouse. In time these concessions were extended to Mobile, the Mississippi River, and elsewhere, as Spain in effect conceded Panton, Leslie, and Company a monopoly of trading with almost all Indians of the Old Southwest. Forbes returned from London to replace Panton in Nassau; other members of his firm supervised warehouses on the St. Johns River, at St. Marks, and on the Mississippi River. Panton's residence in Pensacola had much to do with the fact that after the Revolution that port replaced Charleston as the center of the southern Indian trade. Obviously Panton was pleased.[28]

Miller, however, was furious. At the end of the Revolution the Indian commerce of the Old Southwest had been up for grabs — a game of musical chairs with only one chair. When the music stopped, Panton sat in that chair, and it was located in Pensacola. Miller, Bowles, and Panton's other rivals, wringing their hands, were left standing. When Panton moved from East Florida to Pensacola he assumed Miller's and John McGillivray's former trade. Miller understood what was happening, but for a time imprisoned by Spain, he was almost powerless. Miller had pinned his hopes on Britain rather than Spain; he hoped that at the end of the Revolution Britain would end up with both Floridas and, like Canada in the north, use them as a refuge for loyalist exiles. If this happened, as for a time seemed possible, Miller might return to West Florida and resume his career interrupted by Gálvez.[29] None of this came to pass, and after Spain released him, he returned to Nassau near the end of 1784.

Panton had stolen a march on Miller. Even so, Miller might have his day, reestablish himself in West Florida, and get back at both Panton and Spain. There were several courses of action: one was to discredit Panton, Leslie and Company and force Spain to turn to Miller and his associates. Miller's old friends from British West Florida, Arthur Strother and James Mather, already had won permission from the Spanish governor in New Orleans to import Indian goods into Spanish West Florida. During the 1780s, Panton battled furiously with Strother and Mather over the West Florida Indian trade, and, briefly, Strother and Mather seemed to have the upper hand. Panton relied on his influence with the Spanish governor of East Florida, while Strother and Mather looked to the Spanish governor in New Orleans. In the end Panton won out. Miller was closely associated with Strother and Mather, but the degree of their collaboration in the 1780s is unclear.[30] There were other ways for Miller to retaliate against Panton. Miller could send out his own vessels from Nassau to trade clandestinely with the southern Indians; at the same time he could prod Britain to use force or diplomacy to expel Spain and its minions, Panton, Leslie and Company, from the Floridas and install Miller and his friends in their stead.

Miller began smuggling goods into the Floridas, which, considering their extensive coastline, was easy enough. Nassau was important to both Miller and Panton: manufactures destined for the southern Indians passed through the Bahamas as did deerskins exported from the mainland en route to Britain. Panton rather than Miller, of course, was entrenched in Pensacola, yet Miller enjoyed advantages by remaining in Nassau. As a member of the council he was influential in the government, and at one point he was considered for lieutenant governor. More important was that his friend and fellow Scot, Lord Dunmore, became governor in 1786. They held common views about profits awaiting on the mainland from the Indian trade, about kicking both Spain and Panton out of the Floridas, and about having Britain control all the Mississippi Valley from the Gulf Coast to Canada.[31] Panton, Leslie and Company was an obstacle, a competitor — an enemy. Miller and his friends feuded with Thomas Forbes and Panton's other partisans in Nassau. Miller's party was the Old Settler faction, while Forbes's friends were known as the New Settlers. One could follow the strife in the Nassau legislature and newspapers and also in London as both Miller and Forbes periodically went there to present their case and malign their rivals.[32]

When it extended to the Floridas, the two main protagonists of this conflict were William Panton and William Augustus Bowles. After Gálvez had captured Pensacola, Bowles had gone first to New York and then to the Bahamas. From time to time one catches glimpses of him in the Bahamas as he acquired land, acted, painted, and made voyages over to the mainland. We can only assume that Bowles had originally met Miller in Pensacola and renewed his friendship in Nassau after the war. Miller's first step in getting back at Panton and reestablishing himself as a dominant figure in the southern Indian trade was, in defiance of Panton and Spain, to trade clandestinely with the Florida Indians. Miller therefore turned to Bowles who, he knew, had contacts with the Indians, a native family, and aspirations of becoming a ruler, director-general, potentate, or whatever over the Indians. The firm of Miller, Bonamy, and Company supplied Bowles with trading goods, while councilman Miller and Governor Dunmore helped Bowles organize expeditions which, on several occasions in the 1780s and 1790s, sailed over to the Floridas to the great annoyance of Spain and Panton.[33]

Before 1781, both Miller and Panton—especially Miller—had many commercial dealings with the McGillivrays: Lachlan, John, Daniel, Alexander, and others. Alexander McGillivray, born in the Upper Creek country, was one of Lachlan's mestizo offspring. After the Revolution, Alexander asserted he was the principal chief or spokesman for all the Creeks, and, though he exaggerated, his influence was considerable. During the Revolution, when they were in East Florida, Panton and Superintendent Brown had employed Alexander as a commissary among the Upper Creeks, and when Panton moved to Pensacola he still looked to Alexander, making him an associate in his firm. During the 1780s, Bowles and Miller attempted to lure Alexander away from Panton, and for a time Alexander wavered.[34] But in the long run, the efforts of Panton, Leslie, and Thomas Brown, along with presents and emoluments bestowed by Spain, outweighed the arguments and trading goods of Bowles and Miller. McGillivray, like Panton, became Bowles's bitter enemy in Florida; the fact that both Bowles and McGillivray had served together in the British defense of Pensacola counted for little.

Gálvez's conquest of West Florida transformed the careers of our three subjects, forcing them either to leave the province or, in Panton's case, creating a situation where for the first time it seemed appropriate to move there. By considering the effects of the explosion in the Queen's Redoubt and the sweeping changes of the ensuing general peace, we can readily understand why Panton's house, rather than Miller's, was the biggest in Pensacola. Panton's impressive residence, which was also a warehouse, long stood, remaining intact until 1848, well into the American period, when it burned. According to tradition, when Alexander McGillivray died in 1793, he was buried in Panton's garden. There is some question about this, but there is no doubt that Alexander was not laid to rest in John Miller's garden. Before 1781, Miller had been the most prominent Scottish merchant in Pensacola with a McGillivray connection; after 1781, it was Panton.

Bowles had been in Pensacola when the Queen's Redoubt exploded, though he did not remain in the West Florida capital long after Gálvez's triumph. It was not that he did not aspire to come back, either leading the forces of Muskogee to seize Pensacola or maneuvering to have Spain replace Panton with Bowles and Miller. Although, in the long run, Bowles failed in every respect, he did almost return to Pensacola in 1792, as he was sailing from St. Marks to New Orleans. He had captured Panton's warehouse in Apalachee, and Spain wondered if Panton, Leslie and Company was losing its grip on the Indians. Bowles asserted that it was in Spain's interest to employ him and Miller rather than Panton. Spanish authorities in West Florida and Spain did not trust Bowles and the Scottish merchants associated with him, but neither did they trust Panton and his fellow Scots. The Spaniards were never sure whether to take Bowles's arguments seriously and treat him as the true leader of the southern Indians—the State of Muskogee—or to accept Panton's denunciations that Bowles was a thief, that the Indians called him "captain liar," and that he should be disposed of like a common criminal. In 1795, largely because of international changes stemming from the French Revolution, Panton had his way, and Spain sent Bowles as a prisoner from Madrid to the Philippines. This exile did not last; Bowles escaped and returned to Florida. Between 1799 and 1803, the polyglot army and navy of his State of Muskogee harassed the Spaniards, seizing their ships and capturing the fort at St. Marks. All the while, General Bowles was squinting at Pensacola.[35] Miller, who was in London, pressed on the government the importance to Britain of the Floridas and of Bowles's enterprises.[36] Ultimately Spain recaptured Bowles, closely confining him in Havana's Morro prison where, in 1805, he died.

Panton had met his end four years earlier. Sick and somewhat discouraged, in 1801, he sailed from Pensacola for the Bahamas; he succumbed near Berry Island before reaching Nassau.[37]

Miller, who was in the Bahamian capital, never saw Panton, and we can only guess at his reaction to Panton's death. Perhaps there was sympathy for a fellow Scottish loyalist whose life had been uprooted by the American Revolution; probably there was bitterness and envy that the largest house in Pensacola was Panton's and not Miller's.

Panton was gone, but his partners, relatives, in-laws and associates kept the firm alive, and as always Pensacola remained the focal point. The reorganized firm, first under the leadership of John Forbes and later under that of the Innerarities, continued in operation until the mid-nineteenth century. Despite the confiscation of his property and his exile from South Carolina and Georgia, at the end of the Revolution Panton had seen his opportunity, outwitted his rivals, and firmly planted himself in Pensacola. His successors, displaying the same business acumen, willing to accommodate new friends and to abandon—some might say sell out—old ones, collaborated as circumstances dictated with Catholic Spaniards, American republicans, anxious Indians, forces of His Britannic Majesty, or whoever. The firm long prospered, or at least endured, and one cannot comprehend the history of Pensacola without taking William Panton into account. Bowles died in 1805, but he too left a legacy, that of a pro-British Indian protectorate on the Gulf Coast. For a period in 1814—when British troops in Pensacola were arming and drilling southern Indians—it seemed that Bowles's dream might be realized. But Jackson defeated the British forces and put an end to that. It was Panton, not Bowles or Miller, who in the long run made the greatest impact on the port of Pensacola and on its hinterland.

---

*Professor of History, Florida State University, Tallahassee, Florida.

[1] Lydia Parrish Papers, Harvard College Library (microfilm Florida State University Library), 404-08.

[2] Robert R. Rea and Milo B. Howard, Jr., eds., *The Minutes, Journals, and Acts of the General Assembly of British West Florida* (University, Ala., 1979), 246.

[3] Ibid., 394; West Florida council minutes, Oct. 3, 1777, C.O. 5/631.

[4] See West Florida Papers, Library of Congress (microfilm Florida State University Library); Andrew Rainsford, Alexander McCullagh, and David Holmes to Charles Stuart, Pensacola, May 3, 1779; C.O. 5/80.

[5] Lachlan McGillivray's affidavit, May 21, 1784, Audit Office 13/26, no. 1528, f. 560, PRO.

[6] Brief of proofs taken . . . 1780-81, Papers Relating to West Florida, 1763-82,

George Chalmers Papers, New York Public Library.

[7] Entries dated Nov. 1774, Mar. 1777, Oct. 1777, Dec. 1777, Jan. 1778, Jan. 1775, Mar. 1776, Dec. 1776, West Florida Papers, reel 3; and Nov. 6, 1776, Feb. 15, 1776, Feb. 9, 1776, Feb. 10, 1776, ibid., reel 4.

[8] D. Clayton James, *Antebellum Natchez* (Baton Rouge, 1968), 19.

[9] Miller to Lord Sydney, Middle Temple, May 3, 1787, Liverpool Papers, Additional MSS. 38222, British Library, London. The best account of the Revolution in West Florida is J. Barton Starr, *Tories, Dons, and Rebels: The American Revolution in British West Florida* (Gainesville, 1976).

[10] Miller memorial, New Providence, July 24, 1782, Sir Guy Carleton Papers, PRO (microfilm, Florida State University Library), no. 10,000; memorial of A. Warwick and John Morris, n.d., ibid., no. 10,044.

[11] J. Leitch Wright, Jr., *William Augustus Bowles: Director General of the Creek Nation* (Athens, 1967), 1-11.

[12] Benjamin Baynton, *Authentic Memoirs of William Augustus Bowles, Esquire, Ambassador from the United Nations of Creeks and Cherokees, to the Court of London* (1791, reprint ed., New York, 1971), 6-14.

[13] Ibid., 25.

[14] Wright, *Bowles*, 16-25.

[15] William S. Coker and Thomas D. Watson, "Narrative History of Panton, Leslie, and Company," MS, John C. Pace Library, University of West Florida, 21-27.

[16] Journal of council of safety, June 26, 1776, Allen D. Chandler, ed., *The Revolutionary Records of the State of Georgia* (Atlanta, 1908), 1:146.

[17] Patrick Tonyn to Dartmouth, St. Augustine, Feb. 26, 1776, C.O. 5/556; account of rations and rum to Creek and Cherokee Indians, Sept. 6 – Dec. 23, 1783, by Panton, Leslie and Co., Treasury 1/601, PRO.

[18] Verner W. Crane, *The Southern Frontier* (Durham, 1928), 108-36; J. Leitch Wright, Jr., *The Only Land They Knew: The Tragic Story of the American Indians in the Old South* (New York, 1981), 126-75.

[19] John R. Alden, *John Stuart and the Southern Colonial Frontier: A Study of Indian Relations, War, Trade, and Land Problems in the Southern Wilderness, 1754-1775* (Ann Arbor, 1944), 170-71.

[20] Alexander Cameron and Charles Stuart to John Campbell, Pensacola, March 26, 1779, C.O. 5/50; Germain to Henry Clinton, Whitehall, June 25, 1779, Sir Henry Clinton Papers, William L. Clements Library, Ann Arbor, Mich.

[21] Proceedings and minutes of governor and council of Georgia, May 5, 1780, *Georgia Historical Quarterly* 35 (1951):150.

[22] *East Florida Gazette*, Feb. 22 – Mar. 1, 1783.

[23] Arthur P. Whitaker, ed. and trans., *Documents Relating to the Commercial Policy of Spain in the Floridas, with Incidental Reference to Louisiana* (Deland, 1931), xxvi-xxx.

[24] Randy F. Nimnicht, "William Panton: His Early Career on the Changing Frontier" (M.A. thesis, University of Florida, 1968), 71-73.

[25] Forbes to Bernardo del Campo, London, Sept. 28, 1783; John W. Caughey, ed., *East Florida, 1783-1785. A File of Documents Assembled and Many of Them Translated by Joseph Byrne Lockey* (Berkeley, 1949), 161; petition of Forbes to George III, London, July 15, 1785, Chatham Papers, 223, PRO.

[26] McLatchy to Arturo O'Neill, Apalachey, Mar. 4, 1784, AGI, PC, leg. 36:955.

[27] Coker and Watson, "Panton, Leslie and Company," 46.

[28] Details of Panton's arrival in Pensacola and the development of his firm are in the Panton, Leslie Papers, John C. Pace Library, University of West Florida. This extensive collection eventually will be available on microfilm.

[29] Petition of merchants formerly trading to West Florida, London, Oct. 31, 1782, Shelburne Papers, 66:771-73, William L. Clements Library.

[30] Ibid.; Arthur P. Whitaker, *The Spanish-American Frontier, 1783-1795: The Westward Movement and the Spanish Retreat in the Mississippi Valley* (Gloucester, 1962), 41-42.

[31] J. Leitch Wright, Jr., *Britain and the American Frontier, 1783-1815* (Athens, 1975), 47-49.

[32] John Miller and legislative committee of correspondence memorial, New Providence, June 17, 1785, Board of Trade 6/263, PRO (microfilm Panton, Leslie Papers); see also Thelma Peters, "The American Loyalists and the Plantation Period in the Bahama Islands" (Ph.D. dissertation, University of Florida, 1960).

[33] Wright, *Bowles*, 30-67.

[34] Whitaker, *Spanish-American Frontier*, 112.

[35] Wright, *Bowles*, 115ff.

[36] Miller to Hobart, London, June 22, 1802, C.O. 23/42.

[37] Marie T. Greenslade, "William Panton," *Florida Historical Quarterly* 14 (1935):125-28.

SPANISH HISTORIANS AND THE GULF COAST CAMPAIGNS

Light T. Cummins*

Shortly after three o'clock on the afternoon of May 8, 1781, His Britannic Majesty's commander at Pensacola had seen enough of battle and bloodshed. He decided to run up the white flag. Writing to his adversary Don Bernardo de Gálvez, he implored:

> In order to prevent a further Effusion of Blood, I propose to your Excellency a Cessation of Hostilities until to morrow at noon, in which Time Articles of Capitulation shall be considered of & prepared, provided your Excellency is disposed to accede to Terms honourable to the Troops under my Command, and such as may afford Safety, Security and Protection to the Inhabitants.[1]

Thus did General John Campbell surrender and the Gulf Coast campaigns of Bernardo de Gálvez come to an end.

The siege of Pensacola was one of the last major victories for Spanish arms during the long history of Spain's colonial empire in the Americas. It was also of significance in resolving the War of Independence in favor of the United States. Even so, this important chapter of history has yet to receive its full due attention from American historians concerned with the development of the United States. Two major textbooks commonly used in advanced college history classes dealing with the American Revolution make no mention of Bernardo de Gálvez or the battle of Pensacola.[2] Notice of the battle, or even peripheral discussion of the Gulf Coast campaigns, is conspicuously absent from many survey textbooks used in introductory United States history courses.[3]

The historical literature of the last several decades has begun to change this situation. Beginning with John Caughey's monumental work of the late 1920s, concerned specialists have come to appreciate the significant role which Bernardo de Gálvez played in the genesis of the United States of America. As a result of these early studies, Gálvez was chosen as an appropriate subject for inclusion in the *Dictionary of American Biography*.[4] More than a generation of subsequent scholarship, detailed research, and clear writing has expanded our specialized knowledge about the Gulf Coast campaigns of Gálvez. Concerned students and individuals outside the Gulf Coast region (where Gálvez has always been a local historical celebrity) can now take advantage of a rich and growing body of scholarship which will eventually make the name of Bernardo de Gálvez as familiar to the average American as those of Paul Revere, Sam Adams, Baron Pulaski, the Marquis de Lafayette and other heroes of the revolutionary generation.

An examination of these studies reveals that most of them are solidly based on extensive archival research. The work of Caughey, Kathryn Abbey Hanna, John Richard Alden, Samuel Flagg Bemis, James A. James, Cecil Johnson, Lawrence Kinnaird, J. Leitch Wright, Jr., and J. Barton Starr comes to mind. All these scholars, and many others, have added substantially to a more complete understanding of the important role which Spain played in the American Revolution. In so doing, they have naturally highlighted the Gulf Coast campaigns of Bernardo de Gálvez.[5]

Although many of these studies make use of Spanish archival holdings, it is somewhat curious that some of them give little attention to the literature generated by several generations of Spanish historians. Caughey's *Bernardo de Gálvez in Louisiana* pioneered in the use of Spanish manuscripts — while citing only six studies produced by Spanish scholars. More recent studies of Spanish participation in the American Revolution have overlooked this literature. The purpose of this essay is not to criticize an accomplished group of American historians, nor is it to present a detailed bibliographic survey of all works by Spanish historians dealing with either the Revolution, Bernardo de Gálvez, or the Gulf Coast campaigns. That would be an impossible task within the present limits. Instead, it seeks to select some of the major Iberian studies and suggest the general interpretations that Spanish scholars have brought to bear on Bernardo de Gálvez and the Gulf Coast campaigns.

It is the conclusion of this essay that Spanish historians of this century who have written on Spain and the American Revolution fall into two categories based on certain criteria. First, a number of Spanish scholars have approached the topic from what might be styled a peninsular viewpoint, taking as a frame of reference the role which Spain played in world affairs. Those writing with this orientation have been concerned primarily with the sweep of Spanish history in a nationalistic sense. Some, interested in the reforms of Charles III, have looked to the era as a significant period in the history of Spain. It seemed to them to be a period in which national glory and international power were at least partially realized after a long era of decline. The Gulf Coast campaigns and Spanish successes in the wars of the American Revolution played a significant role in this story. It may be noted that most studies exhibiting this viewpoint have had a tendency to use archival sources emanating from the national councils of Spain. The archives at Madrid and Simancas, with the records of the councils of state, have been the special reference of Spanish writing with the peninsular viewpoint.

Second, another group of Spanish scholars writing of the American Revolution and the role which their country played in it have taken a slightly different orientation, although it does not preclude the conclusions of the peninsularists. This group has a Latin American frame of reference. Few of their studies are concerned with the sweep of premier place in European events, or the diplomatic maneuverings of the court of Madrid. Instead, they see Spanish participation in the revolt as an event of more significance to the New World than to Spain. Their perspective is focused on events in the Americas as the decisive part of the drama, rather than as results and by-products of European-motivated policies set in motion at Madrid, London, or Paris.

Some of the most distinguished writing of Spanish historical literature can be found among the works of peninsular-oriented scholars. Their interpretations have influenced much of the conventional wisdom about Spanish participation in the American Revolution. One of the earliest of this viewpoint was the nineteenth-century historian Manuel Dánvila y Collado. His monumental six-volume study of King Charles III set a tone for subsequent analysis of this rather significant monarch and his era. Although this study was based on limited sources and is dated by modern standards, it clearly established the point of departure for most subsequent studies of Spanish international relations during the late eighteenth century. Dánvila y Collado saw Spanish involvement in the Revolution as one interlocking chapter in the complete revitalization of Spanish foreign relations under the Bourbon monarchs. Even though not specifically concerned with the Gulf Coast campaigns, this study created the framework for subsequent scholars dealing with the campaigns of Bernardo de Gálvez.[6]

Rafael Altamira y Crevea, writing in 1911, became one the first Spanish historians to place participation in the English colonial conflict within the peninsular perspective. He saw Spanish reaction to the revolt as part of a grand scheme of diplomatic goals held by Charles III and his court. Altamira emphasized the attempts at mediation sponsored by the Spanish government as proof that the court of Madrid sought to turn the war to its own advantage. The Spanish crown entered the conflict, in 1779, after three unsuccessful attempts to initiate a cease-fire. Altamira realized that Pensacola played a significant role in the Spanish war goals. He took a strong geopolitical view of its importance, noting that "the return of Gibraltar, along with Pensacola, and all of Florida, the restitution of Minorca, the fort at Mobile, the expulsion of the English from Honduras, and also from Campeche" were all equally important war aims for Spain. It is not surprising that he called Bernardo de Gálvez one of the "most determined and fortunate [generals] of the war in America."[7]

Major Spanish historians writing in the peninsular framework during the years prior to World War II expanded on the role which Bernardo de Gálvez played in furthering the concerns of Spanish empire and power in the New World. Gálvez's actions were seen as the successful implementation of a policy formulated and executed at the Spanish court. Antonio Ballesteros y Beretta found this to be young Gálvez's only motivation. Ballesteros portrayed Bernardo as an aggressive commander in the Americas whose successes were of importance, but no more so than those won by a half-dozen other Spanish generals during the wars of the Revolution. Roberto de Rivas Betancourt, José Rosado, Francisco Peneiro, and Bernardo's father Matias also won strategic victories for Spanish arms.[8] Justa de la Villa, writing in the *Diccionario de historia de España*, firmly established Bernardo de Gálvez's status as a significant historical figure for those concerned with Spanish history. She called the taking of Pensacola an heroic act against overwhelming odds. Of Gálvez, she noted: "His triumphs were perhaps the most unique gained by Spain in the North American war of Independence. He was a typical example of the Enlightenment man because of his philanthropic, reforming, and progressive spirit."[9]

One of the first specialized monographs dealing with Spanish participation in the revolt firmly exhibited the peninsular orientation regarding the Gulf Coast campaigns and their role in fulfilling Spain's international policy. This study, written by Manuel Conrotte, in 1920, emphasized the diplomatic significance which Pensacola played in the delicate negotiations between the Continental Congress and the Spanish government. He detailed the work of Juan de Miralles in attempting to arrange at the Congress for a joint conquest of the British garrisons in Florida. So concerned was Conrotte about the diplomatic role of Pensacola in Spanish policy that he deemphasized the actual taking of the location by Bernardo de Gálvez.[10]

The first peninsular-oriented study of Spanish participation to devote an extensive amount of its narrative to an analysis of Bernardo de Gálvez was *España ante la independencia de los Estados Unidos*, by Juan F. Yela Utrilla. Although dated and surpassed by subsequent scholarship in English, this work still remains today one of the most useful and complete Spanish language studies of Spain's role in the American Revolution.[11] Yela Utrilla made extensive use of sources at the *Archivo Histórico Nacional* and the *Archivo General de Indias*. Unlike earlier studies, his examination of Spanish involvement focused on Louisiana and the role that province played in the war.

This study began as Yela Utrilla's doctoral thesis at the University of Madrid, in 1922, where he worked under the direction of the distinguished historians Eduardo Ibarra Rodríquez and Antonio Ballesteros y Beretta. The author spent several years expanding his documentary base before publication. His two volumes present a narrative analysis of Spain's role in the revolt, along with a documentary section which contains relevant sources drawn primarily from the archives of Madrid, Simancas, and Sevilla.

España ante la independencia de los Estados Unidos was the first Spanish study to give equal weight to European diplomatic negotiations and to events in the New World, especially along the Gulf Coast in Louisiana and Florida. One entire section of the study deals with events in New Orleans and the activities of Bernardo de Gálvez. Yela Utrilla placed special emphasis on the relationship between Oliver Pollock, the North American merchant, and the Louisiana govenor. "Gálvez did not only protect the Americans in New Orleans," Yela Utrilla noted, "but he also gave them supplies."[12] Although this study was the first to emphasize the New World complexities of Spain's participation in the revolt, it viewed Bernardo de Gálvez primarily as the local agent of Spanish imperial power and policy. It failed to consider factors rooted in the Americas which influenced the Gulf Coast campaigns. Frequent contact between Spaniards and American rebels, intraregional rivalry between English and Spanish citizens along the Gulf Coast, and the personal motivations of Bernardo de Gálvez, spurred on by his uncle José, were all ignored by Yela Utrilla. Like other peninsularist studies, this one tended to overlook the details of the battles fought by Gálvez and to emphasize instead the significance of the campaigns in relationship to general Spanish diplomatic policy.

More recent studies by Spanish historians have continued this interpretive school of historical literature. Fernando de Armas Medina, in a study of Louisiana and Florida during the reign of Charles III, termed the taking of Pensacola the single most important military objective gained by Spain. He chronicled the campaigns commanded by Gálvez, noting the victories at Manchac, Baton Rouge, and Mobile. Pensacola's fall to the Spanish completed the successful achievement of Spain's war aims.[13] Armas Medina based his assessment on accounts and sources contained in the *Documentos históricos de la Florida y la Luisiana*, published in 1912, particularly the *"Relación de la Campaña que hizó don Bernardo de Gálvez contra los ingleses en la Luisiana."* Spanish students of the Gulf Coast campaigns were considerably assisted in 1959 with the publication of a full version of Bernardo de Gálvez's diary of operations at Pensacola. Although Gálvez's diary first saw publication in 1781, it was not widely disseminated to the Spanish scholarly community until the 1950s when, through the interest of the Madrid publisher José Porrua Turanzas, it was made available in an inexpensive and accurate edition.[14] Although technically a primary source for historians, most Spaniards concerned with the Gulf Coast campaigns place heavy reliance on Gálvez's own account of the battle of Pensacola.

In the mid-1970s, the Commission for Cultural Exchange between the United States and Spain sponsored an ambitious and successful scholarly project to mark the bicentennial celebration. This project, in addition to providing funds for publication of an extensive guide to Spanish archival holdings relating to the United States, also underwrote individual scholarly projects seeking to examine the role which Spain played in the American Revolution. From this project has emerged the most complete and best documented peninsular-oriented study of Spanish participation in the revolt. María Pilar Ruígomez de Hernandez's *El gobierno español del despotismo ilustrado ante la independencia de los Estados Unidos de América* is a successful effort to assess the complex diplomatic negotiations which propelled Spain into the war and which determined the nature of Spanish participation.

Based on research in the archives of Madrid and Simancas, the author has surveyed and considered almost all of the relevant secondary literature published both in the Spanish and English languages. She views the American Revolution as the first stage in an era of revolution, a period in which Spain played a signal role. Heavily influenced by the French *annales* school, her study attempts to place Spanish involvement in the Revolution within the broad context of economic, political, social, cultural, and ideological concerns. Her narrative blends together political, institutional, and diplomatic themes which center on the problems in policy-formation faced by Charles III and his ministers. In so doing, she considers the commercial relationships Spain maintained in the late eighteenth century, the goals of enlightened thinkers, Franco-Spanish relations, and Anglo-Hispanic rivalries. The Mississippi Valley and the Gulf Coast become for her a regional microcosm where these forces play against one another during the American Revolution. The Gulf Coast campaigns thus become the method whereby Spain sought to regain control of the "American Mediterranean." In the middle of these powerful international forces stood Bernardo de Gálvez, the New World representative of Spanish imperial policy. Giving little support to the view that Gálvez's campaigns might be seen as an expansionist move on the part of Spain, the Gulf Coast campaigns are characterized in this study as the "most efficient and decisive form of support which Spain gave to the United States." Ruígomez, in fact, criticizes American Patriot leaders at the Continental Congress for failing to understand the full significance of Gálvez's victories.[15]

Studies which approach the Gulf Coast campaigns from the peninsular orientation might be said to have several common characteristics. First, little attention is given to the battle as an historical event. Discussion of the Gulf Coast campaigns center on their subsequent significance in international relations. Second, Bernardo de Gálvez is almost always portrayed solely as an agent of Spanish policy. His relations with rebel Americans, which were considerable, are ignored as casual factors. Only Yela Utrilla, for example, even notes the activities of Oliver Pollock. Third, the peninsular perspective always stresses what might be termed the global view of the American Revolution as a worldwide war. Some studies expend more effort in placing the Spanish Gulf Coast campaigns in context with other considerations of Spain's military activities than in examining the battles themselves.

A second more recent and comparatively smaller group of Spanish historians has brought a new perspective to the body of historical literature dealing with the Gulf Coast campaigns. Influenced by North American scholars, these studies give greater attention to the actual events of the campaigns. The emphasis is often on Louisiana and Florida as provinces, rather than on implementation of Spanish imperial policy in the region. Indeed, they may be said to have a Latin American rather than a peninsular frame of reference. Much of the scholarship sponsored by the *Escuela de Estudios Hispanoamericanos* in Seville falls within this broad category. In addition, an active group of Spanish historians centered at the University of Zaragoza use the forum of the *Estudios* published by that institution as an organ to disseminate studies of Spanish Louisiana and Florida which consider nonimperial aspects of those colonies.[16]

A good study with which to note this changing orientation is the analysis of Spanish colonial society in the eighteenth century by Mario Hernández Sánchez-Barba as part of the *Historia de España y América: social y económica* directed by Jaime Vicens Vives. Although not specifically concerned with Bernardo de Gálvez's Gulf Coast campaigns, this study made an extensive analysis of American problems in the Indies and assessed historical events of the era in a New World perspective rather than from a peninsular viewpoint.[17] Luis Navarro García of the University of Seville expanded this perspective into a fuller, more complete study of Spanish America in the eighteenth century.

Navarro García, in a short overview of the Gulf Coast campaigns, assigned most of the credit for the military victories to Gálvez personally. He departed from the peninsularist orientation by noting that, at least in terms of diplomatic support and material assistance provided by Spain, the Spanish court was not as generous with the rebel Americans as it might have been. Bernardo de Gálvez thus remains the most supportive figure of Spanish involvement as far as the American rebels were concerned.[18]

Additional studies, some not specifically concerned with the Gulf Coast campaigns but with larger related topics, have carried forward this orientation. Carlos M. Fernandez Shaw's *Presencia española en los Estados Unidos*, written in 1972, serves as a good example. Within the last ten years, some Spanish scholars working from a nonpeninsular perspective have begun to consider the problems of Florida and Louisiana during the American Revolution. Juan José Andreu Ocariz has examined Spanish Louisiana from this point of view. He concentrated almost entirely on nonimperial matters in assessing the Gulf Coast campaigns. He stressed the boundary problems between neighboring Spanish and English provinces and the pressures placed on both by the American rebels in the Mississippi Valley. He also noted the influence of commercial considerations in motivating Anglo-Spanish rivalry in the region. Unlike studies in the peninsular orientation, Andreu Ocariz devoted a good deal of effort to assessing the internal development of Louisiana in setting the stage for a discussion of the colony's role in the revolution. "The war was popular among the Louisiana Creoles," he noted, "and this allowed the Governor to count on their cooperation from its beginning." He commented also on the role which Spanish Indian allies played in the campaigns: "Gálvez developed an active Indian policy which brought him a certain measure of success." In perhaps the greatest departure from the peninsular interpretation, Andreu Ocariz frankly admitted that although the Gulf Coast campaigns were of immense regional significance to the stablization of the American west, they were of "secondary importance to the war" as far as Spain was concerned.[19]

Studies which focus even more closely on events in the Gulf Coast area are being produced by Spanish scholars at an expanding rate. José Montero de Pedro, marqués de Casa Mena, has been influenced by North American scholarship. His recent volume *Españoles en Nueva Orleans y Luisiana* is a fine example of a nonpeninsular view of the Gulf Coast campaigns. He details the events with some attention, and his treatment of Bernardo de Gálvez and the battle of Pensacola certainly places him among recent scholars writing with the Hispanic-American orientation. He said of the victor at Pensacola:

> Gálvez is the star figure, not only in the historical galaxy of Spanish Louisiana, but also in the much larger and general firmament of our participation in the genesis of the United States. This Spanish governor had a decisive role in that undertaking, and unfortunately has not been recognized and appreciated as he should have been.[20]

Other studies of the last several years have also placed greater emphasis on the career of Gálvez. José Rudolfo Boeta's biographical analysis examined the Louisiana governor's character in addition to recounting his accomplishments.[21] The net result of these studies is the elevation of Bernardo de Gálvez from a mere agent of Spanish empire to a significant figure in the development of a new historical era. Perhaps the marqués Casa Mena expressed this most concisely when he wrote: "Without a doubt because of his accomplishments Gálvez merits a place of honor in the history of the Americas and must be considered . . . as the most valiant friend that the United States has had in the course of her history."[22]

It may be said that the Latin American interpretation has several characteristics which distinguish it from the peninsular orientation. First, it emphasizes the role of events in the Americas apart from their contributions to the aims of Spanish international policy and the diplomatic goals of the Revolution. Factors of personality, commerce, geopolitical pressures in the region, Indian relations, and contact with rebel Americans are considered as important factors influencing the Gulf Coast campaigns. Second, these studies generally use a broader base of primary and secondary sources, often with heavy reliance on studies by North American scholars. Third, it seems that since the bicentennial celebration, the prevailing orientation of Spanish scholars falls within the nonpeninsular framework. Indeed, the recent study of José de Ezpeleta by Padre Francisco de Borja Medina may be seen as the most recent contribution to this growing interpretive school. Although Spanish historical literature has yet to produce a major monographic study of the Gulf Coast campaigns of Bernardo de Gálvez, North American historians now have available to them a rich and expanding series of works by Spanish historians dealing with Spain's participation in the American Revolution.

*Chairman, Department of History, Austin College, Sherman, Texas

[1] John W. Caughey, *Bernardo de Gálvez in Louisiana, 1776-1783* (1934; reprint ed. Gretna, La., 1972), 210.
[2] Oscar T. Barck, Jr., and Hugh T. Lefler, *Colonial America*, 2d ed. (New York, 1968); Curtis P. Nettles, *The Roots of American Civilization* (New York, 1938).
[3] Richard N. Current, *et al.*, *American History: A survey*, 4th ed. (New York, 1975); Dexter Perkins and Glyndon G. Van Deusen, *The United States of America: A History to 1876* (New York, 1968); Robert Kelley, *The Shaping of the American Past* (Englewood Cliffs, N.J., 1978).
[4] The sketch was prepared by Arthur P. Whitaker, Gálvez is also noted in Mark M. Boatner III, *Encyclopedia of the American Revolution* (New York, 1966), 410.
[5] The two most recent studies are J. Leitch Wright, Jr., *Florida in the American Revolution* (Gainesville, 1975); J. Barton Starr, *Tories, Dons, and Rebels: The American Revolution in British West Florida* (Gainesville, 1976).
[6] Manuel Dánvila y Collado, *Reinado de Carlos III*, 6 vols. (Madrid, 1893-1896).
[7] Rafael Altamira y Crevea, *Historia de España y de la civilización española* (Barcelona, 1911), 4:69.
[8] Antonio Ballesteros y Beretta, *Historia de España y su influencia en la historia universal*, 9 vols. (2d ed.; Barcelona, 1943-53).
[9] Justa de La Villa, "Bernardo de Gálvez," *Diccionario de historia de España desde sus orígenes hasta el fin del reinado de Alfonso XIII* (Madrid, 1952), 1:1198-99.
[10] Manuel Conrotte, *La intervención de España en la independencia de la América del Norte* (Madrid, 1920).
[11] Juan F. Yela Utrilla, *España ante la independencia de los Estados Unidos*, 2 vols. (2d ed.; Lerida, 1925).
[12] Ibid., 1:110.
[13] Fernando de Armas Medina, "Luisiana y Florida en el reinado de Carlos III," *Estudios Americanos* 19 (1960):67-92.
[14] Bernardo de Gálvez, *Diario de las operaciones de la expedición contra la Plaza de Panzacola concluidas por las armas de S.M. Católica baxo las ordenes del Mariscal de Campo Don Bernardo de Gálvez* (Madrid, 1959).
[15] María Pilar Ruígomez de Hernandez, *El Gobierno español del despotismo il-*

ustrado ante la independencia de los Estados Unidos de América: una nueva estructura de la política internacional 1773-1783 (Madrid, 1978), 307, 309.

[16]Fernando Solano Costa, "*Preocupaciones economicas y militares de O'Reilly en el gobierno de la Luisiana,*" *Estudios* (1977), 7-16; Jesús Lorente Miguel, "*El comercio exterior de la Luisiana, 1775-1783,*" *Estudios* (1977), 17-24; Juan José Andreu Ocariz, "*Los intentos de separación de la capitania general de Luisiana de la Cuba,*" *Estudios* (1978), 397-431; José Antonio Armillas Vicente, "*Europa y la revolución americana; un nuevo mito,*" *Estudios* (1976), 61-77.

[17]Mario Hernández Sánchez-Barba, "*Las Indias en el siglo XVIII,*" *Historia de España y América: social y economica,* ed. Jaime Vicens Vives, 4:261-460.

[18]Luis Navarro García *Hispanoamerica en el siglo XVIII* (Seville, 1957), 140-41.

[19]Juan José Andreu Ocariz, "*Luisiana española,*" *Estudios,* pt. 2 (1974), 161-92, 174, 176.

[20]José Montero de Pedro, marqués de Casa Mena, *Españoles en Nueva Orleans y Luisiana* (Madrid, 1979), 34-35.

[21]José Rudolfo Boeta, *Bernardo de Gálvez* (Madrid, 1977); Guillermo Porras Muñoz, "*Bernardo de Gálvez,*" *Miscelanea americanista* 3 (1952):575-619; Isidro Vazquez Acuña, "*El conde de Gálvez,*" *Revista historia militar* 5 (1961):51-89; Sebastián Souviron, *Bernardo de Gálvez, virrey de Méjico* (Malaga, 1947).

[22]Casa Mena, *Españoles in Nueva Orleans,* 36.

INDEX

Aguas Frías, 5
Alabama River, 59, 91
Alderete, Miguel (Cdr.), 129-130, 133-134, 137; captures *Port Royal*, 135; plans naval bombardment, 138; promotion for, 139, 142n22
Alexander, William, 186
Alligator (Creek leader), 23
Alston, John (Olsen, Jean), 163, 175n36, 175n41
Álvarez, Eugenio, 161, 163
Álvarez, Julián (Lt.), 153
Amherst, Jeffrey, 85
Amite River, 42
Amoss, James, 30
Apalache: 190; destruction of, 18, 186; detachments at, 22, 150; trade, 60. See San Marcos de
Apalachicola River: 21; divides East and West Florida, 17; Indians offer land on, 21; Indian settlements along the, 18
Aragón, Francisco (Ensign), 152
Aristizábal, Gabriel de, 128-129; Admiral, 140n8; sights the *Ulysses*, 134;
Arkansas Post, 8, 161, 165, 167, 169; attacked, 11, 158, 171; boats and soldiers arrive to reinforce the, 163, 166; seizure of, 160, 167, 169-70; threatened, 158, 160;
Arkansas River, 5, 163, 168-170
Arnold, Benedict, 154n6
Atkin, Edmond, 76
Aubry, Phillipe, Gov., 26
Augusta, 65, 72, 87, 103, 179; British capture of, 67; traders from, 91
Autrán de la Torre, Pedro (Capt.), 128, 138

Bahamas: 18, 180, 188, 190-191; British loyalists move to, 181, 183, 187; canoes voyage to the, 20;
La Bahía, 157n52
Balderrama, Andrés de (Lt.), 28
Balize, 27, 37
Barbour, Philip, 47

Barrancas Coloradas (Red Cliffs): 112-113, 115, 136; attack on, 110, 131-33, 137; battery on, 109, 114, 116, 130, 135, 146; deserters from, 111; occupied by Spanish troops, 120
Barrancas de Margot: expedition to, 11; troops and Indians at, 4;
Barrow, Robert, 30
Bartram, William, 20-21
Basset (merchant), 33
Bassot, Juan Antonio, 153
Baton Rouge: 46, 145, 149, 152-154, 159, 180, 199; strengthened, 8
Baynton, Wharton and Morgan, 30, 45
Bayou Manchac, 47
Bayou St. John, 26, 35
Beekman, New York house of, 26
Benjamin, Samuel, 175n41
Berry Islands, 190
Bethune, Farquhar, 173n3; Choctaw agent, 95-100, 102
Billet, Anselmo, 171
Bird, Henry, 7; expedition of, 9
Blackwater Bay (Middle River), 42, 135
Blackwell, Jacob, 45
Blanco, Diego (Sub.-Lt.), 164
Blommart, John, 162-63, 167, 169, 175n36, 175n41; arrested, 159
Boiderut (Boiderant) Mr. de, 143n39
Bon Secour Bay, 115
Bonet, Juan Bautista (Adm.), 126-27, 140n6; on flagship *Guerrero*, 134; with expeditionary force, 107, 129;
Bonet, Miguel (Capt.), 140n6
Bote, María, 139n1
Bouligny, Francisco, 25, 35, 44, 153
Bowker, Thomas, 47
Bowles, William Augusta: as ensign, 183; at Queen's Redoubt, 177, 181, 190; A.W.O.L., 182; captures fort at *San Marcos*, 190; death of, 191; in the Bahamas, 181, 188-89; Indian trader, 182, 184, 187, 190
Bradley, John, 30

Bradley, Richard, 52n54
Bright, Lewbridge, 40
Brims (Creek leader), 58-59
Browne, Montfort (Gen.), 180
Brown, Thomas (Col.): 68, 81, 87, 184, 186; Indian Supt. for Atlantic Dist., 67, 82, 92, 103, 185, 189
Bucarelli, Antonio, 28
Burdon, George (Lt.), 35
Burney, Simon, 175n33

Cádiz: 125, 151-53; diaries arrive in, 139; fleet from, 108
Cádiz Bay, 125
Cagigal de la Vega, Francisco Antonio (Gen.), 141n18
Cagigal, Juan Manuel de: 137, 141n18, 143n41, 153; Field Marshal, 118; invasion of Bahamas, 141n18; plans naval bombardment, 138; reconnoitered Fort George, 136; replaces Navia, 129; join Gálvez, 134-35
Cahokia, 8
Caloosahatchee River, 20
Calvé (Indian leader), 9
Calvert, Joseph, 37, 39, 41
Calvo de Irazábal, José (Capt.): 115-116, 123n29, 126-28, 130, 142n22, 142n29, 142n33; commands flotilla, 129; offers sailors, 131; orders ships not to move, 132; sails for Havana, 133
Cameron, Alexander: Ensign in Independent Regulars, 77; returns to Creek country, 87, 102; Supt. Southern Indian Dept., 54, 66-69, 71-72, 76-80, 82-87, 92-103
Campbell, Donald, 52n54
Campbell, James (Maj.), 120
Campbell, John (Gen.): 54, 72, 79-80, 93-94, 96-102, 116, 132, 134, 136, 159, 167; calls for Indian help, 69-71, 86-87; capitulation, 87, 119-21, 132, 138, 194; disagrees with Cameron, 81-84; expedition up the Miss. from Mobile, 7;
policy to Indian auxiliaries, 85-86;y siege of Pensacola, 106, 116, 121, 135-37, 158; using of Indians, 94, 99
Campbell, John, 37-38, 47, 52n54; takes loyalty oath, 39, 41
Campbelltown, 46
Campeche, 17, 26-27, 31, 129, 147; Bank, 127-28
Canada, 15, 180, 187-88; British threat in, 14; troops from, 8
Canary Islands, immigrants organized in, 149; Islanders imported, 4
Cape François, 46
Cape San Antonio, 134
Cape San Blas, 135, 150
Cape Sicié, 125, 142n33
Caribbean: 18, 125-26, 147; French in the, 129; militia units for, 149; provisions brought to ports in, 2; Spanish officials in, 13-14
Carleton, Guy, 5
Carondelet, Baron de, 153
Carpenter, Ephraim, 32
Carradine, Parker, 163
Carrizosa, López, 138-39
Cartabona, Francisco, 10
Casa-Calvo, Marqués de, 153
Castejón, (Marquis de González de), Pedro, 132, 138-39, 142n33
Cayo Sal, 19
Cerré, Gabriel, 5
Chacón, José María (Cdr.), 130
Charleston, 45, 66, 72, 76-77, 179, 183; as a port, 184-85, 187
Charlotte Harbor, 18-20, 23
chasseurs, 118
Chattahoochee River, 59, 182
Chester, Peter (Gov.): 32-33, 38, 43, 60-61; appoints a Board of Indian Commissioners, 79, 82, 92; capitulation, 120; welfare of civilians, 137
Chickasaw Bluffs (Memphis): 171; Colbert at, 161-62, 167; deserted, 163-64, 173n6; rebels at, 164, 168; vessels arrive at, 162

Chickasaw River (*Margot*), 162; rebels on, 166, 170
Chief Angaska (Quapaw), 167
Chief Oja (Sioux), 12
Chief Patrimeny (Quapaw), 175n39
Chief Paulous (Choctaw), 165
Chief Payamataha,(Chickasaw), 160, 165, 171
Clark, George Rogers: 6, 8; aided by Leyba, 5; at the Ohio, 7; captures Kaskaskia, 4; supplies reinforcements for St. Louis, 9
Clark, Malcom, 169, 175n37
Classin, Pedro, 176n43
Clonketin, James, 175n33
Codrington, Edward, 45
Colbert, George, 158
Colbert, James, 101, 158, 171, 176n45
Colbert, James Logan: 160, 164-67, 170-71, 173n3; at Chickasaw Bluffs, 161-62, 168-69; attacks Arkansas Post, 11, 168; Chickasaw deputy, 100-102; demands release of rebels, 163; depredations on the Mississippi, 159; hinders navigation, 11, 161-63; in Mississippi Valley, 158; ordered to turn over prisoners, 170; plundering by, 168; retreats from Arkansas Post, 169; Spanish action against, 164
Colbert, Joseph, 158
Colbert, Levi, 158
Colbert, Samuel, 158
Colbert, William, 158
Collart, (Capt.), 37
Comite River, 45
Comyn, Phillips, 28, 45
Comyn, Stephen, 45
Comyn, Thomas, 28, 45
Comyn, Valens Stephen, 30, 45
Continental Congress, 34, 63, 198, 200
Coosa River, 59, 66
Cornwallis, Lord, 13, 185
Cruzat, Anicanova Ramos de, 161-63, 173n3
Cruzat, Francisco (Lt. Gov.): 9-11, 161-62, 164-66, 173n3; Indian trade, 13; orders attack on St. Joseph, 10-11; receives little support from Headquarters, 12
Cuba: 17-19, 21, 27-28, 126, 133-34, 186; canoe voyages to, 20; trade between, 22, 39-40; troops in, 148
Cusseta, 67

Dalziel, Archibald, 37
Dartmouth, Lord, 33
Dauphin Island, 153, 157n52
Davis, John (Capt.), 43, 45, 47, 52 n54
Deans, Robert, 135
Des Moines River, 5-6
Detroit (*El Estrecho*), 15, 85
Donnithorne, Nicolas, 45
Dorion, Pierre 12
Douget (trader), 10
Dubreuil, Jacobo (Capt.): 170; commandant at Arkansas Post, 166-68; Indians come to assistance of, 169; reinforces St. Geneviève, 164, 173 n6; expedition into Chickasaw territory, 11
Ducharme, Juan María, 8
Dunbar, William, 52n54
Duncomb, David, 40
Dunmore, Lord (Gov.), 188-89
Du Quindre, 10

Eason, William (Utoy, William), 163, 175n36, 175n41
East Lagoon, 42
East River, 42, 45-46
Equía, Francisco de (Capt.), 153
El Heturno (Milwaukee chief), 10-11
Emistisiguo (Creek leader), 65
Escambia Valley, 60
Escobar, Juan Bote de, 139n1
Escootehabe (Creek leader), 23
Eslava, Fidel (Cdr.), 128
El Estrecho (Detroit), 15
Ezpeleta, José (Joseph) de: at Queen's Redoubt, 106-107, 119, 149;

Capt.-Gen. of Cuba, 153; forces of, 116, 149; gets command at Pensacola, 118; Governor of Mobile, 94, 99, 107-110, 112-14, 118, 120-21; joins expedition, 115; Maj. Gen., 117; need of reinforcements, 111; titles of, 122;

Falconer, John, 30
Falkland Islands, 22; affair, 1
Fanning, Sylvester, 30
Fitzpatrick, John, 29-30, 34-35, 40, 42-43, 45, 48; New Orleans agent, 28
Flint River, 59
Florida(s): 3, 8, 23, 25, 43, 47, 57, 90-91, 180, 183, 187-90, 197-98, 201-202; British in, 17, 62, 66, 180; coast of, 18; Council, 34, 43; exchange of, 17; fishing in, 19; Indians in, 71; Indians from, 20; loss of, 60; needs of, 28-30; Northern, 20; Spain's recovery of, 14-15; Straits, 134; trade, 22, 61-62, 102; trade between Cuba and, 22; East: 17, 56, 68, 72, 87, 177, 183-88; as a refuge, 185; ceded to Spain, 14, 174; defense of, 65; designated, 17; Indian trade in, 183, 189; trade with, 60, 64; West: 25-26, 28-30, 32, 41-44, 46-49, 54-56, 68-69, 72, 81, 91-92, 101-102, 107-108, 122, 159, 177-83, 185, 187, 190; Assembly, 40, 46, 178; boundaries of, 18, 183; campaign of, 107, 145; ceded to Spain, 14, 177; Council, 34, 43; defense of, 65, 121; designated, 17; English in, 1, 26, 181, 183; Indian Congresses held in, 91; Legislature, 45; merchants in, 27, 32, 38, 44-45; reinforced, 4; resistance in, 160; trade with, 60, 64, 92; 1778 Willing raid in, 93; wrest from British rule, 3
Florida Keys: 17; canoe voyages to, 20; considered as part of Cuba, 18; fishing in, 19

Flor, Manuel de, 153
Folch y Juan, Vicente, 152
Forbes, John, 191
Forbes, Thomas, in Havana, 187-88; partner of Panton, 186
Fort Bute, 145, 149, 153n3
Fort Carlos III (Charles III), 5, 160
Fort Charlotte (Fort *Carlota*), 108, 111; surrender of, 107, 126
Fort George: 110, 118, 125, 135; attack at, 151; bombardment of, 130, 137-38; English troops moved to, 132; fall of, 106, 136, 138-39, 158, 179; Indians at, 101
Fort Jefferson, 101; Indian attack, 159, 173n3
Fort New Richmond, 145
Fort Panmure de Natchez, 152, 159
Fort Pitt, 34, 41
Fort Prince George, 77
Frazer, Alexander, 101
Frederica, 183
French & Indian War, 17, 85
Frenchumastabe, 87, 99-101
Furlong, William, 40

Gage, Thomas (Maj. Gen.), 21, 63-64, 80, 158
Galphin, George, 63-66, 78
Gálvez, Antonio, 140n7
Gálvez, Bernardo de (Gov.): 3-4, 6, 14, 38-39, 46-47, 49, 54, 68-70, 87, 93-94, 101, 103, 107, 109-115, 117, 119, 121-22, 142n29, 145, 147, 152, 155, 159, 163, 170, 177, 180, 186-87, 194-95, 197-204; appoints Cruzat Lt. Gov., 9-10; campaign of, 145; captures Mobile, 82, 126; conquest of West, 189; crushes Campbell, 13, 76, 107, 120, 138-39, 146, 177, 188-89, 194, 198; expedition under, 111, 115-16, 128-38, 149-51, 153; instructs against British incursions, 5; learns of West Florida's defenses, 4, 7; leaves for Havana, 108, 130; men under, 102, 148-49; opposed by

Indians, 87, 102; orders seizure of British vessels, 37; pardons Natchez rebels, 170; sails for New Orleans, 106-107; sails for Pensacola, 181; size of siege units of, 136-38; takes over for Unzaga, 3; wounded, 100, 117-18
Gálvez, José (Joseph) de, 11, 13, 140n7, 145-46, 199
Gálvez, Matías, 140n7, 197
Gálvez, Miguel, 140n7
Galveztown, 4
Garden, William, 52n54
Gelabert, Francisco (Lt.-Engineer), 131, 142n29
Georgia: 44, 56-57, 60-61, 63-65, 68, 72, 81, 87, 90-91, 159, 177-79, 183-85, 191; Americans in, 13; Creeks from, 18; Indians in, 69, 86, 92, 101-102, 184; Indian villages moved from, 19; Patriots, 183; population, 55, 60; prices of clothes in, 20
Germain, George (Lord): 6, 67, 86; advises steps to counter Spanish, 6; makes changes in Indian Dept., 79-80, 83-84, 87
Gibault, Fr. Pierre, 5
Gibraltar, 136, 151, 197; siege of, 126, 149
Gibson, George (Capt.), 34, 36, 154n6
Girón, Gerónimo (Lt. Col.), 149, 152
Goicoechea, Miguel (Cdr.), 128, 130, 136
Goimpy, Du Maitz de, 143n39
González, Manuel (Lt. Col.), 150
Goutyrs, Mr., 169
Gradinigo, John, 30
Grand Lagoon, 114
Grand-Pré, Carlos de, 161, 163
Grant, James (Gov.), 22
Grasse, François de (Adm.): intervention of, 13; requests cash, 14
Gratiot, Charles, 5, 8
Grayden, Alexander, 41
Green, John, 163
Grevembert, Jean-Baptiste, 27

Grimarest, Enrique (Capt.), 111, 121, 153, 165
Guanajuato, 153
Guarico, 134, 136

Haldimand, Frederick (Gen.), 6
Hall, Ricardo, 175n33
Hamilton, Henry (Gov.), 5-6
Hammond, Thomas (Capt.), 28
Hanxleden, J. L. W. von (Col.), 98
Harris, Robert, 27
Havana: 14, 19, 21, 108-109, 111-13, 126-29, 133, 138, 150-52, 181, 187,190; capture of, 17; center of activity at, 2; English occupied, 22; expedition from, 111-12, 115, 127, 130, 134, 146, 150; Indians visit, 21; settlers taken to, 17; supplies from, 133; troops from, 113, 115-116, 118, 135, 146-49, 151-52
Havana Bay, 126, 136
Hayton and Williams and Co., 30
Henry, Patrick, 3
Hesse, Emmanuel, 7
Hickory Ground, 66
Hildago, (Sgt.), 33
Hill, Wills, 21; Earl of Hillsborough, 62
Hispaniola, 27, 46, 125
Hodge, David, 47
Holmes, Joseph, 163
Holsten, Juan, 175n33
Holston, Judith, 163, 165
Horn Island, 27
Hortiz, Joseph, 161-62, 164
House of Gardoqui, 2
Howe, William (Sir), 65
Hutchins, Anthony (Col.), 45, 171, 180

Iberville River (canal), 34, 180
Illinois: 11, 161-62; Creoles in, 6; forts in, 6; garrisons in, 7; Indians of the, 7; merchants in, 15, 29-30; posts in the, 6; Spanish: 4, 9, 11,

160-70

Illinois River: 7; detachments up the, 10; traders retreat up to, 9

Indians: 4-13, 15, 19-20, 31, 33, 58, 61, 63-65, 67-69, 71, 76, 79, 84-87, 90-96, 98, 103, 110-111, 113, 117, 120, 135, 145, 148, 169, 180, 184-186; as allies, 54, 63, 69; attack Cahokia, 8; attack St. Louis, 9; British stationed spys among the, 6-7; English traders among the, 4, 9, 227; friendship of, 5; hostile traders control the, 15; jobs on fishing crews, 20; medals awarded to, 91, 93-95, 99; organized against Americans, 4; raided Spanish settlements, 11; served the British, 71, 152; Cherokees (Cheerake,56): 64-65, 71, 77-78, 82, 92, 95, 184-85; Chickasaw (Chikkasah, 56): 11, 67, 71, 74n34, 78, 80-82, 84, 94-95, 97-98, 100-101, 160, 162-63, 166-68, 170-72; 185; led by Colbert, 158-59, 164, 172; trade with, 91-92; villages, 91, 162, 166, 169; want peace, 165; Choctaws (Choktah, 56): 23, 54, 61-63, 67, 71, 74n34, 78, 80-82, 84, 87, 90-91, 93-99, 101, 165, 185; East Party, 90, 95; Six Villages, 90, 93, 95, 97; trade with, 91-92; West Party, 90, 95; Creeks: 18, 20, 54-56, 58-59, 61-72, 74n34, 81-82, 86, 91, 95-98, 100-103, 183-85; in Pensacola, 87, 91; Lower, 21-23, 60, (Cowetas), 63, 92-94, 182, 189; Lower Towns, 59-60, 63, 67, 69, 91; McGillivray principal chief, 189; merchants, 57; trade with, 92, 183-84; Upper, 21, 59-60, 63, 65, 67, 73n12, 78, 92-94; Upper Towns, 59-60, 63, 66-67, 69, 91, 93; Cusseta, 67; Fox, 7, 9, 12; Kaskaskia, 164; Koasati, 66; Loup, 164; Milwaukee, 10-11; Muskogee (Muskohge), 56, 190; Okfuskees, 63, 66-67; Ottawa, 12; Peoria, 164; Quapaw, 160, 165-70, 175n39; Sac, 7, 9; Seminoles, 20, 65, 183-84; Shawnees, 64-65, 95; Sioux, 7, 9, 12; Tallapoosa, 101; Tallassee, 67; Tiger Clan, 72n22; Wind Clan, 66

Innerarities [James & John], 191

Jackson [Andrew], 191
Jamaica: 19, 22, 37, 41, 43-44, 46, 170; plans to invade, 114, 146; reinforcements from, 70, 99, 118, 134; slaves from, 40
James, Benjamin, 100-101
Jefferson, Thomas, 3
Johnson, Guy, 77, 84
Johnson, William (Sir), 76-78; Indian trader, 182-83
Johnstone, George (Gov.), 33
Johnston, William (Capt.), 84
Jones, Evan, 30, 42-43, 45, 49
Jones, James, 42-43, 45
Jones, John (Dr.), 42
Junta de Generals, 108-109, 129, 134

Kaskaskia: 5, 8; capture of, 4; rebels at, 7
Key West, 19
King Charles III (Carlos), 2, 17, 117, 122, 145-47, 196-97, 199-200
King George III, 17, 25, 33, 184
Kingston, Jamaica: 39, 44-45; merchants of, 40
King's Warehouse, 19
Knox, William, 86

L'Abbadie, Sylvestre, 161, 164; captured, 167; issues I.O.U., 162-63; reaches Chickasaw Bluffs, 162
Lafayette, Marquis de, 195
Lafon, Carlos, 166
Lafon [Carlos?], Monsieur, 164
La Framboise, Baptista, 167
La Grange, François, 162
Lake Pontchartrain: 26, pine forests on, 31; trade regulations on, 35

Langlade, Charles (Capt.), 7
Law, Robert, 26
Layones, Anselmo, 169
Le Fleur, Henry, 30
Leslie, John, 186-87, 189
Leyba, Fernando de: 13; aided Americans, 5; appointed Lt. Gov. of Spanish Illinois, 4; death of, 9; prepares against British attack, 8-9
Little Tallassee, 66, 78
Llano, Antonio de (Lt. Col.), 152
Logan, Terry and Company, 26, 42
Lombard, Jean, 38
Longinos, Antonio, 176n43
Longoria Flores, Francisco de (Col.), 117, 130, 132, 151-52
Lords of Trade, 18
Louis XVI, 146
Louisiana: 3, 25-26, 29, 31-32, 34, 36, 38, 49, 44, 48-50, 107-108, 122, 146-47, 150, 198-99, 201-201; British merchants in, 44; commerce, 33; creoles of, 145, 202; defenses of, 2, 8; divided, 17; English ordered to leave, 3; French, 1; forces from, 107, 112; immigration to, 4; plan to capture upper, 7; Spanish control over, 14; trade rules, 28; trading with, 35, 37, 43, 49; troops in, 148-49; Spanish: 28, 49-50, 68, 178, 180, 201-203

McCrugh, James, 39
McGillivray, Alexander: 66-67, 69-70, 74n26, 74n33, 78, 87, 98, 102, 163, 171, 174n17, 176n46; arrives with Creeks, 71, 100, 74n38; Commissary of Upper Creeks, 189; death of, 190; member of Panton, Leslie & Co., 189; to arrive with Indians, 86-87, 94, 97, 100
McGillivray and Struthers, 30
McGillivray, Daniel, 178, 189
McGillivray, Donald, 178
McGillivray, James, 178
McGillivray, John: 178-79, 187, 189; John Miller and Company, 178
McGillivray, Lachlan, 178-79, 189
McGillivray [McGilvery, William], 169-70
Mchim, Jame, 175n33
McIntosh, Alexander, 30
McIntosh, James, 178
McIntosh, John, 98, 100, 173n3
McIntosh, William, 52n54, 69, 94
McLatchy, Charles, 186-87
McMin, Thomas, 30
Maar, Patricio, 175n33
Malaga, 4
Malliet, Jean Baptiste, 10, 12-13
Manchac: 1, 31, 33-34, 37, 40, 44, 145, 154n3, 180, 199; district, 1; strengthened, 8
Margot River (Chickasaw River): 162; rebels on, 166, 170
Marigny, Pedro de (Pierre), 147, 149
Marshall, William, 30
Martinique, 126, 152
Mather, George, 48
Mather, George, Jr., 48
Mather, James: 34, 37-38, 47-48, 52n54, 187-88; see Morgan and Mather, 37
Mathews, Ziblan, 175n33
Mayorga, Martín de, 146
Mease, Edward, 43
Mérida, 26
Meson, Joseph, 162
Miami River, 19
Michilimackinac, 7, 12, 15
Middle River (Blackwater Bay), 42, 135
militia, 2, 8, 10, 55, 63, 110, 145, 148-49, 164, 166
Military Adventurers, 43
Miller, Bonamy, and Company, 189
Miller, John: 47, 177, 182, 189, 190; business in Pensacola, 180-81, 191; elected to West Florida Assembly, 178; Indian trader, 184; moved to Bahamas, 181, 183, 187-88, 191; partner of McGillivray, 179, 189; smuggling by, 188

Miller, John and Company, 178
Miller, John, Peter Swanson, and Company, 178
Miralles, Juan de, 198
Mirando, Francisco, 152
Miró, Estevan (Esteban), 11, 153, 163, 166-67, 169-70, 172; acting gov., 161; at Mobile, 115; leaves for Natchez, 164-65
Mississippi River, 1, 5, 8-10, 13, 17, 22, 25-26, 28, 30, 32-34, 37-40, 44, 46-48, 50, 67, 150, 159-60, 163, 165-67, 169-70, 172, 179-80, 184, 187; boats seized on the, 166; British license canoes on the, 12; British posts on, 180; British subjects on, 172; campaign along the, 149; closure of, 14; depredations on, 159; English vessels on, 3; establishment of new forts on, 163; forts on, 145-46; Indians join British on, 6; Indians on, 101, 160; Indian trade on, 179, 184; Loyalist settlements on, 3-4, 7; new border at, 1; permits needed for, 27; piracy on, 10, 22; Pollock sends supplies up, 41; sanctuary of boats on, 36, 38, 90; slave shipments to, 45; Spanish colonies on, 7-8, 90; Spanish navigation on, 158, 161; Spanish posts on, 160, 163; Tory settlers on, 159; traders on, 34, 43, 46
Mississippi Valley: 3, 16n, 188, 200, 202; campaign of, 7; defense of, 7; peace negotiation of, 14; rebellion in, 11; rivalry in, 3; Spaniards in, 158
Missouri River, 6, 12, 15
Missouri Valley: fur trade of the, 7; monopoly of Indian trade, 15; posts captured, 13
Mobile: 7, 26, 30, 47-48, 59, 62, 65, 68, 70, 82-83, 03, 99, 107-12, 114-16, 120-21, 126-28, 132-33, 153, 165, 170, 178-80, 183, 197, 199; additional men from, 112, 116; as a port, 184; besieged, 85; campaigns against, 13, 148-49; Collector of Customs at, 45; conditions of, 86; conquered, 8, 182-83; defense of, 107; expeditions against, 146, 153, 182; fall of, 8, 69, 72, 93-94, 131, 182-83; fishing regions, 18; Gálvez ordered to conquer, 7; Indians at, 78, 83, 96-97, 101, 158-59, 165; Indians trade with, 91; meat & fish scarce in, 20; merchants in, 29, 43; militia units at, 149; secret agents sent to, 4; ships in, 129; trading houses in, 26, 30, 187; troops from Havana for, 113, 150; under British rule, 145
Mobile Bay: 115, 127, 138, 152; expedition arrived at, 107, 113; fishing along, 19; shallow sandbars, 150; Spaniards in, 69, 96
Mobile River, 47
Mohawk Valley, 77
Monbrun [Monbreun], Etienne Boucher de, 10, 13
Moniac, Jacob, 66
Monsanto, Isaac, 26
Monteill, Chevalier de: 155n12; arrives in Havana, 129; joins the siege, 135; meets with Solano, 133; on board *Palmier*, 134, 143n39
Montgomery [Alabama], 66
Montgomery [John (Capt.)], 8-9
Moore, Philip, 52n54
Moore, William (Capt.), 27-28
Morgan and Mather (see James Mather), 37-38, 45-48
Morgan, George, 154n6
Morgan, Patrick (see Morgan and Mather), 37-38, 46-49
Morro Castle, 152, 190
Motard, Joseph, 162

Naquiguén (Milwaukee leader), 10-11
Nash, John, 32-33
Natchez: 1, 31, 40-41, 153, 161, 163-69, 170-72, 180; district, 1, 45, 47, 180; expeditions to meet at, 7, 164; fall of, 160; merchants in,

29-30; post at, 5; rebellion at, 102, 158-60; sends representatives to West Florida Assembly, 40; spy in, 162; strengthened, 8; threats of seizure, 163; troops sent to, 11

Natchitoches, 28

Navarro, Diego José (Capt. Gen. Cuba), 129

Navarro, Domingo José (Capt. Gen.), 113, 129

Navarro, Martín, 149-50

Navia, José de (Marquis de Santa Cruz de Marcenado), 140n5

Navia y Ballet, Victorio de (Gen.), 113, 129, 140n5, 141n18, 148; sails for Havana, 126, 151; troops under, 149, 152

New England Company of Military Adventurers, 43

Newfoundland, cod from, 19

New Orleans: 11-12, 22, 26-28, 31-32, 35, 38-42, 45-48, 90, 94, 107-108, 112-13, 145, 149-50, 159, 161, 163, 165-67, 169-70, 188, 190, 198; activity at, 2; as a free port, 3; British attack on, 7-8; convoy from, 116, 169; Creeks in, 95; defense of, 7; expedition from, 149; French traders leave, 27; help from, 8; inhabitants of, 36-37, 43, 162; men from, 112, 116, 133, 147; merchants in, 5-6, 25, 29-30, 34, 36; militia from, 110, 148; plans to seize, 20; ships in, 129; Spanish attack, 6; Spanish control, 90; spy system in, 4; traders in, 43-44; Willing in, 4

New York: 22, 26, 28, 32, 46-47, 76, 84, 183, 188; traders in, 27, 42-43, 182

Nicholson, Robert (Capt.), 42

Noriega, Joseph, 153-54

Obregón, Pedro (Cdr.), 128

Oconee River, 18, 60

O'Conor, Hugh, 153

Ogeechee River, 60

Ogilby, Hannah, 36, 38

Ogilvie, Francis (Maj.), 17-18

Ohio, 6, 34; 36, 76, 158-159, 164, 167, 179, 184-85

Okfuskee, 63, 66-67

Olivier Bay, 115

Olsen, Jean (Alston, John), 175n36

O'Neill, Arturo (Lt. Col.), 151, 153

Opaymataha (Chickasaw), 94-95

O'Reilly, Alejandro (Alexander): 1, 25, 30, 141n18, 142n33, 149-50; arrival of, 29; hands over governorship, 31; to establish Spanish rule in Louisiana, 1

Ozcoydi, Manuel (Sgt.), 119, 121

Palao, Antonio, 153

Panis, Jacinto, 4

Panton, Leslie and Company: 171, 188; Indian trade monopoly, 187-90

Panton, William: 48; at St. Augustine, 184-85; death of, 190-91; Indian trader, 183-84, 186, 188-90; in Pensacola, 177, 187, 189; moves to Georgia, 185; moves to the Bahamas, 181, 183, 187; residence of, 189-91

Parent, Joseph Baptist, 13

Parker, Sir Peter (Adm.), 129

Parscau, Duplessis, 143n39

Pascagoula River, 41, 44, 90-91

Pastor, Alejo (Sgt.), 168

Peace River, 23

Pearl River, 35, 90

Pell, John (Capt.), 27

Peneiro, Francisco, 197

Pennsylvania Loyalists, 106

Pensacola: 6-7, 19, 28, 31, 34, 36, 38-40, 42-44, 46-48, 59-60, 62, 65, 67-72, 78-79, 84, 86-87, 90-91, 93, 95-96, 98-101, 111, 114, 116, 120-22, 133-34, 139, 149-50, 152, 160-61, 181-83, 187, 194, 197-99; as a port, 179, 184-85; assault of, 126, 129; blockade of, 109-110; British vessels in, 27, 135; by-passed, 22; Cameron ordered to, 92; campaigns against, 13, 145-49, 197; communications between, 178; defense of, 70, 76, 94, 177; depots at, 63; deserters from, 110; enforcements for, 134; expedition against, 108, 127-30; expedition from, 8; fall of, 8, 54, 76, 102, 106-107, 117, 119, 151, 153-54, 158, 186, 199; Folch as governor of, 152; Gálvez ordered to conquer, 2, 7-8; harbor of, 18, 113, 179; Indians in, 71, 81-85, 94-100, 102, 152, 159; invasion of, 133; lack of barracks in, 22; low on ammunition, 86; march to, 109, 112; meat and fish scarce in, 20; merchants in, 29, 41, 45, 190; neutrality of, 132; sea expedition from, 8; secret agents sent to, 4; ships at, 135; strength of, 130, 148; trading houses in, 26, 183, 188, 191; under British rule, 87, 145, 182, 194

Pensacola Bay: 109, 113-14, 136, 150, 181-83; forces arrived at, 116; open the entrance of, 107-108, 110, 113, 115, 130

Perdido Bay & River, 109-115, 133, 178

Pereda, José, 127

Philadelphia, 2, 30, 36, 43-45, 181

Pickles, William (Capt.), 34, 37, 52n49

Piernas, Pedro (Lt. Col.), 108, 114, 160

Pierrefue, Deidier de (Capt.), 138, 143n39

Pilcher, Benjamin, 32

Pino, Antonio, 167-68, 176n42

Pointe Coupé (Coupée), 42, 47, 169

Pollock, Oliver: 36, 47, 154n3, 199, 201; supplies American forces, 3-6, 41

Pontiac's Rebellion, 85

Pouré, Eugenio (Capt.), 10, 161, 163

Poushauma, 95

Prairie du Chien: traders from, 12-13; traders retreat to, 9

Prevost, Augustine, (Gen.), 86
Prince of Wales Redoubt, 136-37
Proud, William, 32
Puebla, Mexico, 153
Puente, Juan Elixio de la, 17-18
Puerto Príncipe, 114
Pulaski, Baron, 195
Putnam, Israel, 43

Queen's Redoubt: 118, 136; assault on, 119, 138, 149; explosion of, 76, 106, 138, 177, 181, 183, 189

Rada, José Fermín de (Joseph), 128, 150
Rae, Robert, 63-64
Ravenel, Chevalier de, 134, 143n39
Rebolo, Luis (Col.), 117
Red Cliffs (*Barrancas Coloradas*): 112-13, 115, 136; attack on, 110, 131-33, 137; battery on, 109, 114, 130, 135, 146; deserters from, 111; occupied by Spanish troops, 120

Regiments or Units: *Agenois*, 143n39 (*Angenois*), 146); *Aragón*, 141n19, 143n41, 151-52; *Catalonia*, 116, 152; *2º Cataluña*, 143n41; *Cambresis*, 143n39, 146; *du Cap*, 146; East Florida Rangers, 184; *España*, 116, 141,10, 143n41, 152; *Flanders*, 141n19, 143n41; *Gatinois*, 143n39, 146; *Guadalajara*, 141n19, 143n41, 152; *Havana*, 116, 143n41, 150; *Hibernia*, 141n19, 143n41, 151; Independent Rangers, 77; Louisiana, 108, 148-49; *Mallorca*, 152; Maryland Loyalists, 181; *Naples*, 153; *Navarra*, 116, 141n19, 143n41 (*Navarre*), 106, 111, 119, 149, 154; Orleans, 143n39; Pennsylvania Loyalists, 106; *Poitori*, 143n39, 146; *Príncipe* Lombardy), 116, 141n18, 141n19, 150-51; *Rey* (King's), 141n19, 143n41, 151; Royal Artillery, 84, 153, 166; *Soria*, 141n19, 143n41, 149, 151; *Toledo*,

153; Waldeckers, 98
Reid, William, 34
Requerols, Salvador (Capt.), 152
Revillagigedo, Viceroy Conde de, 150
Rhode Island, 32-33
Riaño, Juan Antonio de, 131, 153
Ringuet, Baptista, 167
Río Grande River, 22
Ritson, John, 30
Rivas Betancourt, Roberto de, 197
Rochambeau, Jean Baptiste (Gen.), 13-14
Rock River, 9
Rodney, George (Adm.), 126, 129, 136
Rodríguez, Manuel (Sgt.), 153
Rogers, Patricio, 175n33
Rojas, Rafaela Ignacia Ortíz de, 125
Romans, Bernard, 21
Rosado, José, 197
Ross, Alexander, 52n54
Ross, David: 45-47, 49, 52n54; and Company, 38-39; lost schooner *Sally*, 37; takes loyalty oath, 39
Ross, George, 37-38, 45, 52n54
Ross, Robert: 37-38, 41, 45; acquires property in Pensacola, 40; takes loyalty oath, 39
Rousseau, Pedro de (Capt.), 132, 135
Royal Navy Redoubt: 111, 113, 115, 118, 131, 136, 148; assault on, 132-33, 137; battery on, 114, 116, 130, 135, 146; occupied by Spanish troops, 120
Rozas, Domingo Ortíz de (Count de Poblaciones), 139n3
Rumsey, James, 45

Saavedra, Francisco de: 123n29, 155n17; meets with Solano, 134-35; raises funds, 14
Sabine River, 22
Saint Domingue, 49
Salla, Cayetano de (Lt. Col.), 149-51
San Antonio (town), 157n52
San Bernardo (settlement), 149
San Luis (settlement), 134, 138

San Marcos de Apalache (St. Marks), 17, 19-20
San Martín, José de, 150
San Miguel (arroyo), 117
Santa María de Loreta (settlement), 19
Santa Rosa Island: 131, 133-34, 150; battery on, 151; expedition sails to, 115-16, 130, 135; garrison at, 132
Santo Domingo, 125-26, 146
Savannah: 28, 86-87, 179, 183, 185; as a port, 184; rebels at, 63
Scotchie (see John Stuart), 77
Selby, Prideaux, 46
Serrato, José (Cdr.), 130, 136, 139
Seven Years War, 1, 3, 76, 125, 149
Shakespear, Stephen, 44
Ships: *Africa* (brig), 27-28; *Andromaque* (frigate), 134, 127-38, 143n36, 143n39, 144n51; *Ann*, 34; *Astuto* (ship-of-line), 128; *Belle Savage*, 27; *Berwick* (brig), 37; *Bienfaisant* (brig), 143n36; *Bostonian* (schooner), 52n49; *Caimán* (frigate), 128-30, 139; *Camilla* (brig), 37; *Concepción* (schooner), 127; *Destin* (ship-of-line), 143n36, 143n39; *Dispatch* (schooner), 39; *Dragón* (ship-of-line), 128, 138; *Duque de Cornwallis*, 126; *Dutton* (frigate), 129; *Eleanor* (schooner), 44; *Galveztown* (brig), 116, 131-33, 135, 150; *Guerrero* (ship-of-line), 128, 134; *Gustave* (brig), 143n36; *Hannah* (brig), 37; *Hercules* (brig), 37; *Hope* (sloop), 32; *Intrepide* (ship-of-line), 143n36, 143n39; *Jesse* (brig), 37; *Julie*, 47; *La Hermosa Limeña*, 28; *Liberty* (sloop), 40; *Licorne* (frigate), 143n36; *Lièvre* (brig), 143n36; *Little Bob*, 27; *Live Oak* (sloop), 28, 38, 42; *La Mamie*, 38; *Matilde* (frigate), 142n22; *Mentor* (frigate), 130, 135; *Norton* (brig), 34, 37; *Nuestra Señora de la O* (frigate), 128-29, 134; *Palmier* (ship-of-line), 134, 143n36, 143n39; *Peggy*

(sloop), 37; *Petite Minerve* (schooner), 143n36; *Polly*, 38; *Port Royal* (frigate), 130, 135; *Rayo* (ship-of-line), 125; *Rebecca*, 39; *Resource* (frigate), 129; *Sally* (schooner), 37; *San Juan Nepomuceno* (flagship), 126-27; *San Pió* (brig), 116, 128-30; *San Ramón* (flagship), 115-16, 123n29, 126-33; *Santa Cecilia* (frigate), 128-30, 137-38, 144n51; *Santa Clara* (frigate), 129-30, 133, 137-38, 144n51; *Santa Rosalía* (frigate), 127, 150; *Serpent* (cutter), 135, 143n36; *Souris* (schooner), 143n36; *Steady Friend* (brig), 37; *St. Peter* (brig), 28; *Sylph*, 38; *Tritón*, 138, 143n36, 143n39; *The Two Pollies* (sloop), 132-33; *Ulysses* (frigate), 129, 134; *Unicornio* (frigate), 134; *Valenzuela* (sloop), 131; *Velasco* (ship-of-line), 128; *William* (brig), 27; *York* (brig), 27
Sigüenza Point (*Punta de Sigüenza*), 115-16, 130, 132-33, 151
Sinclair, Patrick (Gov.), 7
Sinnot, Pierce A., 20-21
slaves, 34, 36-37, 39-42, 44-45, 47-49, 54, 106, 149, 158, 161, 169-70
Smith, John, 163
Solano, Agustín, 139n1
Solano, María Isabel, 139n2
Solano y Bote, José (Vice Adm.): 127-30, 135, 137, 141n18, 142n22, 142n33; arrives in Havana, 150; forces of, 136; in Venezuela, 125-26; Marquis del Socorro, 125, 139, 150; meets with officers, 133-35; ordered to meet Gálvez, 134; plans bombardment, 138; promotion for, 139, 144n57; sails with fleet, 125-27, 134, 152; Viscount of *Feliz Ardid*, 126
Soler, Antonio (Sub.-Lt.), 166, 174n25
Sonda de Tortuga, 127-28
Soto, José de, 153
South Carolina, 13, 56-57, 68, 76-78,

81, 102, 114, 159, 179, 183-84, 191
Starn, Joel, 175n33
St. Augustine: 19-20, 60, 65, 67-68, 92, 170-71, 184, 186-87; as a military post, 22, 150; as a port, 184-85; attacked, 146; British forces at, 17-18; depots at, 64
Steer, Samuel, 44-45, 49
Ste. Geneviève: militiamen from, 8; rebels at, 7; reinforced, 164
St. Francis River, 160, 167
Stephenson, John, 28, 40, 137
St. Johns River, 183, 187
St. Joseph (Fort St. Joseph): attack on 10-11; campaign of, 15; expedition against, 12
St. Louis: 4, 12-13, 162, 164-66, 170; attacked, 9; boats escorted to, 170; fear of British attack on, 8; merchants in, 5; monopoly of Indian trade north of, 14-15; plans to capture, 7-8; supplies to, 160-61; warnings to, 10
St, Marks (*San Marcos de Apalache*), 17, 150, 186-87, 190
St. Marys River, 183
St. Maxent, Francisco Maximiliano de, 153
Strachan, Charles, 26
Strother, Arthur, 46-48, 187-88
Struthers, William (see McGillivray & Struthers), 30, 47, 178
Stuart, Charles, 30, 62, 79
Stuart, John: 22, 61-68, 71-72, 73n22, 80-81, 83; called Scotchie, 77; death of, 79, 86, 92; rumor of charges against. 79; Supt. of Indian Affairs, 20-21, 61-62, 76-78, 86, 158, 185
St. Vincent, 41-42
Sutton's Bayou, 135; Lagoon, 117
Swallen, Betnigo, 175n33
Swanson, Peter, 178
Swanson, William, 52n54

Tacón, Andrés (Cdr.), 127
Taitt, David: 66-67; joins Cameron,

86; readies Indians for assistance, 78; storehouse of raided, 78
Tallassee, 67
Tallapoosa River, 59, 66
Tampa Bay, 18-19, 23
Tangipaho, 26
Tartar Point, 116, 181
Tensaw (Tensa) River, 60, 180
Terry, Jeremiah (see Logan, Terry & Co.), 42
Teste Island, 38
Thomas, John (Dep. Comm. Indian Affairs), 34
Thompson, James, 47
Thompson's Creek, 42
Tombigbee River, 90-91
Tonyn, Patrick (Gov.), 65, 72, 184
Treviño, Phelipe, 153
Turner, John, 161, 163

Ulloa, Antonio de (Gov.): 1, 26-29
Unzaga, Luis de (Col): as Gov., 1, 31-34, 36-37, 154n6; Capt.-Gen. of Venezuela, 140n7; leaves office, 3, 34; requests instructions from Spain, 2-3; Va. asks for trading privileges from, 2
Utoy, William (Eason, William), 175n36, 175n41

Vallé, Carlos (Lt.), 164
Vallé, François, 161, 163, 173n11
Valliere, Joseph (Capt.), 169-70, 172, 175n39
Vásquez, Benito, 167
Velasco, Luis de (Cdr.), 151
Velasco, Santiago, 128
Velasco, Santiago Muñoz de, 128
Velázquez, Diego de (Gov.), 150
Veracruz, 22, 26-27, 146-47
Vergennes, Comte de 2
Vicksburg (Walnut Hills), 34
Vidal, Luis, 127
Vigo, Francisco, 5-6
The Village, 96, 98, 113, 152, 183
Villa, Justa de la, 197

Villars, Louis de (Lt.): captured, 168; commandant (temp.), 165-66, 173n11, 174n25, 175n32; released, 169-70
Villars, María Luisa Vallé de, 168
Villiers, Balthazar de (Capt.), 8, 160-61, 173-174n11
Villebeuvre, Juan de la (Capt.), 152
Vincennes, 6-8, 12

Wabasha (Sioux leader), 7, 9
Wales, Henoc, 167-68
Walker & Dawson (London firm), 47
Walker, John (Capt.), 27
Walker, William, 41-43, 49
Wallace, Alexander, New York firm of Hugh and Wallace, 46
Walnut Hills (Vicksburg), 34
Waugh, John, 37, 47
Weir, John 46
West Indies: 47-49; British, 40-41; French, 34
Whipple, Christopher, 31
Williams and Company (see Hayton and Williams and Co.), 30
Williams, David, 52n54
Williams, William, 175n36, 175n41
Willing and Morris (firm), 36
Willing, James: plundering on Miss. River, 167; raids by, 3-4, 38-39, 44, 67, 93, 167; supplied by Spaniards, 38; vessels seized by, 46
Windright, William, 175n33
Winfree, Jacob, 163, 175n36, 175n41
Wright, James (Gov.), 61, 73n22

Xaramillo, Juan (Lt.), 152

Yazoo River, 158, 161, 172
Yorktown, 13, 185
Yucatan: 31, 150; ships headed for, 127; trade with, 39-40

Zúñiga, Mauricio de, 153